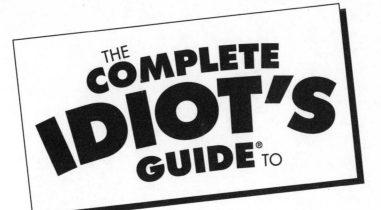

THE COMPLETE IDIOT'S GUIDE® TO

Alchemy

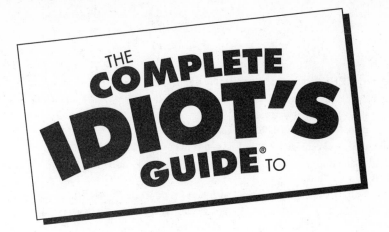

Alchemy

by Dennis William Hauck

ALPHA

A member of Penguin Group (USA) Inc.

ALPHA BOOKS

Published by the Penguin Group

Penguin Group (USA) Inc., 375 Hudson Street, New York, New York 10014, USA

Penguin Group (Canada), 90 Eglinton Avenue East, Suite 700, Toronto, Ontario M4P 2Y3, Canada (a division of Pearson Penguin Canada Inc.)

Penguin Books Ltd, 80 Strand, London WC2R 0RL, England

Penguin Ireland, 25 St. Stephen's Green, Dublin 2, Ireland (a division of Penguin Books Ltd.)

Penguin Group (Australia), 250 Camberwell Road, Camberwell, Victoria 3124, Australia (a division of Pearson Australia Group Pty. Ltd.)

Penguin Books India Pvt. Ltd., 11 Community Centre, Panchsheel Park, New Delhi—110 017, India

Penguin Group (NZ), 67 Apollo Drive, Rosedale, North Shore, Auckland 1311, New Zealand (a division of Pearson New Zealand Ltd.)

Penguin Books (South Africa) (Pty.) Ltd, 24 Sturdee Avenue, Rosebank, Johannesburg 2196, South Africa

Penguin Books Ltd., Registered Offices: 80 Strand, London WC2R 0RL, England

International Standard Book Number: 978-159257-735-4
Library of Congress Catalog Card Number: 2007939745

10 09 08   8 7 6 5 4 3 2 1

Interpretation of the printing code: The rightmost number of the first series of numbers is the year of the book's printing; the rightmost number of the second series of numbers is the number of the book's printing. For example, a printing code of 08-1 shows that the first printing occurred in 2008.

Printed in the United States of America

Note: This publication contains the opinions and ideas of its author. It is intended to provide helpful and informative material on the subject matter covered. It is sold with the understanding that the author and publisher are not engaged in rendering professional services in the book. If the reader requires personal assistance or advice, a competent professional should be consulted.

The author and publisher specifically disclaim any responsibility for any liability, loss, or risk, personal or otherwise, which is incurred as a consequence, directly or indirectly, of the use and application of any of the contents of this book.

Most Alpha books are available at special quantity discounts for bulk purchases for sales promotions, premiums, fundraising, or educational use. Special books, or book excerpts, can also be created to fit specific needs.

For details, write: Special Markets, Alpha Books, 375 Hudson Street, New York, NY 10014.

Publisher: *Marie Butler-Knight*
Editorial Director: *Mike Sanders*
Senior Managing Editor: *Billy Fields*
Executive Editor: *Randy Ladenheim-Gil*
Development Editor: *Lynn Northrup*
Production Editor: *Kayla Dugger*
Copy Editor: *Nancy Wagner*

Cartoonist: *Steve Barr*
Cover Designer: *Bill Thomas*
Book Designer: *Trina Wurst*
Indexer: *Johnna Vanhoose Dinse*
Layout: *Ayanna Lacey*
Proofreader: *Aaron Black*

Contents at a Glance

Contents

Introduction

My initiation into alchemy came while I was attending the University of Vienna. I had gone there to study mathematics in the tradition of the Viennese logician Kurt Godel. However, within three months of my arrival, I was sidetracked into studying a much older tradition.

Four hundred years earlier, Vienna and nearby Prague were at the heart of European alchemy, and hundreds of alchemists flocked to the area to study. I was unaware of Vienna's rich alchemical tradition until one day when I stumbled into a basement room in the university library that was full of old alchemy books.

The German and Latin manuscripts were in antique typesetting that was very difficult to read, but the drawings in those books were strangely profound and resonated deeply with me in ways I could not put into words. All I knew was that whatever was going on in those drawings was more real than anything that was going on in my life at the time, and I wanted to be part of it.

I resolved to learn as much as I could about alchemy and began translating the old manuscripts I found in Vienna and Prague. My research led me to even larger collections of alchemy books in Switzerland, Germany, and Holland. Finally, an Italian friend directed me to Merus Favilla, a practicing alchemist living in Prague who occasionally took on new students.

After some painstaking negotiations, Merus agreed to take me as a student. Every Wednesday for over a year, I took the train from Vienna to Prague to be initiated into the mysteries of the ancient craft. The cost of my weekly tuition was a carton of Camel cigarettes for my master and a box of Mozart Balls (chocolates) for his wife.

I learned much during my strange apprenticeship in Prague—mostly about the hidden signatures and correspondences of things. But the most important thing I learned was that the real trick to grasping alchemy was making it come alive within me. As the German alchemist Gerhardt Dorn once put it: "You must transmute yourselves from dead stones into living Philosophical Stones."

Unlike academic disciplines, alchemy can actually take root in you and grow into something that is more than the sum of its parts. This is when the true secret teachings of alchemy begin and when the magic happens. There is some sort of energetic connection to the principles of alchemy that is very empowering. True alchemists know exactly what I am talking about, and I hope you will, too, by the time you are done with this book.

The objective of this book is to teach you the alchemists' coded language so you can appreciate and work with the ancient wisdom they have passed down to us. For my part, I promise to be honest and direct, with no unnecessary secrecy, no pompous theorizing, and no special allegiance to any particular tradition or organization. My focus in this book is to help you understand the principles of alchemy and apply them in practical ways in the modern world.

So let *your* apprenticeship begin with this book. All you have to do is assume the role of a "complete idiot" and become an empty vessel. Forget everything you thought you knew about alchemy and alchemists. You are now at the beginning of a new path toward enlightenment. And don't worry—you have everything you need hidden away inside you. Just come as you are.

How This Book Is Organized

This book is divided into six sections:

Part 1, "Introduction to Alchemy," traces the roots of alchemy into the distant past and shows how the discipline developed from the mythic writings of godlike beings into the practical treatises of the Alexandrian alchemists. From alchemy's origins in ancient Egypt to the founding of the Great Library, the basic tenets of alchemy were well developed long before the heyday of the medieval alchemists.

Part 2, "The Principles of Alchemy," takes a look at the fundamental concepts of alchemy and traces their development in the Hermetic arts, philosophy, religion, psychology, and other traditions down through the last 5,000 years. We'll also decipher the coded language the alchemists used to describe their work to other alchemists.

Part 3, "The Operations of Alchemy," reveals the secret processes alchemists used to transform substances in their work. These fundamental operations worked not only in the practical work in the lab but also on the mental and spiritual levels.

Part 4, "Practical Alchemy," focuses on what went on in the alchemist's workshop. We learn exactly how the alchemists made their tonics, tinctures, and elixirs and how they worked with the metals to transform lead into gold.

Part 5, "Spiritual Alchemy," looks within to see how alchemical principles work to transform the hidden essences of soul into the pure light of spirit. We also investigate the mysterious connection between the spiritual work and the success of alchemical experiments.

Part 6, "Modern Alchemy," looks at alchemy in the world today. We discover how alchemical principles are being applied in our everyday life in the workplace, in personal relationships, and in society in general. We also investigate the amazing similarities between the concepts of alchemists and those of modern scientists.

You'll also find two helpful appendixes: a list of resources that includes recommended books, alchemy websites and organizations, and sources for herbs and laboratory supplies; and a glossary of words and terms used by alchemists to help in your understanding of alchemy.

A Note About Style

Following the style of the alchemists, major philosophical concepts are capitalized to differentiate them from more mundane meanings. For example, "sulfur" refers to the flammable yellow chemical also known as brimstone, while "Sulfur" refers to the underlying principle of fire, passion, and energy that the alchemists associated with that substance. Similarly, the terms "Above" and "Below" are philosophical concepts related to our ideas of heaven and Earth.

Guideposts Along the Way

A variety of special sidebars are scattered throughout this book to elaborate on the text and help you understand the material better.

def•i•ni•tion

Check these boxes for definitions of words and terms that may be unfamiliar to you.

From the Alchemist

Check these boxes for anecdotes, ancient wisdom, quotes, surprising facts, and other entertaining elaborations on the text.

Tread Carefully

Here you'll find cautions and information about misconceptions in both the practical and spiritual work in alchemy.

Thoth's Tips

Thoth, the father of alchemy, offers tips, shortcuts, suggestions, and sources of more information to enhance your understanding of alchemy.

Acknowledgments

I wish to thank the International Alchemy Guild (IAG) for allowing me access to their extensive archives and graphics files in the preparation of this work. I am also forever indebted to Merus Favilla for his loving initiation into the secrets of the craft.

Trademarks

All terms mentioned in this book that are known to be or are suspected of being trademarks or service marks have been appropriately capitalized. Alpha Books and Penguin Group (USA) Inc. cannot attest to the accuracy of this information. Use of a term in this book should not be regarded as affecting the validity of any trademark or service mark.

Part 1

Introduction to Alchemy

The roots of alchemy are buried in the shifting sands of ancient Egypt as the craft developed from writings attributed to divine beings who are said to have come to Egypt over 10,000 years ago. The scribe Thoth, considered the first alchemist and also the father of music, mathematics, astronomy, and agriculture, recorded the wisdom of the ancient visitors and sealed his writings in two great pillars that became known as the Pillars of Hermes. According to legend, the pillars were rediscovered thousands of years after the Great Flood and hidden away in an isolated temple in western Egypt. The city of Alexandria was founded to study and translate the sacred texts, and from there the ancient spiritual technology of alchemy spread throughout the world.

Your Apprenticeship in Alchemy

In This Chapter

- ◆ Alchemy: the art of transformation
- ◆ Why alchemy is still relevant today
- ◆ Understanding the six types of alchemy
- ◆ The fundamental philosophy behind alchemy
- ◆ Learning alchemy

Just what is alchemy? This question can present a bewildering variety of answers, because alchemy is at the root of so many different traditions and disciplines. And that's unfortunate, for the one simple thing about alchemy is its definition. So, to avoid confusion in your study of this subject, remember this basic definition right from the start: alchemy is the art of transformation. Alchemy is about how to change one thing into another, and the goal of alchemy is to perfect or evolve the substance at hand. Alchemists try to change something that is inferior, imperfect, or unacceptable into something that is better, more perfect, and closer to what they desire.

It doesn't matter whether we're talking about metals, chemicals, or herbs or about our bodies, minds, or souls. Nor does it matter whether we're talking about chemistry, biology, medicine, religion, sociology, politics, software, or psychology. The word "alchemy" is always about how to accomplish some sort of creative transformation.

So there you have it. You've already made a giant leap toward understanding alchemy, and you've only just begun to read! And you'll be making many more giant leaps soon—I promise you. Alchemy may seem confusing and arcane and, at times, even deliberately misleading, but once you understand their secret, coded language, the alchemists' words will all fall into place for you. And this book will teach you that ancient code of symbolic images, special terms, and secret ciphers in as straightforward a manner as possible.

Why Study Alchemy?

But why should you spend your time trying to penetrate the alchemists' coded language and learn the age-old secrets of alchemy? What relevance does alchemy have today?

Surprisingly, this ancient discipline, which dates back at least 2,000 years, has much to offer the modern world. The universal principles, which the alchemists discovered, apply to all levels of the physical, mental, and spiritual realms. Whether you are working in an artist's studio or a boardroom, in a lab developing healing tinctures or in a clinic as a therapist, or in the inner laboratory of your own soul and spirit, alchemical techniques will help you make the transformations you desire.

The art of transformation reveals the hidden chemistry of change underlying an enormous variety of subjects ranging from psychological transformation and personal relationships to the formation of stars and planetary systems. In fact, alchemy has achieved more respect today from the general public and among scholars than at any time in the last 400 years.

Swiss psychologist Dr. Carl Jung (1875–1961) is credited with returning alchemy to its rightful stature in academia with his development of depth psychology, which he based on the universal symbols of alchemy that appeared in his patients' dreams. Jung made the ancient operations of alchemy viable tools in helping his patients achieve psychological wholeness.

Even in such unexpected areas as economics, one can find many serious works crediting the effectiveness of alchemical principles. Recently, H. C. Binswanger, director of the Institute for Economics and Ecology at the University of St. Gallen, Switzerland, wrote a breakthrough book called *Money and Magic* in which he urged economists to stop using the term "mainstream economics" and substitute "alchemical economics" as a more descriptive name. He contends that economics developed more as a form of alchemy than finance.

While putting the job title of "alchemist" on your resumé may not bring in a flood of offers, thinking of yourself as a practicing alchemist in the workplace can bring unexpected rewards and advancement. So let's look at the different kinds of modern alchemy and see how they can help you get ahead in the world.

> **Thoth's Tips**
>
> An entertaining way to grasp the basic principles of alchemy is to read some of the many novels devoted to the topic. Among the best are Paulo Coelho's *The Alchemist*, Russell House's *The Portal*, Patrick Harpur's *Mercurius*, Fidelis Morgan's *Unnatural Fire*, Maria Szepes's *The Red Lion*, J. K. Rowling's *Harry Potter* series, Margaret Mahy's *Alchemy*, and Michael Scott's *The Alchemyst*.

The Kinds of Alchemy

Because in the most basic terms, alchemy is the art of transformation, the best way to study the different aspects of alchemy is to focus on what is being transformed and then devote our attention to these types of alchemy throughout the rest of the book.

Spiritual Alchemy

The most popular reason for studying alchemy today is to reconnect with spiritual realities. In this approach to alchemy, the gold of the alchemist is not common metal gold, but an inner spiritual gold. Using meditation to penetrate the symbolic imagery of alchemy, the seeker attempts to transform the dark, heavy, *karmic* lead of the soul into the bright, purified, and incorruptible gold of spirit. I discuss the techniques of spiritual alchemy in Chapter 19.

def•i•ni•tion

> **Karmic** is a term that comes from the Hindu word *karma*, which means actions, and refers to the cumulative effects our deeds have on ourselves and others. In spiritual alchemy, karma is the burden of the soul carried from past incarnations as well as the effects of our present actions. By becoming free of karma through special meditations, good deeds, and purification of thoughts, a person can overcome original sin and return to a golden state of innocence and incorruptibility.

Psychological Alchemy

Alchemy not only gave birth to chemistry but also to modern psychology. The alchemists were the first to treat psychological problems as chemical imbalances in the body. They believed the powers of the metals were expressed in humans as our basic instincts and emotions, and these could be transformed into the nobler aspects of reason and enlightenment through alchemical processes. Carl Jung did groundbreaking work in this area of alchemy, and you learn more about his work in Chapter 18.

Artistic Alchemy

Throughout history, alchemy has had a tremendous influence in the creative arts. Early Egyptian alchemists were experts at capturing essences in oils and perfumes and applying colors and metals to jewelry and sculptures. Today, many artists working with metal, glass, enamels, perfumes, and other media consider themselves part of the alchemical tradition and adhere to its principles. Alchemical art tends to use materials in ways that make them appear to be something else, thus revealing their essence in unexpected ways. We can also find similar transformative staging in alchemical literature, music, and even software games.

Many filmmakers follow the principles of alchemy to add psychological depth and archetypal power to their films. Workers from Paramount studios even set up an "Alchemy in Film" panel in the late 1990s to assist writers in understanding alchemy. Films like *2001* and *2010*, *Like Water for Chocolate*, *The Fifth Element*, *The Matrix*, *Revelation*, *Fullmetal Alchemist*, and *The Da Vinci Code* are just a few examples where the creators have made conscious use of alchemy in the plotline.

Social Alchemy

In the last century, the term "alchemy" became the slogan and rallying point for a variety of movements driven by the human desire to change adverse conditions. These endeavors included trying to change slavery into freedom, sin into grace, folly into wisdom, poverty into wealth, fear into courage, war into peace, sterility into fertility, bureaucracy into democracy, disease into health, and death into immortality. All these social movements borrowed alchemical terms and principles to focus their efforts at changing the status quo. Chapter 22 tells you more about social alchemy.

Practical Alchemy

Practical alchemy deals with the production of tinctures, tonics, oils, compounds, and elixirs that capture healing energy. Such laboratory work also focuses on creating mineral transformations and perfecting the metals commonly associated with changing lead into gold. Practical alchemy reached its heyday in Europe in the Middle Ages, but in the last 50 years this kind of work has staged a noticeable resurgence. In fact, according to the International Alchemy Guild (IAG), more licensed practical alchemists exist today than at any time in history. In Part 4, we delve into this intriguing topic and teach you a bit of kitchen alchemy along the way.

Therapeutic Alchemy

During the last century, we have seen the proliferation of a new breed of alchemical practitioners, who focus on ancient healing modalities. Techniques such as alchemical hypnotherapy, dream therapy, and shamanic journeying use imagery to direct or stimulate healing energy. Oriental alchemical arts like yoga, aikido, Tai Chi, Chi Kung, tantra, acupuncture, and reiki have seen a profound increase in Western culture. Alchemical bodywork like chiropractics, Rolfing, Feldenkrais, bioenergetics, and polarity therapy have their origin in the work of nineteenth-century alchemists seeking to isolate the life force. Most modern holistic disciplines like homeopathy, herbology, naturopathy, ayurveda, Chinese medicine, aromatherapy, and reflexology trace their origins in ancient alchemical teachings, and even New Age astrologers, numerologists, and Tarot readers owe their livelihoods to Egyptian and Babylonian alchemists. We study some of these fascinating traditions in more detail in Chapter 2.

Tread Carefully

Don't be confused by the wide variety of possible alchemical transformations. For an alchemist, no real distinction exists between the different kinds of transformations, because the myriad of things in our world are all manifestations of just one thing—the universal mind at the source of creation. By focusing on this single divine spark in all things, the alchemist hopes to reveal the essence of a substance or situation and guide its growth to a natural state of perfection. We learn much more about this philosophy in Part 2.

The Perennial Philosophy

One of the reasons for the endurance of alchemy through the ages is that it's based on a fundamental philosophy that has itself exhibited tremendous staying power in the human mind. The alchemists call it the "One True Philosophy of the Whole World" and believe it was first revealed to humanity in ancient Egypt. It is also known as the "Perennial Philosophy" because, down through history, it has always resurfaced in some form despite many successful attempts by orthodox authorities to suppress it.

To perform his transformation, the alchemist attempts to understand and connect with the unseen reality behind the manifested world.

The basic idea of the Perennial Philosophy is that there are certain universal truths common to all cultures and systems of knowledge. The German mathematician Gottfried Leibniz first used the term in this sense, when he defined it as the eternal philosophy that underlies all religions. The term, further refined by twentieth-century philosopher Aldous Huxley, has come to mean the most basic and everlasting universal truths sensed by all human beings.

In other words, down through history, people in many different cultures and times have experienced similar feelings about the nature of reality and the meaning of existence. Differences arise only when some authority attempts to control or adapt these basic ideas into a rigid system of behavior. In this view, the world's nations and religions are constantly fighting each other over minor, cultural variations in the same basic belief system. Unlike dogmatic religion, which encourages these petty sectarian disputes, the Perennial Philosophy states that there are as many roads to God as there are people in the world.

The three fundamental tenets of alchemy and the Perennial Philosophy of which it is part are:

1. The material world is not the only reality. Another hidden level of reality exists that determines our existence. The physical world is a shadow or projection of a higher reality that cannot be grasped by the senses. Only the higher faculties of the human mind and spirit can perceive it.

2. The basic duality of material versus nonmaterial realities is mirrored in human beings. Our material body is subject to the physical laws of birth and death; our nonmaterial body (called soul or spirit) is not subject to decay or loss and carries the essence of who we are. This divine energy at the heart of everything is known as the Quintessence, the Fifth Element, in alchemy, or the life force in most other traditions.

3. All human beings possess the capacity to perceive these separate levels of reality, both in themselves and in nature, but we are taught to ignore the subtle clues to this greater reality. The perception and application of this ultimate truth is the goal of human beings and the purpose of our existence.

What makes alchemy different from other mystical systems that are part of the Perennial Philosophy is that alchemy attempts to apply this wisdom in practical ways in the everyday world. No other discipline has taken such a down-to-earth and in-your-face approach to working with these mystical principles.

That approach, unfortunately, got a lot of alchemists burnt at the stake, but it also makes alchemy a unique and powerful discipline—a combination of religion and science that makes a lot of sense to people trying to remain true to themselves in the modern world. You find more about being alchemists in today's world in Part 6.

Becoming an Alchemist

In the past, becoming an alchemist began with a long apprenticeship or training period that traditionally involved a very specific path of initiation. In the ancient mystery schools, the teachings were arranged into three levels of mastery:

◆ The Philosophicum (knowing what is really there)

◆ The Theoreticum (knowing how it works)

◆ The Practicum (knowing how to do it)

def•i•ni•tion

Adept is from the Latin word *adeptus,* meaning having attained mastery of a subject. Alchemists coined the term in the 1660s to refer specifically to someone who had learned the secret of transforming base metals into gold; today it is used to mean anyone who is skilled in the secrets of anything.

Obviously, initiatory alchemy was a very personal process that usually involved a one-on-one relationship with an *adept* that lasted many years.

Modern teaching of alchemy takes place at a faster pace on all three levels of initiation at once. On the philosophical level, the objective is to achieve an awareness of the lower and the higher worlds in which the alchemist works. The goal of the theoretical work is to understand how to interact and control the unseen energies of those realms. The practical work is concerned with learning the personal and laboratory techniques of transformation and is, in turn, presented in three phases: the plant work, the mineral work, and the animal work.

This kind of total immersion program takes commitment on the part of both teacher and student, and the biggest danger is that the student will not be fully initiated. Unfortunately, there is no Hogwarts School of Alchemy prepared to give students the kind of personal attention they need for true initiation.

Nonetheless, we do have a number of workable alternatives for persons seeking formal instruction in alchemy. The International Alchemy Guild (IAG) is a good place to inquire about practicing alchemists who take on students in your area. (Find contact information for the Guild and other groups mentioned here in Appendix A.)

Some graduates of the Paracelsus Research Society still take on students. The institute, originally based in Colorado, was formed by alchemist Albert Reidel (known as Frater Albertus and author of *The Alchemist's Handbook*). Unfortunately, the premier school for practical alchemy in the United States closed its doors in 1984 when Reidel died. Dr. Joseph Lisiewski, who founded Paracelsus College in 1982, carried on his work in Australia. The school has a seven-year curriculum of plant, mineral, and animal alchemy.

Before it closed in 2000, the Philosophers of Nature (PON) offered a two-year course in plant work and a seven-year course in mineral work. The course manuals are still available from Triad Publishing. French alchemist Jean Dubuis wrote the material which was taught by American alchemists Russ and Sue House.

The Institute for Hermetic Studies (IHS) of Pennsylvania, under the direction of author Mark Stavish, offers seminars on mineral and plant alchemy, as do practicing alchemists Paul Bartscher and Micah Nilsson of Al-Kemi in Oregon. John Reid offers a free online course on plant alchemy, and Scottish archivist Adam McLean offers several online courses in deciphering alchemical symbols. The Rosicrucian Order (Ancient Mystical Order Rosae Crucis, or AMORC) in San Jose, California, sometimes offers summer classes in plant and mineral alchemy, though they are open to members only and membership is very expensive.

The largest school of alchemy in the world, with over 500 students in 12 countries, is Flamel College of California, whose Director of Practical Alchemy is Robert Allen Bartlett, a student of Frater Albertus and his Chief Chemist. Flamel College offers certification in Practical and Spiritual Alchemy, a diploma in Alchemy, and is the only organization actually hiring alchemists. Although it occasionally holds on-site classes, most of the instruction is done by correspondence study. The seven modules in its Alchemy Home Study Program include all necessary labware, herbs, and chemicals.

The Least You Need to Know

◆ The simplest and most accepted definition of alchemy is that it is the art of transformation.

◆ Today the principles of alchemy can be found at work in psychology, business management, art, literature, filmmaking, software development, and many other creative endeavors.

◆ Modern alchemy consists of six branches: spiritual, psychological, artistic, social, practical, and therapeutic.

◆ Alchemy is part of the Perennial Philosophy, the basic tenet of which holds that certain universal truths are common to all cultures and belief systems.

◆ One can receive formal training in alchemy, though the apprenticeship tradition has largely given way to correspondence and online training.

2

The First Alchemists

In This Chapter

- ◆ Ancient alchemical manuscripts
- ◆ A gift from the gods?
- ◆ Thoth, the father of alchemy
- ◆ The mysterious Pillars of Hermes
- ◆ Secrets of the Emerald Tablet
- ◆ The line between myth and reality

The roots of alchemy are buried in legend and mystery; allegedly the earliest books on alchemy appeared all at once, as if they had been locked away for safekeeping and were suddenly released. At the beginning of the first millennium, all around the world alchemical principles exploded into human consciousness, and these same ideas continue to inspire us to this day.

However, alchemists point to the heavens—not books—for the origin of their craft, and ancient Egyptian writings seem to back them up. Three-thousand-year-old scrolls describe "visitors from the firmament" who came to Egypt and shared their knowledge of the universe, including the art of alchemy.

One document contains a succinct summary of that ancient wisdom. It was engraved on a green crystalline tablet that became known as the Emerald Tablet, and in this chapter, we use the Emerald Tablet to grasp the philosophy behind alchemy.

Lost Gems of Knowledge

The first known alchemy books appeared almost simultaneously in Egypt, Mesopotamia, India, and China over 2,000 years ago, and most modern historians date the birth of alchemy to that period. This was the era of the great library at Alexandria, and ships visiting the busy Egyptian port carried alchemical manuscripts around the world. However, those early writings quote even more ancient texts and refer to a lost tradition that goes back to the dawn of civilization.

All we can say with certainty is that by 300 C.E., the principles of alchemy were widely accepted by philosophers, priests, and craftsmen in civilized nations around the globe. Hundreds of parchment scrolls, clay tablets, and papyri existed that dealt with alchemical principles and processes. Yet, to this day, the true source of that knowledge remains unknown.

Although references to alchemical principles are found in Egyptian scrolls dating back to 1500 B.C.E., the original canon of texts from which those principles were derived has vanished. The early alchemy manuscripts that have survived are remarkably similar in style and seem to originate from a common source. All are written in a strange, convoluted style with obscure references to pre-existing concepts and are filled with secret ciphers and cryptic symbols for which no explanation is given.

The Gods of Alchemy

Despite the difficulty in pinning down the historical source of alchemy, the answer to the question of where alchemy came from is almost unanimous among alchemists.

Most alchemists agree that their art originated in Egypt during a time known as *Zep Tepi*. In this tradition, alchemy is literally a gift from the gods.

According to legend, a contingent of godlike beings settled in Egypt and exhibited an advanced spiritual technology that enabled them to transform matter. These angelic visitors were the first alchemists; they practiced their art in Hormanouthi, a temple hidden near the Nile River.

def•i•ni•tion

Zep Tepi is an ancient Egyptian phrase, meaning First Time. It refers to an epoch over 12,000 years ago when divine beings arrived "through the Void" to settle in Egypt. The gods shared their wisdom and civilized the primitive humans.

According to hieroglyphic texts, the visitors originated from different levels in the firmament, and their bodies were more subtle than humans. Whether for purposes of breeding or out of sheer lust, the visitors were described as unable to resist the temptations of the flesh and desperately wanted to marry young women and have children. The results of these unions were described as giants who had dominion over the earth and its creatures.

Oddly, the idea of angelic visitors lusting after humans is part of many religious texts around the world. Genesis 6:1–5 describes fallen angels who wanted to have children with the daughters of men. In exchange, they taught men magic and metallurgy and how to make tinctures to capture the essence of plants. The story is elaborated in considerable detail in the Old Testament apocryphal *Book of Enoch*.

Who were these mysterious visitors to Egypt? Zosimus, the father of Greek alchemy who lived in Alexandria around 300 C.E., wrote that fallen angels who had children with humans taught mankind alchemy and "all the arts of nature," and he insisted the legends predated history and were literally true. Tertullian and many early Hermetic writers spoke of this same superhuman race and their interactions with humans. The alchemist Clement of Alexandria said the visitors "laid bare the secrets of the metals, understood the virtues of plants and the force of magical incantations, and their learning even extended to the science of the stars."

In an ancient Egyptian text called "Isis the Prophetess to Her Son Horus," Isis begins teaching her son the principles of alchemy and tells him how she acquired her skills. According to her story, she had gone to Hormanouthi to learn the Sacred Art and met one of the visitors, who was overcome by physical lust for her. Isis agreed to satisfy his hunger if he would disclose the secrets, but he refused. Eventually, she met a visitor named Amnael who agreed to her demands, and Isis was initiated into the mysteries of alchemy.

According to legend, Isis, her brother and sister, her husband Osiris, and five similar divine beings settled at Heliopolis, which became the center for alchemy in Egypt. The myths of Isis and Osiris help explain the mysteries of alchemy and are retold many times in the writings of alchemists. We cannot determine whether these ancient myths contain any literal truth, but there is no doubt that the alchemists felt they imparted deep wisdom about the true origin of their craft.

Thoth's Tips

Over 150,000 books have been published on alchemy, and it is estimated that through history, more books have been written on alchemy than any other topic. If you're interested in learning more, the books listed in Appendix A are a good place to start.

Thoth: The Father of Alchemy

Thoth was one of the godlike beings who came to Egypt during the time of Zep Tepi. However, there is an important difference between Thoth and the other gods of Egypt. Thoth exists on all levels of time and space, in heaven and on Earth and in between. He has always existed and always will. He spoke the first Word of creation, and all he has to do is name a thing to bring it into existence. Thoth brought the very first gods into being, yet he is content to serve both the gods and mankind. Thoth is the divine intermediary between spirit and matter that makes alchemy possible.

The Egyptians considered Thoth the first scribe, the inventor of language and writing who recorded the ancient teachings in hundreds of books. Because of this, Thoth is considered the father of many disciplines, including alchemy, mathematics, agriculture, music, magic, religion, science, and medicine. Most of the scrolls attributed to him were preserved in the great library at Alexandria. In the writings of Thoth, alchemy is presented as a unique spiritual science, a merging of science and religion that requires a balanced blending of heart, body, and mind.

Most often depicted as a man with the head of an ibis (a tall wading bird with a long curved beak), Thoth was also associated with baboons and apes, which is taken as a symbol of his divine mission to raise our animal nature to new levels of enlightenment. Thoth was known as the "Revealer of the Hidden" and "Lord of Rebirth" and was considered the initiator of human transformation.

One of Thoth's scrolls from which fragments remain is called *The Book of Breathings*, which teaches humans how to become gods through spells and control of the breath. Thoth is also considered the author of *The Book of the Dead*, which guides the departed through the underworld into the light. It is said the lost *Book of Thoth* was written in his own hand. The script consisted of strange symbols that elevated the reader's consciousness to directly experience the "presence of the gods." The book revealed the true story of the creation of mankind and described an afterlife in the stars for those who followed his teachings.

The Pillars of Hermes

According to legend, Thoth preserved his canon of writings inside two great pillars just before the Great Flood inundated the world. Thousands of years later, the pillars were rediscovered. According to existing texts written by Egyptian priests, one of the pillars was discovered outside the city of Heliopolis, and the other was unearthed near Thebes.

The massive columns were covered with sacred hieroglyphics. When first discovered, they were referred to as the "Pillars of the Gods of the Dawning Light." The pillars were eventually moved to a secret temple dedicated to the First Gods. Some texts indicate that this location was the Temple of Amun in Siwa, which is the oldest temple in Egypt. Only priests and pharaohs were allowed to view the sacred objects and scrolls.

Some evidence suggests the pillars really existed. Not only were they described in scrolls dating back to 1550 B.C.E., but they also were periodically put on public display and have been mentioned by credible sources throughout history. Solon, the Greek legislator and writer, studied them firsthand and noted that they memorialized the destruction of an ancient advanced civilization. The great historian Herodotus encountered the two pillars in a secret Egyptian temple he visited in 400 B.C.E. "One pillar was of pure gold," said Herodotus, "and the other was as of emerald, which glowed at night with great brilliancy." Because Hermes is the Greek name for Thoth, he named them the "Pillars of Hermes."

The mysterious Pillars of Hermes were said to have been viewed by Alexander the Great, Achilles Tatius, Dio Chrysostom, and Laertius, and other Roman and Greek historians have described them in detail. In *Iamblichus: On the Mysteries*, Thomas Taylor quotes one ancient writer who noted that the two pillars were created before the Great Flood. The Alexandrian scribe Manetho recorded that the pillars contained 36,525 manuscripts written by Thoth, although it should be noted that this figure is the exact number of days in 100 years, which symbolized perfect completion to the Egyptians.

The Emerald Tablet

When opened, Thoth's pillars were said to contain not only many priceless manuscripts, but also a marvelous artifact that has become known as the Emerald Tablet. The green crystalline tablet carried a succinct summary of the Thothian writings and outlined a new philosophy of the Whole Universe.

The priests of Amun kept the tablet and other texts in hiding, but its philosophy filtered down into other writings. Phrases from the Emerald Tablet can be found in the Papyrus of Ani (1250 B.C.E.) and chapters from the *Book of the Dead* (1500 B.C.E.), the Berlin Papyrus No. 3024 (2000 B.C.E.), and other religious scrolls dating between 1000 and 300 B.C.E. One papyrus known as "An Invocation to Hermes," which dates from Hellenic Egypt, actually refers to the tablet: "I know your names in the Egyptian tongue, and your true name as it is written on the Holy Tablet in the holy place at Hermopolis, where you did have your birth."

Not until Alexander the Great conquered Egypt and became its Pharaoh in 332 B.C.E. did knowledge of the tablet's existence spread. Historical documents show that Alexander traveled to Siwa, where he retrieved the writings of Thoth and the tablet. He then took the items with him to Memphis and then on to Hermopolis.

The Emerald Tablet.

The Emerald Tablet

In truth, without deceit, certain, and most veritable.

That which is Below corresponds to that which is Above, and that which is Above corresponds to that which is Below, to accomplish the miracles of the One Thing. And just as all things have come from this One Thing, through the meditation of One Mind, so do all created things originate from this One Thing, through Transformation.

Its father is the Sun; its mother the Moon. The Wind carries it in its belly; its nurse is the Earth. It is the origin of All, the consecration of the Universe; its inherent Strength is perfected, if it is turned into Earth.

Separate the Earth from Fire, the Subtle from the Gross, gently and with great Ingenuity. It rises from Earth to heaven and descends again to Earth, thereby combining within Itself the powers of both the Above and the Below.

Thus will you obtain the Glory of the Whole Universe. All Obscurity will be clear to you. This is the greatest Force of all powers, because it overcomes every Subtle thing and penetrates every Solid thing.

In this way was the Universe created. From this comes many wondrous Applications, because this is the Pattern.

Therefore am I called Thrice Greatest Hermes, having all three parts of the wisdom of the Whole Universe. Herein have I completely explained the Operation of the Sun.

The Treasures of Alexander

The Pillars of Hermes were said to contain over 300 scrolls in addition to the Emerald Tablet, and reports indicate that Alexander moved them to the Temple of Heliopolis in 332 B.C.E. and put them on public display. Researcher Manly P. Hall found fragments of a letter from one traveler who had seen the Emerald Tablet in Heliopolis. "It is a precious stone, like an emerald," wrote the man, "whereon these characters are represented in base-relief, not engraved into the stone. It is esteemed above 2,000 years old. Plainly, the matter of this emerald had once been in a fluid state like melted glass, and had been cast in a mold, and to this flux the artist had given the hardness of a natural and genuine emerald, by his art."

Hermetic scholars believe that Alexander built the great library at Alexandria primarily to house and study the Thothian materials, and the writings of a scribe from the Temple of Heliopolis confirmed that view. His name was Manetho, which means "Gift of Thoth," and he was one of the first scribes allowed access to the contents of the pillars. He wrote that the writings were more than 9,000 years old and contained the sum of all knowledge. Unfortunately, only a few of Manetho's works survived the burning of the great library at Alexandria. Some of his letters to Ptolemy II survived, as well as one of his books, called *Sothis*. In that book, Manetho wrote: "After the Great Flood, the hieroglyphic texts written by Thoth were translated from the sacred language into Greek and deposited in books in the sanctuaries of Egyptian temples."

def•i•ni•tion

Hermetic refers to the writings of Hermes, the Greek god and mythic alchemist associated with Thoth. Known for his ability to keep secrets, Hermes had the magical power to seal treasure chests so that nothing could get inside. Our term hermetically sealed (meaning airtight or impenetrable) refers to this ability.

Manetho wrote that the magical *Book of Thoth*, written in the hand of Thoth himself, was kept in a locked gold box in the inner sanctuary of the Temple at Hermopolis, and only one priest at a time was entrusted with the key. According to some historians, an occult brotherhood known as the "Sons of Horus" was formed before the Arab invasion of Egypt to preserve Thoth's book and his other teachings, as well as the complete works of Manetho. The alchemist Clement of Alexandria was given access to the secret documents around 170 C.E., but that is the last recorded reference to this original material.

The Fate of the Emerald Tablet

When Alexander left Egypt in 331 B.C.E., he headed north to Cappadocia and Mesopotamia. According to some reports, he took the treasures from the Pillars of Hermes and stored them in an underground cavern in Cappadocia. Alexander went on to conquer all the remaining territory from Babylonia to India, but died on the return trip in 323 B.C.E. Alexander's final wish was to be buried near the temple at Siwa in Egypt, but his tomb has never been found.

The legend picks up again in Cappadocia in 32 C.E., when a young boy named Balinas was exploring caves outside the city of Tyana and discovered the ancient texts hidden by Alexander. The precocious lad took a five-year vow of silence as he absorbed the materials and then sought out teachers versed in Hermetic philosophy to complete his education. He became known as Apollonius of Tyana and was renowned for his magical skills and healing abilities. He is said to have returned the tablet to Alexandria around 70 C.E. and made the enlightened city his home. He wrote most of his books in Alexandria, though he continued to travel the world, inspiring everyone he met with his great wisdom.

As for the Emerald Tablet, a few reports record it was buried for safe-keeping in a vault on the Giza plateau around 400 C.E., but no trace of it has ever been found. No one knows for sure if there is such an artifact as the Emerald Tablet, but several expeditions have been undertaken to search for it.

From the Alchemist

The earliest surviving translation of the Emerald Tablet is in the Arabic *Book of Balinas the Wise on Causes,* which was written around 700 C.E. Several Arabic translations made their way to Europe with the Moorish invasion of Spain in 771 C.E. The first Latin translation appeared in 1140 in a book by Johannes Hispalensis called *Book of the Secrets of Creation.* After the alchemist Albertus Magnus issued several more translations in the mid-1200s, the Emerald Tablet spread like wildfire. Most European alchemists had a copy and constantly referred to "the secret formula" it contained.

The Legend of Thoth/Hermes

In the history of alchemy, the line between myth and reality has always been blurred. To the Egyptians, Thoth, the father of alchemy, was a divine being, the custodian of all knowledge, and intermediary between heaven and Earth. However, several modern authors have looked at the evidence and concluded that Thoth was a real person—a survivor from the lost continent of Atlantis or even an extraterrestrial. Yet his mythic status cannot be denied. The Romans identified Thoth with Mercury, their winged god who carried messages between gods and men. In fact, nearly every ancient culture has some mythic figure that can be associated with Thoth.

To the Greeks, Thoth became Hermes, a priest, philosopher, and alchemist who lived in Egypt around the time of Moses. His Latin name, Hermes Trismegistus, means "thrice greatest Hermes" and refers to his unique mastery of all three levels of reality—the physical, spiritual, and mental planes of Earth, heaven, and everything between. He was viewed as a gentle teacher, much more accessible than Thoth. In fact, 13 manuscripts known as the "Corpus Hermeticum" are attributed to him. These alchemical and esoteric teachings from the Alexandrian period were unknown in the West until 1471, when the Italian astrologer Marsilio Ficino translated them into Latin.

Many alchemists believed Hermes Trismegistus was a real person who supposedly lived for centuries and traveled throughout the world. Because so many later authors wrote under his name, it may have seemed like Hermes lived for hundreds of years. Nevertheless, historical documents attest to his presence in Ceylon, India, and Babylonia, where the Arabs venerated him as the first person to have shared his knowledge of the art of alchemy.

The Staff of Hermes

The primary symbol of Hermes is the *caduceus*, and a strange Greek legend relates how he came to possess it. One day a Greek seer named Tiresias was hiking on Mount Kyllene and discovered two snakes copulating alongside the road. In an effort to sepa-rate the snakes, he stuck his walking staff between them. Immediately, Tiresias was turned into a woman and remained so for seven years, until once again he found two copulating serpents and separated them with his staff. At that moment, Tiresias transformed back into a man. The magical staff, complete with the entwined snakes, was considered too dangerous for anyone to use and was hidden in a cave on Mount Kyllene. The cave, marked by an upright stone phallus, would eventually become the birthplace and home of Hermes. While still a young man, he found the caduceus and eventually learned to harness its power for healing.

def•i•ni•tion

The **caduceus** is a staff with two serpents entwined in opposite directions around it. They were considered the most fundamental form and, because they shed their skins, were thought to possess the secret of immortality. The coiled serpent symbolizes the divine fire or reservoir of life force in the body. The caduceus is often shown with two wings, which represents the purified or ascended life force.

The caduceus bears a striking resemblance to the double-helix of proteins that make up DNA, which is the basic blueprint of all life. Several modern authors have suggested that this similarity is a clue that Thoth or someone associated with him manipulated our genetic structure to speed up human evolution within the last 40,000 years.

Today, Hermes' staff has become the chief logo of the medical profession, and there are certainly more representations of the Hermetic symbol in the world today than at any other time in history. Scholars insist it all began with the Greek healer Asclepius, who adopted the caduceus to symbolize healing, though the connection goes back much farther to the original Hermes. The Ebers Papyrus, a 68-foot-long scroll that is the oldest surviving book in the world, tells us: "Man's guide is Thoth, who bestows on him the gifts of speech, who makes the books and illumines those who are learned therein, and the physicians who follow him, that they may work cures."

Hermetic Philosophy

The esoteric teachings of Thoth and Hermes make up the philosophical foundations of alchemy, and these ideas are summarized in the Emerald Tablet. Take a moment to read the tablet, and try to absorb its meaning before consulting any other sources. It often helps to rewrite the tablet in your own words. Nearly every medieval alchemist from Albertus Magnus to Isaac Newton had his own version of the Emerald Tablet that guided him in his work.

Perhaps the easiest way to grasp the principles expressed in the Emerald Tablet is by viewing them pictorially. Renaissance alchemists spent many hours meditating on the Hermetic symbols depicted in a stunning engraving called "Tabula Smaragdina," which is Latin for "Emerald Tablet" (see the following figure). Created by artist Matthieu Merian, it was first published in 1618 in Daniel Mylius's *Opus Medico-Chymicum* (*The Medical-Chemical Work*).

The Emerald Tablet engraving.

Let's take a short tour of this engraving to gather some basic insights to deepen your understanding of the Emerald Tablet. The first thing you notice about this engraving is its sharp division into the Above and the Below sections. The Above is the spiritual realm of light and divine union, while the Below is the material realm of matter and duality.

Next, we see two great suns rising over the horizon. The larger sun in the background is the ineffable One Mind, whose rays encompass the whole universe. In front of this is a smaller sun known as "Mind the Maker." This we can think of as the mind of nature or the physical laws of the created world.

"Mind the Maker" is an important and controversial Hermetic concept that would have gotten you burnt at the stake if you had spoken of it in the Middle Ages. It implies that the ultimate god does not directly participate in our world. Instead, the Word of God was projected into our reality like a template or computer program—what the Emerald Tablet calls the Pattern. In the drawing, these crystallized thoughts of God are represented by the angels embedded in the smaller sun.

This humanistic concept does not mean the alchemists did not believe in God. On the contrary, they sought to reveal and perfect the original divine light in everything. This is the true nature of the Great Work, and it begins Below in the duality of matter.

From the Alchemist

The principles in the Emerald Tablet are recognized by many modern movements, such as Eckankar and *The Secret,* and are a part of the teachings of most esoteric organizations, such as the Rosicrucians and Golden Dawn. For instance, one famous text on Freemasonry, *Morals and Dogma,* says: "He who desires to attain the understanding of the Grand Word and the possession of the Great Secret … must take, for the key of the allegories, the single dogma of Hermes, contained in his Tablet of Emerald."

We see the duality of our existence in the division of the Below into left and right sections. On the left is the daytime realm of Solar energy and masculine symbols. On the right is the nighttime realm of Lunar energy and feminine symbols.

At the center of the Below is the hermaphroditic Hermes, who wields two starry axes. He has cut the chains that bind us to world Below and realizes the full power of the archetypal forces Above.

At the heart of the engraving is a bull's-eye target depicting the One Thing of the universe. The seven layers of this sphere must be peeled away like an onion to reveal the hidden essence or soul of matter.

The Least You Need to Know

◆ The mythic origins of alchemy go back to ancient Egypt during a period known as Zep Tepi.

◆ Thoth is considered the father of alchemy, and his teachings were passed down to us sealed in the fabled Pillars of Hermes.

◆ Hermes is the Greek god associated with Thoth and was known as Hermes Trismegistus in medieval Europe.

◆ The Emerald Tablet is a succinct summary of Hermetic philosophy and alchemical principles.

3

The Land of Khem

In This Chapter

- ◆ The early history of alchemy
- ◆ Alexandria: world center of alchemy
- ◆ The destruction of alchemy manuscripts
- ◆ The growth of alchemy in China and India
- ◆ The Arabs saved alchemy

The word alchemy derives from the Arabic phrase *Al-Khemia*, which literally means from the land of Khem. *Khem* is an Egyptian term that describes the fertile black soil found in the Nile River delta. So the Arab Al-Khemia referred to the origin of alchemy in Egypt and alludes to the mysterious and secretive black arts of the ancient Egyptians. Our word chemistry did not appear until the seventeenth century; it derives from the same root but has come to be associated with only the laboratory side of the alchemist's work.

The Land of Khem was the birthplace and home to alchemy for at least 5,000 years. Specifically, scholars consider Egyptian alchemy to span the centuries from 5000 B.C.E. to 350 B.C.E. This was followed by a period of Greek alchemy in Egypt from the arrival of Alexander the Great in

332 B.C.E. to the Arabian invasion in 642 C.E. Arabian alchemy flourished for another 500 years before the heyday of alchemy began in Europe.

The inhabitants of the Land of Khem were amazingly advanced in metallurgy and chemical knowledge. Egyptian goldsmiths had mastered their craft by 3000 B.C.E., and sophisticated operations such as the smelting, fusion, alloying, and precise weighing of gold and other metals are depicted on tomb walls dating from 2500 B.C.E.

Egypt's eastern desert is rich in gold deposits, and maps dating back to 1400 B.C.E. show gold mining regions there. By 1300 B.C.E., Egyptian craftsmen were producing gold and copper of greater than 99.9 percent purity. From the earliest times, Egyptians were also skilled at such alchemical processes as extraction of essential oils from plants; dying and glass-tinting; and the fermentation of fruit juices, honey, and malt beverages. How the Egyptians became so advanced in such a short time is one of the greatest mysteries of alchemy.

Secrets of Priests and Craftsmen

To the priests and craftsmen of ancient Egypt, the principles of alchemy were a divine revelation whose secrecy they had to maintain at all costs. Ostracism and death were the punishments for sharing the sacred wisdom with the common people. Even the pharaohs had to pass through levels of initiation before the secrets were shared with them.

As stated in Chapter 2, the ancient teachings of Thoth were kept concealed from the people until Alexander the Great became pharaoh of Egypt in 332 B.C.E. According to early historians, Alexander made the dangerous journey across the Libyan Desert to the Temple of Amun at Siwa where the writings of Thoth were hidden, took the tablets and scrolls to the temple of Heliopolis near modern Cairo, and stored them in the sacred archives there.

After securing the scrolls, Alexander personally laid out the boundaries for the new city of Alexandria, where a library would be built to house and study the texts. He then assembled a diverse group of priests, alchemists, and other scholars to prepare Greek translations.

Alexandria: Center of Ancient Alchemy

Alchemists from around the world visited Alexandria to consult the library's scrolls and confer with other alchemists. Even the earliest Greek alchemical writings from

Alexandria are full of references to Chinese, Indian, Babylonian, Hebrew, and Persian alchemists and their traditions. Eastern influences of meditation, mind development, Vedic astrology, and Oriental magic are obvious in the writings of the Alexandrians. This high-minded merging of philosophies invigorated and strengthened alchemy, allowing it to survive the coming Dark Ages and bloom in medieval Europe.

The first alchemist of record in Alexandria was Bolos of Mendes, a sorcerer who lived there around 300 B.C.E. He was a follower of Democritus, a Greek philosopher who originated the atomic theory of matter. Bolos wrote important treatises on the techniques of tingeing metals, chemistry, and astrology and presented a system of sympathetic magic based on how deeply aware the sorcerer could become of the hidden forces of nature.

In Bolos's most influential work, *On Natural and Mystical Things*, he describes the discovery of an ancient text hidden within a great column that dealt with the universal harmony of nature. Many believe this is the first recorded reference to the Emerald Tablet (see Chapter 2).

Bolos is credited with creating the science of alchemy by joining philosophy and theory with practical demonstrations and experimentation. He wrote that there existed four branches of practical experimentation: Gold, Silver, Precious Stones, and Dyes.

From the Alchemist

One passage from *On Natural and Mystical Things* became a fundamental motto of alchemists for the next 2,000 years: "Nature rejoices in Nature; Nature conquers Nature; Nature masters Nature." The revered alchemist Zosimus explained how Bolos's motto applies to the work of alchemists, who are themselves part of nature: "We can proceed with the transmutation of common metal into noble metal by working alloys or by purifying the metals, while at the same time basing ourselves on the affinity between metals and knowing their sympathies and antipathies. Raw material, sympathy, transmutation by qualitative change of the colors: we have thus the principles that constitute alchemy."

Another sorcerer-alchemist from Alexandria and a contemporary of Bolos was the Persian Ostanes of Medes. He was one of the first alchemists to identify the elixir of life, which he described as a "divine water" that cured all maladies. He had a great influence on early alchemists and is mentioned many times in early scrolls as an authority on alchemy. He personally taught other alchemists—including Pseudo-Democritus, who wrote many early alchemical texts—and he would eventually become the personal alchemist for Alexander the Great.

The most famous and respected of the Alexandrian alchemists was Zosimus. Arabian alchemists revered him as "the universal wise man with the brilliant flame." In his alchemical experiments, Zosimus worked closely with his sister Theosebeia, and around 250 C.E., he wrote a 28-volume alchemy encyclopedia. Fortunately, most of his encyclopedia survived the burning of the Great Library of Alexandria and provides us with much of our knowledge of how the ancients practiced their art. Zosimus wrote many other books, including *The Book of Images*, and important commentaries on astrology, magic, and theology.

Like Bolos, Zosimus noted that alchemy had its roots in sacred hieroglyphs engraved on ancient pillars, but he emphasized that it was absolutely forbidden to divulge the exact texts to the uninitiated.

Zosimus was a member of the Gnostics, an early group of Christians who formed in the first century. He believed that one could only obtain true knowledge of the divine by direct experience and not from religious authorities. He felt that the Great Work of alchemy was to perfect the alchemist himself, and that such work would bring out the divinity in both man and nature. With Zosimus, Alexandrian alchemy took a new direction that emphasized its mystical principles.

Another important figure in Alexandria was Manetho, a priest and scribe who lived there during the reigns of Ptolemy I and Ptolemy II (323–246 B.C.E.). Records indicate Manetho supervised many important religious projects in Egypt and lived for more than 80 years. Among Manetho's surviving books are *The Sacred Book*, *On Antiquity and Religion*, and the *Digest of Physics*. He also wrote an encyclopedia of Egyptian history that is considered the most complete and authoritative on record.

Manetho's name literally means "Gift of Thoth," but he was also known by the name *Maani Djehuti*, which means "I have seen Thoth." As noted in Chapter 2, Manetho was instrumental in translating and interpreting the ancient scrolls attributed to Thoth and is believed by some to have been the first translator of the Emerald Tablet.

Two female alchemists in Alexandria earned the lasting respect of alchemists down through the ages. The first, Maria Prophetissa (also known as Mary the Jewess), lived around 200 B.C.E. She invented many early alchemical devices, including the *Bain Marie*, "Mary's Bath," which is a double-boiler water bath that evenly distributes heat to substances. She also invented the kerotakis apparatus, a closed vessel in which thin leaves of copper and other metals were exposed to the action of various vapors, such as sulfur and mercury. She discovered hydrochloric acid and was famous for her Mary's Black, which she formed by fusing sulfur with a lead-copper alloy.

Maria Prophetissa.

The second famous female alchemist in Alexandria and a contemporary of Maria Prophetissa was Kleopatra, who should not be confused with Cleopatra the Hellenic Queen of Egypt. This Kleopatra is credited with inventing the chief laboratory apparatus of alchemists down through history—the alembic or stillhead. Distillation allowed alchemists to purify substances into their most essential components and is the most important operation in chemistry.

Kleopatra's philosophical writings on alchemy stressed the importance of bringing inanimate substances and chemicals to life, and she compared the work of alchemy to the creation of a fetus in the womb.

Greek Philosophy and Alchemy

Not only were the Alexandrian alchemists inventing new equipment and improving ancient techniques, but they also fundamentally altered alchemical philosophy.

Alexander's primary instructor in alchemy was Aristotle, whose theory of the Four Elements found full expression among the alchemists of Alexandria (see Chapter 7).

Aristotle's belief that nature strives toward perfection is clearly part of the alchemical idea that all metals grow toward the perfection of gold within the bowels of the earth. Plato's philosophy that matter was fashioned into its forms by qualities imposed on it from an archetypal realm of ideals also fueled the alchemists' belief in the transformation of the metals.

The Greeks taught that the *microcosm and macrocosm* obeyed the same set of universal laws, and that heavenly bodies could influence events on Earth. In the Emerald Tablet, the idea of the macrocosm is represented by the word "Above" and the idea of the microcosm is represented by the word "Below." The philosophy here is that "All Is One"; that is, the same laws apply to all levels of reality.

def•i•ni•tion

> **Microcosm and macrocosm** is a way of expressing the idea that the same patterns of creation and change are present on all levels of the universe from atoms to the stars. Microcosm is from the Greek words for small, *micro*, and world, *cosmos*. Macrocosm is from their word for large, *macro*, and world, *cosmos*.

Another Greek idea that became part of the philosophy of alchemy was the belief that nature itself is alive and aware and participates in changes in its environment. In other words, there is a divine presence in the world responsible for the changes we experience. Thus, the alchemists considered all matter to be alive and believed any substance could be transformed and perfected if that indwelling spirit, which was thought of as a tiny spark of light, could be purified and released. In their writings, the alchemists referred to this spark of life concealed in the darkness of matter as the Magisterium, the Grand Elixir, or the Philosopher's Stone (see Chapter 9).

The Concept of Transmutation

One of the biggest philosophical changes in alchemy took place during the Greek period in Egypt near the end of the fourth century B.C.E. and had to do with the idea of the transformation of metals. Today we refer to the permanent transformation of one metal into another as *transmutation*. However, it is apparent from surviving manuscripts that the Egyptians judged metals by the physical qualities of color, hardness, texture, and weight, and if a metal looked like gold, they considered it gold.

As mentioned earlier, the Egyptians were unsurpassed in the arts of dying fabrics, tinting glass and gemstones, and tingeing metals. To change the colors and textures of metals, they dipped them into acids and other chemical solutions, alloyed or gilded them with different metals, or treated them with a variety of polishes and secret compounds. In changing the appearance of metals, however, the Egyptians were not consciously faking things. They really believed the metals could actually be changed into one another by manipulating their visible qualities.

For instance, in the Leiden Papyrus, an alchemical scroll written in 727 B.C.E., there are numerous recipes for the coloring and gilding of metals, but the concept of actual transmutation does not arise. The same thing is true in Bolos's *On Natural and Mystical Things* and other early alchemical manuscripts.

By the fourth century B.C.E. in Egypt, however, a distinct change occurred in the way alchemists described the transformation of metals. The practical recipes on tingeing and gilding metals were gone. Instead, the coloring and alloying of metals were interpreted in spiritual terms and the consciousness of the alchemist seemed to be taking part in the chemical operations.

In a long commentary to the librarian priest of the Serapeum in Alexandria, the alchemist Synesius described this sudden change in attitude. Although the methods seem obscure and mystical, there's no doubt the new generation of alchemists were convinced their techniques produced genuine and permanent transformation. The concept of transmutation was born.

Of course, the change from the practical to the mystical approach to transformation of metals was probably not as sudden as it appears in the manuscripts. In all likelihood, the change in attitude was the result of a mixing of philosophies in Alexandria that took centuries to assimilate.

Destruction of the Alexandrian Texts

While alchemy flourished around the world at the beginning of the first millennium, the secretive activities of the alchemists and a deteriorating political climate in Egypt spelled disaster for the Great Library at Alexandria.

The first assault came because of a conflict between the Egyptian co-rulers Ptolemy XIII and his sister Cleopatra. The Roman ruler Julius Caesar arrived in 48 B.C.E. to resolve the conflict and named Cleopatra the sole ruler. But her brother blockaded the port of Alexandria and war broke out, resulting in the Great Library catching fire with an estimated 400,000 manuscripts lost. The 300,000 remaining manuscripts of the Great Library were then moved to an adjoining temple called the Serapeum and to a center for scholars known as the Museum. What remained of the library survived another three centuries. Then in 270 C.E., the Queen of Syria invaded Egypt and occupied Alexandria for two years before the Romans drove her out. During the occupation, the Museum was partly destroyed and more books were lost.

By 275 C.E., the mystical and secretive writings of alchemists in Alexandria had caught the attention of Roman authorities. Finally, in 290 C.E., Emperor Diocletian decreed the destruction of all manuscripts on alchemy in Egypt, which resulted in a further loss of precious original works on alchemy.

Then in 312 C.E., Christianity became the official religion of the Roman Empire, and in 391 C.E., Emperor Theodosius banned all pagan sects. Christian zealots immediately attacked the Serapeum temple library, destroyed nearly all the books, and turned it into a Christian church.

The Museum survived until 415 C.E., when Christian mobs dragged the last librarian out into the street and accused her of being a heretic and teaching Greek philosophy. Using abalone shells, they scraped the flesh from her body while she was still alive.

What remained of the Great Library of Alexandria consisted of fewer than 30,000 volumes, which were moved into a new building for safekeeping. The final straw for the library came when the Arabs conquered Egypt in 642 C.E., and Caliph Umar instructed his men to burn all the remaining books. According to historical accounts, he told his generals: "If these writings of the Greeks agree with the Book of Allah, they are redundant and need not be preserved; if they disagree, they are blasphemous and ought to be destroyed."

The Growth of Alchemy in Asia

Meanwhile, alchemists in China and India, who had been inspired by the writings of the Alexandrians, made great strides in their craft, and from 300 B.C.E. onward, alchemy became very popular throughout Asia. However, both Chinese and Indian alchemy were well developed centuries before the rise of Alexandria.

Alchemy had surfaced in China around 500 B.C.E. and had its roots in Taoism, a system of philosophy that originated with a Hermes-like sage known as Lao Tsu. His teachings became the basis for a tradition of inner alchemy that focused on the transformation of the practitioner's life force (known as *Chi*). The basic premise of this kind of biological alchemy is that humans have only a limited supply of the life force in their bodies. This leaks away through the day-to-day activities of living, but it's possible to accumulate the life force and live for centuries if one understands alchemy.

From the Alchemist

Taoist alchemy rests on the same basic principles revealed in the Emerald Tablet, and there are many possible explanations for these similarities. According to legend, Hermes traveled throughout Asia and lived in what is now Ceylon for some time. There are even some references to Hermes' presence in ancient Indian religious texts. In terms of the Emerald Tablet, the life force or Chi is the One Thing, which is transformed by the "meditation of One Mind." This idea shows up in Taoist alchemy in the principle of Chi follows mind. By learning to focus the light of consciousness, the practitioner hopes to transform and control the life force.

Lao Tsu's alchemy must have worked, for many reports say he lived nearly 200 years. His followers developed a huge body of writings that consisted of over 1,500 manuscripts. Of these, about 500 deal with alchemy.

The Taoist alchemical texts discuss recipes for creating various mineral elixirs, provide descriptions of alchemical apparatus, and give rituals and meditations for purification and focusing of the mind of the alchemist. Taoist alchemists also experimented with the life-giving properties of gold, cinnabar (a sulfur-mercury ore), jade, pearls, lapis lazuli, rubies, and many other minerals, as well as thousands of herbs.

By 300 B.C.E., Chinese alchemists were attempting to transmute base metals into gold but not necessarily for material wealth like so many of their counterparts in the West. The Chinese were focused on extending life and saw gold as an essential ingredient in the much-sought Golden Elixir of Immortality.

One of the most famous Chinese alchemists was Ko Hung, who lived from 283 to 343 C.E. As a child, he was trained in the strict moral doctrines of Confucianism but embraced Taoism as a young man. He became an alchemist and spent the rest of his life searching for the elixir of life. His gentle philosophy was a blend of Confucian ethics and Taoist mysticism that he described in a monumental work called *He Who Holds to Simplicity*.

In one of his alchemical treatises, Ko Hung described the three kinds of alchemy practiced in China. The first, he said, concerned the preparation of a drinkable gold liquid that produced longevity. The second was about producing an artificial cinnabar or red stone that could be projected to perfect any substance instantly. The final kind of alchemy concerned the actual transmutation of base metals into physical gold.

Like the Chinese, the Indian alchemists were conscious of accumulating the life force, which they symbolized as kundalini, a serpent of energy coiled at the base of the spine.

Also, like the Chinese, Indian alchemists associated medicinal gold solutions with longevity and immortality.

def•i•ni•tion

Rasayana is a Sanskrit word that literally means the path, *yana*, of the elixir, *rasa*. It is considered the rejuvenation branch of the ancient Indian health tradition of *ayurveda*, which is another Sanskrit word meaning knowledge, *veda*, of the life force, *ayur*. Rasayana alchemists make mercury cures, gem elixirs, herbal tonics, and other alchemical products sold throughout modern India.

Sanskrit texts mentioning alchemical methods and the elixir of life date back to 1000 B.C.E., but very few original alchemy manuscripts from India still exist. We know the alchemical tradition flourished in India from 900 to 1300 C.E. However, except for an oral tradition that survives in the Tamil communities in southern India, a popular system of health tonics and elixir therapy called *rasayana* is all that remains today.

By 1100 C.E., both Chinese and Indian alchemists were clearly becoming less concerned with practical operations and more focused on the spiritual techniques of transformation. The metals had become identified with various parts of the human body, and the purified essences the alchemists sought to work with were to be found within.

In fact, Taoist adepts began seeing themselves as spiritized essences of the noble metals, whose duty was to work their transmutations in a world of base metals or common mortals. Among Taoist alchemists, there was tremendous optimism that changing the world was really possible. But even as the spirit of alchemy soared to new heights in the Orient, it was nearly extinguished in the West during the Dark Ages.

How the Arabs Saved Alchemy

Although the Arabs destroyed what remained of the Great Library of Alexandria, they were ultimately responsible for preserving alchemical knowledge. As the Arabs established a new civilization throughout Persia, Palestine, Syria, Egypt, Arabia, Asia Minor, North Africa, and eventually Gibraltar and Spain, they assimilated a great deal of diverse cultures in a short period of time and were eager to acquire those cultures' knowledge. From its founding around 750 C.E., Baghdad became a center of learning, and manuscripts from all around the world made their way to the city.

While a handful of the Alexandrian manuscripts made their way to Constantinople, most of the more important works ended up in Arabia. Many Alexandrian alchemical scrolls had already been translated into Arabic, and others were smuggled out of

Egypt after Emperor Diocletian's decree of 290 C.E. Around 400 C.E., a mystical group of Christians known as the Nestorians saved many alchemical manuscripts by taking them to Persia and Arabia for safekeeping. The Sabeans of Harran, a Syrian group of astronomers and alchemists, translated many Alexandrian alchemy texts into their native dialect before they were exiled to Mesopotamia in 489 C.E.

Knowledge of alchemy had spread through Babylon to the Orient around 500 C.E. and finally reached Europe with the Moorish invasion of Spain in 711 C.E. At its peak, the Muslim occupation of Europe encompassed Spain, Gibraltar, and most of Portugal and southern France. Cordoba, in Spain, became the new center of alchemical knowledge, and Muslim, Jewish, and Christian alchemists and mystics all flocked to the city.

Notable alchemists who came to Cordoba to live and work included Maslamah ibn Ahmed, Muhammad ibn Umail, and Moses ben Maimon (also known as Robert of Chester). Like Alexandria, the crossbreeding of ideas in Cordoba resulted in a flood of new ideas. Jewish texts like the *Zohar* (*Book of Splendor*) and the Sepher Jetzirah (*Book of Formation*) gave birth to the Kabbalah, and many lost alchemy manuscripts were retrieved after they were translated back into Latin from Arabian. Finally, with the Crusades, the Templars and other travelers who went to fight for the Holy Land further dispersed the Arabian texts on alchemy throughout Europe.

Arabian Alchemy

The Muslims knew the legend of Thoth, the Hermes of the Greeks, and called him Idris or Hirmis. According to Arabian legend, Hermes was exiled from Egypt and came to Babylon to teach. The Babylonian Hermes wrote at least fifteen new books on alchemy and magic, including *The Great Epistle of the Celestial Spheres*.

Many works by Greek philosophers were among the Arabian alchemical translations. Plato, or "Aflatun," was considered by Arabians to be a great alchemist who invented several devices for use in the laboratory. According to the Arab tradition, Pythagoras acquired his knowledge of mathematics and alchemy from the scrolls found in the Pillars of Hermes. Known as "Fithaghurus" in Arabia, Pathagoras's *Book of Adjustments* became very popular among alchemists.

There were also translations of the works of Archelaos, the teacher of Socrates to whom Arabs attribute the great alchemical treatise *Turba Philosophorum*. Also, translations exist of the oral teachings of Socrates, who was considered a practicing alchemist who successfully generated an artificial life form. Socrates never publicly admitted to being an alchemist and was opposed to writing down any alchemical treatises for fear they would fall into the wrong hands.

Aristotle, who the Arabs called "Aristu," was revered as a great alchemist and scholar. Aristotle wrote a book on alchemy for his student, Alexander the Great, which, by order of Heraclius, was translated into Syrian in 618. Several works by Aristotle survived only in Arabic, including a discourse between him and Alexander called *Epistle of the Great Treasure of God*. The book has three chapters entitled "About the Great Principles of Alchemy," "Alchemic Operations," and "The Elixir." In it, Aristotle reviews the alchemical writing of Hermes, Asclepius, Pythagoras, Plato, Democritus, and Ostanes.

The other writings of the Alexandrian alchemists also became popular in Arabia, and many translations were made. The works of Bolos of Mende and Zosimus were especially popular. A group of Hermetic Muslims called the Brothers of Purity compiled an encyclopedia of alchemical theory and practice in the years between 909 and 965 that consolidated the diverse teachings.

The first Muslim alchemist, Khalid ibn Yazid, was initiated into alchemy by Morienus, a Christian hermit and alchemist who flourished in the 650s. His student Khalid lived from 660 to 704 and wrote several original treatises on alchemy. Khalid's castle became a vibrant center for alchemy in the seventh century, with visiting alchemists sharing their books and discussing their ideas with each other.

Thoth's Tips

Did you know that an Arabian alchemist invented the camera? Ibn al-Haytam, also known as Alhazen, lived from 965 to 1039 and is considered the father of photography for building the first camera, which was basically a sealed dark box with a pinhole lens that projected an image on the back of the box. The Arabs had long before discovered the photosensitive properties of silver compounds (such as silver nitrate and silver chloride) and probably took the first crude photographs. Modern scientists have even speculated that Alhazen's camera design could have been used to create the Shroud of Turin.

One influential Arabian alchemist was Al-Razi, who is known in the West as Rhazes. A Persian alchemist and physician who taught in Baghdad, he lived from 866 to 925. Rhazes was an even more prolific writer than Jabir and authored 33 books on natural science, mathematics, and astronomy, and 48 more on philosophy, logic, and theology. He authored 21 books on alchemy, including his influential *Compendium of Twelve Treatises* and *Secret of Secrets*.

Razi was a very accurate and systematic experimenter, who produced the first classification of metals, chemicals, and other substances. Razi was also known as a compassionate teacher and humanitarian, who personally distributed gifts to the poor and nursed the sick back to health with his own preparations.

Not all alchemists fared well in the Arabian lands. Al-Tughari, a widely respected alchemist born in 1063, worked as a civil servant, but politics proved his undoing, and he was publicly executed in 1121. Before he died, Tughari wrote many important books and poems on alchemy. He claimed to have gotten his esoteric knowledge directly from Hermes, and indeed, his work is very sophisticated and can only be understood by advanced students. Tughari's most famous work is *The Lamps and the Keys*, in which he presents ancient Hermetic teachings and theories of alchemy.

Thanks to Arabian alchemy, the basic laboratory methods of distillation, sublimation, dissolution, calcination, and crystallization were greatly improved and better understood. The refining of metals and alloys was also perfected. Overall, the greatest contribution was the development of chemical apparatus and experimental techniques. The Arabs were meticulous and untiring in their experimentation and made careful written observation of their results. They designed their experiments to gather information and answer specific questions, which represented the true beginning of the scientific method.

The Gibberish of Jabir

The greatest Arabian alchemist was Jabir ibn Hayyan, who lived from 721 to 815 and wrote an astonishing number of books that dealt with every aspect of alchemy. Among his most important works are *Book of the Kingdom, Little Book of the Balances, Book of Mercury,* and *Book of Concentration.* He also translated dozens of alchemy manuscripts and saved many original texts that had been lost when the Great Library of Alexandria was destroyed.

Jabir was a fanatical experimenter, and his practical guides to alchemy included the refining of metals and preparing steel, dying of cloths and leather, the making of varnishes to protect cloth and iron, writing with gold ink from pyrites, glassmaking using manganese dioxide, distilling acetic acid from vinegar, and producing lead carbonate, arsenic, and antimony from their sulfides. Jabir corrected experimental errors and references in the works of Pythagoras, Plato, Aristotle, and other Greek philosophers and developed his own complex numerological system of scientific alchemy.

Jabir the alchemist.

However, Jabir was so careful to conceal the true principles of alchemy that his works rarely made sense to outsiders, and the term "gibberish" originally referred to his writings. Nonetheless, to the initiated, Jabir is still held in the highest esteem.

Jabir believed the metals formed from two primeval forces or exhalations deep in the bowels of the earth. The dry exhalation became sulfur, and the wet exhalation was mercury. The various metals then formed by differing purities and concentrations of sulfur and mercury, and gold formed from the purest and most balanced combination of these two elements. To transform base metals into gold, one must purify and balance their sulfur and mercury. He also popularized the idea of a Philosopher's Stone that would instantly combine the mercury and sulfur of base metals to make gold, and his lifelong quest was to find it.

Tread Carefully

The works of Jabir became widely known in Europe under his Latin name *Geber*, and his works were translated into Latin in the fourteenth century by someone historians now call Pseudo-Geber. Unfortunately, Pseudo-Geber became so enthused about the original Jabir's work that he decided it wouldn't hurt if he published a few of his own books under the illustrious name of Geber. So be forewarned: while Jabir is always Jabir, Geber is not always Jabir.

Jabir's Mercury-Sulfur Theory of the metals was the single greatest advance in alchemical philosophy of the Arabian era. Alexandrian alchemists had planted the seed with their observations of the actions of sulfur and mercury in the kerotakis apparatus. The preparation of the stone of cinnabar (a brilliant red sulfide of mercury) was made by the union of sulfur and mercury in the apparatus, and this process always held a powerful fascination for the Greek alchemists who considered sulfur and mercury "tincturing spirits" because of their ability to color and alloy the metals.

Jabir combined the kerotakis observations with Aristotle's theory that the Elements Earth and Water give rise to smoky and vaporous exhalations deep in the earth. The earthy smoke consisted of Earth burning (changing into Fire), and the watery vapor was Water evaporating (changing into Air). Jabir added to the theory the idea that sulfur and mercury formed as by-products of these primordial exhalations. The range of metals formed when sulfur and mercury recombined in various degrees of purity and proportion. Jabir theorized that the two "tincturing spirits" of sulfur and mercury acted like two dyes that could be mixed to produce a range of colors, or in this case, a range of metals.

The Least You Need to Know

◆ Alexandria was the center for ancient alchemy and source of alchemical manuscripts and ideas for the whole world from 300 B.C.E. to 400 C.E.

◆ Many of the world's most important alchemy manuscripts, including the scrolls of Thoth, were lost in the successive burnings of the Great Library of Alexandria.

◆ The Arabians copied and translated many Alexandrian texts and introduced them to Europe with their invasion of Spain.

◆ The teachings coming out of Alexandria inspired Chinese and Indian alchemists, but they had also developed their own unique traditions earlier.

Medieval Alchemy and the Quest for Gold

In This Chapter

◆ Alchemy in the Dark Ages

◆ The genius of Roger Bacon

◆ The Church's persecution of alchemists

◆ Alchemists Nicolas Flamel and Sir Issac Newton

◆ Puffers: a new class of alchemists

◆ The demise of alchemy and rise of chemistry

After the tumultuous outpouring of alchemical ideas in Alexandria, the craft of alchemy went into a dormant phase and was actively pursued only in Arabia and the East. The West was in the grip of the Dark Ages, a period of stagnate intellectual growth and lack of innovation that lasted from the fall of the Roman Empire (476 C.E.) to the beginning of the second millennium (1000 C.E.).

Arabian invaders brought alchemy back to life in Europe through the infusion of Alexandrian manuscripts and commentaries they brought with them when they crossed over from Morocco in 711 C.E. and occupied Spain for more than 700 years. The Islamic rulers proved very tolerant, and Spain soon became a haven for Jews and other persecuted minorities. The new rulers also encouraged learning in what some historians refer to as a mini-renaissance in Europe.

The Emerald Tablet and other alchemy manuscripts, first translated into Latin in the early 1100s, quickly spread throughout Europe. Scholars eagerly embraced the new ideas, which resulted in a wide dissemination of alchemy books. However, alchemy proved to be a complex tradition full of special jargon and symbolic images, and the ancient craft was not so easily deciphered. Try as they might, early students of alchemy failed to grasp the deeper meanings of the new ideas and preferred literal interpretations that did not require too much thought. In the cryptic, multilevel language of alchemy, interpreting anything literally spelled disaster, so before long, European alchemists were trapped in a quagmire of gibberish and contradictory concepts. Only one literal fact seemed clear, and that was that alchemy was about making gold.

Nevertheless, the early alchemists' attempts to transform base metals into gold resulted in the discovery of acids, alcohols, alloys, and hundreds of new compounds. Alchemy became the leading intellectual movement in Europe, even to the point where some universities started replacing the works of Aristotle with texts attributed to Hermes. This was the heyday of alchemy.

The Beginning of European Alchemy

The first translation of an Arabian alchemy manuscript in Europe was the *Book of the Composition of Alchemy* by Morienus, who had lived in the seventh century. In 1144, Robert of Chester, who translated the *Koran* and introduced algebra and other Arabian teachings to the West, translated this book into Latin.

Soon after Robert's translations began circulating, the floodgates opened, and by 1200, Europe was inundated with hundreds of Arabian books. So much translating was going on that the Archbishop of Toledo in Spain founded a new college completely devoted to making Latin translations of Arabian works. One of his translators, Gerard of Cremona (1114–1187), single-handedly translated 76 manuscripts, including important alchemy books by Avicenna and Jabir.

Many writers were also ready to interpret the confusing alchemy texts for the eager Europeans. Writers, such as Vincent of Beauvais and Bartholomew the Englishman, added long commentaries to the Latin translations of Arabian alchemy works, and other authors wrote whole books trying to explain what the Arabs were saying.

Jewish scholar Moses Maimonides (1135–1204) wrote a popular commentary on alchemy entitled *Guide for the Perplexed.*

Before long, Europe was producing its own alchemists. The first of these was a Swabian monk by the name of Albertus Magnus (Albert the Great), who lived from 1193 to 1280. Albertus was a true genius, so skilled in all forms of knowledge that he was called "Doctor Universalis." He became an adept in alchemy, and his labwork resulted in the discovery of potassium lye and many other useful compounds.

Through his meticulous observations of the metals, Albertus realized the regularity of properties charted in the modern periodic table, in which the characteristics of the elements repeat in an eightfold cycle. "The metals are similar in their essence, and differ only in their form," he summarized. "One may pass easily from one to another, following a definite cycle."

Albertus taught at several universities, including in Freiburg, Cologne, and Paris, and initiated other Europeans into alchemy. One of his students was St. Thomas Aquinas, who was one of the world's greatest philosophers. Aquinas popularized the works of Aristotle and wrote a monumental compendium of religious philosophy called *Summa Theologica.* He is also thought to have created the influential text *Aurora Consurgens,* which is an alchemical interpretation of the "Song of Songs."

Aquinas was a prolific writer, but after having a mystical experience in December 1273, he never wrote another word. As a result, several of his most important works end abruptly in the middle of a paragraph. He told his fellow monks that during meditation he had seen a vision of Sophia, the divine feminine principle suppressed by the patriarchal Church. He said he had found the Philosopher's Stone in the wisdom of Sophia, and after that profound experience, everything he had written seemed worthless, like so much straw in comparison.

The Wizardry of Roger Bacon

Educated at Oxford and Parisian universities, Roger Bacon was another medieval genius who mastered a number of different disciplines. Like Leonardo da Vinci, Bacon created drawings and models of airplanes, helicopters, tanks, submarines, and other inventions centuries ahead of his time. He drew one of the first complete maps of the world and created the more exact Gregorian calendar we still use today. He also built early microscopes and telescopes and constructed a towering observatory that survived for centuries.

Roger Bacon.

Bacon was initiated into alchemy by a mysterious Frenchman named Master Peter, whom Bacon often referred to as the "Lord of Experimentation." Others suggest that Albertus Magnus may have initiated Bacon in Paris, but whoever taught him, Bacon quickly became Europe's leading alchemist. He shared formulae for numerous useful compounds, including gunpowder, and produced powerful tinctures and elixirs. He is also said to have achieved successful transmutations of the metals.

From the Alchemist

In Mirror of Alchemy, Roger Bacon described his practical view of alchemy: "Alchemy is a science teaching how to transform any kind of metal into another through the use of the proper medicine. Alchemy therefore is about how to make and compound a certain medicine, called the Elixir, such that when it is cast upon metals or imperfect bodies of any kind, it fully perfects them in the very projection. The first principles of this Elixir can be found in nature and are called Sulfur and Mercury, and all metals and minerals are begotten of these two. But I must tell you that nature always intends and strives to the perfection of gold, yet there are many accidents coming between the metals that change their purity."

Unfortunately, Bacon was so far ahead of his time that his contemporaries believed he was in league with the devil, and his antisocial behavior did not help dispel the rumors. He was said to have created a talking head of brass that revealed dark secrets to him and a mirror in which he could see into the future.

Although he was a Franciscan monk with a Doctorate in Divinity from Oxford, Bacon was constantly in trouble with the Church, which kept a close eye on his activities. In 1257, a Church court accused him of practicing sorcery and placed him under house arrest in Oxford for the rest of his life.

Pope Clement IV released him from his sentence in 1267 on the condition that Bacon write down all his knowledge in one book. The result was a vast compendium of mathematics, science, and philosophy called the *Opus Majus* (*The Major Work*). In it, Bacon summarized all branches of science and proposed they were all part of a single true philosophy that had been lost to mankind.

Bacon continued to criticize the Church and even declared that the ancient civilizations of Egypt and Greece were morally superior to the Christian world. Not surprisingly, he was sentenced to prison for heresy in 1278, but was released 14 years later by the head of the Franciscan order after Bacon shared certain alchemical secrets with him. In his typically defiant fashion, Bacon immediately began work on *Compendium Theologiae*, a book about the theological errors and faults of Catholicism. His superiors were incensed at his impudence, but this time, because he had an ally in the head of the Franciscan order, he avoided prison.

The Church never forgave Roger Bacon, and his works are still banned. When he died in 1294, his fellow monks nailed all the books in his library to their shelves and left them to rot unopened.

Alchemy and the Church

Roger Bacon's run-ins with Church authorities were typical of the relationship between alchemists and religious authorities in the Middle Ages and Renaissance. To avoid conflicts, some alchemists deliberately concealed their work in Christian terminology. For instance, the word "Christ" was often used to refer to the Philosopher's Stone, the spark of life concealed in the darkness of matter (see Chapter 9). Other alchemists stopped publishing their ideas or went into hiding.

But many alchemists would not compromise their principles. Alchemist and mathematician Giordano Bruno is a good example. He gave public lectures on the principles of the Emerald Tablet and portrayed the universe as a living presence full of alchemical influences. Declaring the tablet's "Operation of the Sun" as the grand symbol of all natural processes, he boldly asserted that the sun was the center of the cosmos, in direct violation of Church dogma. Then he went so far as to assert that the universe was infinite and contained many other worlds that harbored intelligent life.

That declaration was too much for the Church, and in 1576, they attempted to arrest him on charges of heresy. Bruno, who was a Dominican priest, got wind of the action against him and fled. But the Church pursued him all across Europe as he continued to publish his heretical manuscripts. Finally, the priests of the Inquisition caught up with him in 1592 and began a seven-year trial, during which they listed every single blasphemous statement Bruno ever wrote and demanded he recant each one. When he refused to recant something he had said, they tortured him mercilessly. Still, he refused to take back anything he had said or written. When the Inquisitors realized they could not break him, they sentenced him to death, and on February 8, 1600, a gag was tied tightly around Bruno's tongue, and he was burned alive in public.

The Church was always suspicious of alchemists' preoccupation with meditation and spiritual development. The chillingly unsympathetic position of the Church in that regard was read into court records during the heresy trial of Miguel de Molinos in Rome in 1687. Molinos was an advocate of meditation and quiet contemplation, but he crossed the line when he asserted that anyone could practice prayer and meditation in the presence of God in the privacy of his own home. According to the representative of the Pope, the duty of the Church was only to preserve ritual and maintain the physical presence of the Church and not to invoke the spiritual enlightenment of individuals. The Church banned all of Molinos's writings and sentenced him to life in prison, where he died nine years later.

Of course, the Church's fury was not directed just against alchemists and people seeking spiritual development. Anyone who healed with herbs or extolled the virtues of natural cures was accused of practicing the black arts. The Church had declared that the devil caused all disease, which could only be cured by exorcisms performed by priests. Anyone else was interfering with the will of God.

It has been estimated that more than 3 million people were burned at the stake during the Middle Ages. Girls could be tortured for witchcraft from the age of 9, and boys from the age of 10. Homosexuals were sometimes thrown into the fires of burning witches. In fact, the derogatory term "faggot" originally referred to small logs used to start fires. The Church also proclaimed that all cats were demons to be burned along with witches. Cats were imprisoned alive in the walls of buildings to ward off evil spirits, and at Easter, cats were locked in wicker baskets and thrown into bonfires.

These Church practices killed so many cats that the rat population surged, which contributed to the rapid spread of the Black Death (bubonic plague) in the fourteenth century. Nearly half the population of Europe perished—including at least one Pope and hundreds of Inquisitors.

Medieval and Renaissance Alchemy

The Black Death had another unforeseen consequence. It gave rise to the great need for medicines, and alchemists were at the cutting edge in the search for new cures. These alchemists produced many herbal tinctures and tonics that provided relief to diseased people, and the silver- and mercury-based antibiotics created by alchemists were the only effective tools for the treatment of syphilis, pneumonia, infections, and the plague.

Arnold of Villanova was a Spanish alchemist who became a leader of medical alchemy in the late thirteenth century. His tonics cured many ailments, and his elixirs were said to rejuvenate body tissue and increase longevity. He treated several national leaders and popes, although he was briefly imprisoned in Paris for his heretical views on the alchemical nature of the Holy Trinity.

Paracelsus, one of the greatest alchemists of all time, is considered the founder of modern medicine, because he began using chemicals (drugs) in the treatment of disease. His hybrid of alchemy and medicine, which he named *iatrochemistry*, became very popular in the sixteenth and seventeenth centuries.

def•i•ni•tion

latrochemistry is a branch of alchemy that merged chemistry and medicine. The word comes from the Greek *iatros*, doctor, and literally means doctor-chemistry. latrochemists believed that health was dependent on keeping a specific balance of bodily fluids that could be controlled by understanding the effect of chemicals in the body.

Nicolas Flamel's Powder of Projection

Another alchemist who benefited the infirm and diseased people of the Middle Ages was Nicolas Flamel. However, he was no doctor, nor did he produce miraculous cures. Instead, the penniless bookseller suddenly became very rich and gave huge sums of money and property to charities. He also founded several free hospitals, free schools for the blind, and homes for the poor throughout France. His explanation for his new-found wealth was that he had discovered the secret of making gold.

Nicolas Flamel was well educated in the Hermetic arts, had been initiated into alchemy, and had a driving passion to discover the Philosopher's Stone. His bookstore was full of alchemy books, and he was always on the lookout for new alchemy texts to add to his library. One day, a young Jewish man came to him with a rare alchemy book to sell, and Flamel gladly paid him the requested price of 2 florins. This was during a period in history when Jewish people were being expelled from France and many of them were selling treasured possessions before fleeing to safety in Islamic Spain.

From the Alchemist

The house Nicolas Flamel built in 1407 still stands at 51 rue de Montmorency in Paris. It is the oldest house in the city and was renovated in 2007. The documents of his life still exist in the public records of Paris. His birth and death certificates show he was born in 1330 and died in 1418. His marriage contract to his wife Pernelle, his last will and testament, deeds of properties he gave to charity, financial records of his many monetary gifts, and commissions of monuments to his memory are all recorded for anyone to view.

The curious book had an ancient binding of worked copper, on which were engraved curious diagrams and certain characters, some of which were Greek and Hebrew and others unknown. The pages of the book were not parchment but were the bark of young trees covered with script written with an iron point. The pages were divided into groups of seven and consisted of three parts separated by a page showing a strange and unintelligible diagram.

The edges of the book were covered in gold leaf, and the title page listed the author as "Abraham the Jew—Prince, Priest, Levite, Astrologer, and Philosopher." There were curses against anyone who read the book who was unworthy of its contents, and every page carried the word Maranatha!, which was a Syrian expression used by Jews of the time as a curse on their enemies. It meant literally, "the Lord cometh to execute vengeance on you."

Despite his great learning, Flamel could not make sense of the book. He even copied pages from the book, displayed them in his store, and sent them to experts hoping someone might understand parts of them. After 21 years of trying to decipher the book, Flamel decided to travel to Spain to seek the help of Jewish scholars who had settled there. Flamel left the book in safekeeping with his wife and only took a handful of pages copied from the book. He hoped to entice someone to make the journey back to Paris with him to help translate the entire book.

In Leon, Flamel met an elderly Jewish scholar who was familiar with the book of Abraham the Jew and wanted very much to see it for himself, but the man died on their return journey. Fortunately, the scholar had recognized the script on the copied pages as ancient Chaldean and translated several pages. That was enough for Flamel and his wife to begin translating the remaining pages, and three years later they finished the complete translation.

According to his diaries, Flamel followed the instructions of Abraham the Jew and changed a half-pound of mercury first into silver and then into pure gold. Simultaneously, as Flamel put it, he "accomplished the same transmutation in my soul." After only three transmutations of mercury into gold, Flamel was rich beyond his dreams, yet he kept none for himself. Instead, he gave it away to charity. At nearly all his charities, Flamel commissioned strange stones or plaques containing alchemical symbols. Alchemists still make the pilgrimage to view mysterious symbols at Saint-Jacques-la-Boucherie Church, the Cemetery of the Innocents, and other works commissioned by Flamel.

Flamel continued his lifelong labor of copying manuscripts and studying alchemy, but soon lost interest in making gold. Because he saw his fellow alchemists ruined by the love of gold, he locked away Abraham's book and never shared its contents with anyone. He felt that the physical transmutations in his lab had started a greater spiritual gold growing within him and his wife, Pernelle, that was worth more than any material possession.

So he continued to live the quiet life of a scholar, wrote many important books on alchemy, and along with his wife lived a long, vigorous life into his 80s. He carefully planned how he wanted his wife and himself buried. He also had his tombstone prepared beforehand. It shows a bright sun above a key and a closed book in the middle of various figures. Many have taken this to mean that Flamel chose not to share the key to alchemy with an impure world. His tombstone can still be seen at his gravesite in Paris at the Musee de Cluny at the end of the nave of the Saint-Jacques-la-Boucherie Church. After the death of Flamel and his wife, their house, monuments, and even his grave were nearly destroyed by people searching for gold or alchemical secrets.

Flamel bequeathed his library to a nephew named Perrier, whom he had initiated into alchemy. Perrier kept the family secrets, and Flamel's library was passed down from generation to generation. One of his descendents named Dubois demonstrated what he called his illustrious ancestor's powder of projection in the presence of Louis XIII and successfully transmuted leaden balls into gold.

The ruthless Cardinal de Richelieu heard of the Flamel demonstrations and imprisoned Dubois for questioning. The cardinal eventually condemned him to death and seized all of his property, including the book of Abraham the Jew. He also ordered Flamel's original home searched and his coffin pried open. According to reports from the time, no body was found.

The cardinal built an alchemical laboratory at the Chateau of Rueil, which he often visited to study the manuscript and try to understand the hieroglyphs to discover the secret of creating gold. Fortunately, the ambitious politician never succeeded in cracking the key of Abraham the Jew. After Cardinal de Richelieu died, the book itself was never found, although copies of the drawings and some of the text were made. You can view them online at www.FlamelCollege.org/flamel.htm.

Isaac Newton and the Black Dragon

Famed scientist Sir Isaac Newton was a practicing alchemist who wrote more on alchemy than any other subject. Yet most of his alchemical works were never published, because after his death in 1727, the Royal Society deemed them "not fit to print." Today, most scholars agree that Newton considered himself first and foremost an alchemist, and that the inspiration for his laws of light and theory of gravity came from his alchemical work.

Newton believed that alchemy originated with Thoth and that supernatural visitors to ancient Egypt gave it to mankind. He prepared his own personal translation of the Emerald Tablet and kept it safely hidden away in his laboratory. When he worked on his alchemy experiments, Newton demanded complete secrecy. "He very rarely went to bed sometimes not till five or six in the morning," said one of his servants of his alchemy work, "especially at springtime, at which time he used to employ about six weeks in his laboratory, the fire scarce going out night or day. What his aim might be I was unable to penetrate into."

Newton was always fearful that the secrets of alchemy would leak out into the world and cause fearful political and social consequences, because mankind was not ready for such power. In 1676, after fellow alchemist Robert Boyle announced the discovery of a "special mercury" that became hot and glowed when mixed with gold, Newton was terrified Boyle had revealed too much. He wrote him a letter cautioning him to keep everything about alchemy secret: "Your discovery may possibly be an inlet to something more noble that is not to be communicated without immense damage to the world if there should be any verity in the Hermetic writings," Newton wrote to Boyle, "therefore I question nothing but that the great wisdom of the noble Author will sway him to high silence—there being other things besides the transmutation of metals, which none but the Hermetic philosophers understand."

Newton was a true adept of alchemy who revered the divine pattern spoken of in the Emerald Tablet, while Boyle was one of a new breed of materialistic alchemists who denied the existence of hidden forces, correspondences, synchronicities, and invisible influences of any kind in nature.

Newton's lifelong work in alchemy focused on *antimony*, a brittle, steel-gray metal that tarnishes to a black finish, which usually hides its silvery metallic luster. It is known in alchemy as the "Black Dragon." Newton was fascinated by the regulus of antimony, which is a star-shaped crystalline form produced when heating antimony ore to high temperatures. If antimony has been sufficiently purified, it forms long and slender crystals, which, during cooling, form triangular branches around a central point that looks like a bright silver star. Alchemists named this peculiar signature of antimony after Regulus, the brilliant double star at the heart of the constellation Leo. The name is derived from the Latin *regulus*, meaning lesser king. The regulus of antimony combines readily with gold.

From the Alchemist

The word antimony comes from the Greek words *anti monos*, meaning "not alone," because it is an ore often found combined with other metals. But there is an interesting legend that the metal was really named by the fourteenth-century German alchemist Basil Valentine. As the story goes, Valentine secretly added the powdered metal to the food of Dominican monks in order to study its effects on humans. A natural emetic, the antimony made the monks vomit and suffer from severe nausea, so Valentine named the metal after the Latin words *anti mony*, meaning "anti-monks." The tincture of antimony was used in the Middle Ages to treat venereal diseases.

Newton believed that the spirit of the Black Dragon of antimony was purified and released during the creation of its regulus. He felt the consciousness of the alchemist played an important role in capturing this powerful presence hidden in the black metal. "On a clear, uncloudy, and windless day, the regulus will become starred quite easily when you're ready and sufficiently skilled in the process," he wrote, "The clear weather helps considerably, but more so does the bond between the matters and the operator."

In the star signature of antimony, Newton found the possibility of gaining cosmic knowledge from the spirits of the metals. He went on to create the regulus of iron and regulus of silver and used them as reflecting mirrors in a telescope to peer deep into space. Finally, Newton applied thrice-distilled mercury to the silver regulus to obtain the most perfect reflecting mirror ever used in telescopes. Perhaps Newton's belief that the regulus of metals could provide information about the universe was realized. About this time, he began publishing his breakthrough papers on the nature of light and gravity.

In the mid-1670s, Newton composed a long treatise entitled *The Clovis* (*The Key*), which was the culmination of years of experimentation with the regulus of antimony. He finally admitted he had transmuted antimony into the long-sought Philosophical Mercury that would make gold multiply and grow. "I know whereof I write," Newton said, "for I have in the fire manifold vessels with gold and this Philosophical Mercury. I have such a vessel in the fire with gold thus dissolved, but extrinsically and intrinsically into a Mercury as living and mobile as any mercury found in the world. For it makes gold begin to swell, to be swollen, and to putrefy, and to spring forth into sprouts and branches, changing colors daily, the appearances of which fascinate me every day. I reckon this is a great secret in alchemy."

The Puffers

The fascination with gold during the Middle Ages produced a new class of alchemists known as "puffers." They were called puffers because they constantly sat next to their furnaces vigorously fanning their bellows trying to increase the heat of their fires. They were convinced that extremely hot temperatures alone could transmute the metals.

> **Thoth's Tips**
>
> The gold-making fever peaked in the sixteenth century, and large sections of Paris, Cologne, Vienna, Prague, and other European cities were devoted to alchemical workshops in which alchemists pursued their craft with feverish dedication. Some of the original alchemical laboratories can still be seen in the "Zlata Ulicka" (Golden Alley) of Prague, where alchemists lived and worked during the reigns of Emperors Maximilian II (1564–1576) and Rudolph II (1576–1612).

When their methods failed, the puffers resorted to trickery to produce gold. They covered pieces of real gold with dye or paint that could be easily removed by dipping them in magical elixirs that were really just acidic solutions. Using such tricks, many puffers were able to convince princes, kings, and popes to finance their endeavors, although not a few went to the gallows when they were unable to produce more gold than they consumed. A few heads of state, such as Frederick of Wurzburg, had special gilded gallows built just for hanging alchemists.

The lure of multiplying gold seduced mercenary alchemists like the puffers, who quickly degenerated into charlatans and criminals and eventually brought alchemy into disrepute. In fact, so many people claimed to be making gold that several nations feared it would upset their economies if even a few of the stories of transmutation were true. Many passed laws making the alchemical production of gold and silver unlawful.

Henry IV of England outlawed alchemy in 1404, but Henry VI started issuing licenses in alchemy in 1440. Later, laws were passed that a certain percentage of all gold coins had to use alchemical gold. All gold coins minted during the reign of Edward III are said to have been made entirely of gold produced by alchemists. Respected alchemists like Isaac Newton, Raymond Lully, and Jacque le Cor were appointed the heads of national mints for obvious reasons.

During the Renaissance, however, European royalty began to realize they didn't need alchemists to magically multiply their coffers. They could do it themselves simply by printing paper money. The idea surfaced in the early 1700s in the court of the French prince of Orleans. Like many rulers of the time, he had employed alchemists to produce gold in hopes of paying off his debts, but he promptly dismissed all his alchemists after meeting Scottish gambler and financier John Law, who suggested the prince print worthless paper money to pay off his debts. The promissory notes, each signed by the prince, became legal tender that were traded publicly and never had to be redeemed. The idea caught on as rulers around the world realized that paper could be transmuted into any value much easier than lead into gold.

Alchemy became splintered during this period, torn asunder into the two opposing camps of the true adepts and the pseudo-alchemists. The pseudo-alchemists were the worldly puffers and other uninitiated amateurs who relied on physical methods and trickery to produce material gold. The true adepts were a select fraternity of initiated alchemists to whom the laboratory work was a part of a comprehensive philosophical and spiritual system based on the teachings of Thoth and Hermes. The experiments of the true adepts to transmute metals were carried out as a demonstration of Hermetic principles and not just as a way of accumulating wealth.

Thanks in part to the proliferation of pseudo-alchemists in the Middle Ages, the Hermetic principles and spiritual significance of alchemy were shoved into the background. True adepts suffered along with the puffers in the degeneration of their craft and loss of standing in society. By the late sixteenth century, alchemy was in philosophic disarray and widely regarded as the most confused and difficult system of thought in history. French historian Albert Poisson summed up the situation in his

Tread Carefully

In studying alchemy, it's extremely important to understand the difference between the two types of alchemists who worked during the Middle Ages. True adepts and pseudo-alchemists both wrote treatises on alchemy that differ greatly in their objectives and dedication to the spirit of alchemy. Very often modern writers on the subject overlook the distinctions between these two diametrically opposed groups.

History of Alchemy (1891): "Scholasticism with its infinitely subtle argumentation, theology with its ambiguous phraseology, astrology so vast and so complicated, are only child's play in comparison with the difficulties of alchemy."

The Rise of Chemistry

Modern chemistry actually arose from the purely physical work of the puffers and originated from an entirely different tradition than the Hermetic teachings passed down from ancient Egypt. Puffers were called chemists in popular speech in the Middle Ages, and by the Renaissance, chemistry had become a separate discipline from alchemy. Historians sometimes use the term "chymistry" to refer to the short period in the seventeenth century when alchemy and chemistry were not sharply separated from each other. But by the eighteenth century, alchemy and chemistry had gone their separate ways.

The trend was obvious as early as 1595, when Andreas Libavius published a book called *Alchymia*, a guide for chemists that separated the laboratory aspects of alchemy from its spiritual principles. Then Jan Bantista van Helmont (1577–1644) began working with gases as separate substances and not the single Element of Air. Johann Glauber (1604–1668) continued the trend by treating metals, acids, and salts as everyday things without spiritual or archetypal properties. These "chymists" shared the alchemist's belief in transmutation but no longer felt bound by the Hermetic principles of their craft. A new system that focused only on physical reality slowly supplanted traditional alchemy.

The demise of alchemy began in 1661 with the publication of Robert Boyle's practical laboratory guide *The Sceptical Chymist*. Boyle was both an alchemist and chemist who discovered the mathematical laws that govern the formation of gases. That may not sound earth-shaking to us, but Boyle was actually abandoning alchemy with his idea that mathematical laws and not spiritual principles govern the creation of matter.

Antoine Lavoisier, who developed the mathematical theory of conservation of mass in chemical reactions in 1783, is considered the father of modern chemistry. In 1787, he published his definitive work *Elements of Chemistry* and, two years later, *Characteristics of Chemicals*. In these books, he abandoned any references to alchemical principles and focused only on the physical properties of substances.

The absolute end to any spiritual component in chemistry came with the publication of John Dalton's *Atomic Theory* in 1803. His billiard-ball theory of matter ignored the elegant crystallization of energy idea that was part of the alchemical viewpoint. This crystalline idea would not return until the rise of quantum physics in the twentieth century (see Chapter 23).

In many ways, chemistry can be thought of as materialistic alchemy. The last gasp of alchemy in Europe came when the puffers' methods became mainstream in the eighteenth century with the commercialization of chemistry. Alchemy had degenerated from a practical path of spiritual perfection into a competitive race for commercial products to put up for sale. New drugs and miraculous chemicals had replaced the lure of gold, but the basic techniques and motivation of puffers and chemists were the same.

The practice of alchemy could not survive in the new atmosphere of materialism and industrialization, where the work was solely on the physical level. The key to success in the ancient art had always been the ability to work on all levels of reality—not only on the physical but on the psychological and spiritual levels as well. The alchemist's workshop was "between worlds," and things that took place there could never be reproduced in a chemist's lab.

The Least You Need to Know

- Many alchemists of the Middle Ages had difficulty understanding the alchemy manuscripts being translated for the first time into Latin and focused mainly on making gold.

- The Church persecuted alchemists because of their heretical spiritual beliefs and disregard of Church dogma.

- Those in power employed alchemists to make gold and often executed those who failed.

- Alchemists split into two factions during the Middle Ages, true adepts who followed the ancient Hermetic teachings and the materialistic puffers or pseudo-alchemists.

- Modern chemistry was born of the practical yet spiritually incomplete laboratory work of the puffers.

Part 2

The Principles of Alchemy

Alchemy is based on the precepts of the Emerald Tablet, an ancient artifact attributed to Hermes Trismegistus. The Hermetic teachings describe a dynamic living universe that arose from a primordial soup known as the First Matter. Hermetic concepts permeated ancient philosophy, religion, science, and other traditions and have been passed down to us in an "Underground River" of secret teachings. These teachings were kept hidden because of their great power to tap into universal patterns and transform things in accordance with the deeper laws of nature. The actual methods and operations used by alchemists were concealed in unique ciphers, glyphs, and symbols that they used to communicate with one another.

Chapter 5

The Secret Language of Alchemists

In This Chapter

- ◆ The perfect language of birds
- ◆ Bird symbolism in alchemy
- ◆ Lions, dragons, and other animals in alchemy
- ◆ The mystery of the rose
- ◆ The unspoken wisdom of ciphers

Alchemists communicated with each other in a special language of metaphors, symbols, and unique ciphers. Many of them even invented their own alphabets and secret scripts to keep their work private. Whether or not they needed to keep their writings secret is debatable, for to most outsiders, the writings of alchemists were all gibberish (see Chapter 3).

The tradition of secrecy in alchemy goes back to its origins in Egypt, where priests believed the universal principles contained in the writings of Thoth were so powerful that they must not be shared with those who might abuse them. So they discussed the secrets in riddles, symbols, and images that only the initiated would understand.

To pass the secret teachings down through the ages, the ancients encoded them in sacred writings and symbolic images carved into public monuments and buildings. This tradition of concealing secrets openly in the architecture of buildings was carried on during the heyday of alchemy in the Middle Ages in the sacred architecture of cathedrals and the symbolic sculptures and monuments in the center of cities.

The Language of the Birds

Alchemists used an oblique writing style to communicate with one another publicly while concealing the true subject matter. This method of symbolic writing appears unintelligible unless you have the necessary key to the symbolism to be able to interpret it.

Their style of communication became known as the "language of the birds" and was considered a higher or more perfect language that was the key to true knowledge. It was also known as the "green language" or "living language" to indicate it carried more than just static words. This idea arose from the haunting suspicion that the high-pitched chirping of birds was actually a superior language beyond our comprehension.

Writing has been associated with birds since the beginning of recorded history. Thoth, the inventor of writing and language, was depicted with the head of the long-beaked ibis bird. Some Egyptologists believe the hieroglyphic language originated by tracing the movements of birds in the sky and on the ground. And scholars believe the first known style of writing (cuneiform) may have originated from bird tracks.

It was also believed that certain holy men and sorcerers could converse with birds and thereby learn mystical secrets of nature. King Solomon, the Nordic warrior Siegfried, and St. Francis of Assisi are some of the historical figures who are believed to have understood the language of the birds.

The Birds of Alchemy

The alchemists spoke in the language of birds in the most literal sense, too. They used images of birds to stand for some of their most important concepts, especially those dealing with *volatile* or spiritual processes.

The movements of birds are very significant in alchemical drawings. Ascending birds indicate the volatilization or evaporation of compounds, while descending birds indicate the fixation, condensation, or precipitation of compounds. Birds shown both ascending and descending indicate the operation of distillation.

A standing bird usually indicates the kind of alchemical operation underway. (See Part 3 of this book for a detailed explanation of the operations of alchemy.) The crow or raven indicates Black Phase operations such as calcination or putrefaction, which involve the breaking down of structures by fire or decay. The white goose, white swan, or albatross stand for the White Phase operations of separation and purification. The rooster or cockerel means the operation of conjunction is underway, and the peacock announces the beginning of the fermentation operation.

def•i•ni•tion

Volatile means something is easily changeable or transformed. Volatility is a measure of how quickly something changes. In alchemy, volatility is how easily a chemical evaporates or becomes spiritized. The opposite of volatile is fixed, which means something is stable or unchanging.

The pelican stands for the distillation operation, as well as the beginning of the Red Phase of alchemy. The eagle also stands for distillation, as well as the operation of sublimation. The color of the eagle sometimes indicates the color of the vapors being released during distillation. For instance, a white eagle represents steam. The bennu bird or phoenix, the mythical bird that was reborn in the fire, stands for the final operation of coagulation and the creation of the Philosopher's Stone.

Other bird symbolism in alchemy includes the double-headed eagle, which stands for the Rebis or androgynous state of mercury and the bat, which also signifies dual-natured substances and androgyny. The dove is a symbol of renewed spirit or an infusion of divine energy. Chemically, the dove heralds the purifying transformation from the Black Phase to the White Phase of alchemy.

The basilisk is a symbolic alchemical creature with the head of a bird and the body of a dragon. According to legend, the wingless creature was hatched from a hermaphroditic cock's egg and nursed by a serpent. Chemically, the basilisk stands for the union of mercury (the bird) and sulfur (the dragon) in the mineral cinnabar. Spiritually, it is the melding of our higher and lower natures of spirit (the bird) and soul (the dragon) to create a new incarnation or "Child of the Philosophers."

In alchemy, eggs in general are highly symbolic. They stand for any kind of sealed vessel of transformation, which includes not only closed glass vessels but also such unexpected things as coffins, tombs, and sepulchers. References to eggs and the hatching of birds and serpents abound. For instance, the alchemist's insulated fermenting box was referred to as the "House of the Chick," and the whole cosmos itself was sometimes depicted as a serpent hatching from or entwined around an egg.

Another egg symbol, the Griffin's Egg, is an allusion to the Vessel of Hermes in which the conjunction (alchemical marriage) of volatile and fixed principles takes place. The Griffin is a mythical beast that has the body of a lion and the head and wings of an eagle. Since the lion is considered the king of the beasts and the eagle the king of the birds, their union in the Griffin makes it the most powerful and majestic animal imaginable.

Animal Symbolism in Alchemy

While birds and flying animals generally indicate spiritual or volatile principles, terrestrial animals usually stand for physical or fixed principles. Whenever two animals are found, they signify sulfur and mercury or some relationship between fixed and volatile principles.

Animals also symbolize basic principles of alchemy. For example, they may symbolize the Four Elements in drawings (see Chapter 7). The Earth Element is usually symbolized by an ox or lion, the Water Element by fish or whales, the Air Element by doves or eagles, and the Fire Element by salamanders or dragons.

Serpents represent the life force or the energies being exchanged in alchemical transformations. Two entwined serpents represent the opposing masculine and feminine energies that make up the life force (such as depicted in the caduceus) or the union of opposing substances in the lab. Three-headed serpents or three serpents in a group stand for the three principles of Sulfur, Mercury, and Salt (see Chapter 8). Winged serpents represent volatile substances; wingless serpents represent fixed substances. A crucified serpent represents the fixation of a volatile substance.

In alchemical drawings, frogs and toads indicate the First Matter (see Chapter 6) and the energies of materialization. The black toad symbolizes the First Matter being released by the putrefaction of a substance. The chaining or tying together of a toad on the ground and an eagle in the sky represents the union of fixed and volatile components, such as silver and mercury or soul and spirit (see Chapter 12).

Other animal symbols include two fish swimming in opposite directions, which designate the essences of spirit and soul during the operation of dissolution. Bees, beetles, and butterflies are symbols of purification and the rebirth of soul or essence. The mythical unicorn was a symbol of sublimation and was associated with the white tincture and white powder of alchemy. The noble stag with large antlers was associated with the red tincture and red powder of alchemy. Scenes of the stag and unicorn meeting in the middle of a forest indicate the completion of the work and the successful creation of the Philosopher's Stone.

Wolves symbolize the wild, untamed spirit of man or the chaotic forces of nature. Dogs represent the domesticated spirit of man or natural forces working to assist the alchemist. Chemically, the dog is Philosophical Mercury or the purified benevolent spirit of the metal mercury. The Grey Wolf stands for the metal antimony. The Grey Wolf is a fearsome beast. When molten, it mercilessly devours other metals like lead, tin, and copper. Drawings showing dogs fighting with wolves represent the process of purifying gold with antimony, which was alloyed with other metals to remove them from gold.

The Lions of Alchemy

Lions are important symbols, as they are usually associated with the properties of sulfur or the application of heat or acids to the metals. Chemically, the lion is any salt or fixed substance obtained from the metals. It is black, green, or red according to its state of transformation. The first of the lions is the Black Lion, which represents the black salt, lead ore, or in general, the darkest part of a substance that must be purified and transformed by fire.

In working with minerals and metals, the Green Lion is the root of the essence of the metals or soul of the metals. The Green Lion was known for devouring the metals; the chemical signature that gave it its green color was iron sulfate, and acids made with iron sulfate were called the Green Lion. These included vitriol or sulfuric acid, which dissolved most common metals such as iron and copper, and also nitric acid. When nitric acid was mixed with hydrochloric acid, it produced the greenish acid aqua regia, which could even dissolve gold. Images of the Green Lion devouring the sun refer to this ability. The Green Lion is also associated with the green acetate of lead in its oily or unredeemed form.

When working with plant essences and vegetable matter, the Green Lion represented the life force in the leaves of plants. In this case, the Green Lion eating the sun is the process of photosynthesis that creates the greenness of nature from the pigment chlorophyll. Alchemists understood this process and tried to isolate the life force in plants to use in their experiments and even create artificial life forms.

At the next level of the work, the work with animals, the Red Lion is the life force in blood. In the work with minerals and metals, the Red Lion is the red acetate of lead in its crystallized form. Generally, with the Red Lion we gain control over untamed or unredeemed forces by feeding the Green Lion a seed of gold or purifying it with a catalyst or transmuting agent.

Philosophically, the Green Lion is the raw forces of nature or the subconscious that we are seeking to tame, and the Red Lion is the assimilation or control of those forces. In the final stages of the work, the Red Lion grows wings. The Winged Lion is the volatile or spiritual aspect of a substance, which is the sublimated salt used to make the Philosopher's Stone.

The Dragons of Alchemy

Dragons are another group of important symbols and represent the properties of mercury or the application of life force or energy. Chemically, the dragon is the mercury acid obtained from the metals or acids in general. Like lions, the alchemical dragon is black, green, or red according to its level of transformation.

The Black Dragon is the blackened metallic compound undergoing putrefaction, death, and decay. The Green Dragon is the indwelling spirit or life of the metal, the thing that gives metals their active properties. Philosophically, the Green Dragon is a formerly ferocious and unforgiving dragon that is now tamed. Its energy is contained by having been crystallized. Formerly threatening unconscious elements have now been assimilated into consciousness. The Red Dragon appears at both the beginning and end of the work. It is the chaotic energy of the First Matter at the beginning of the work (see Chapter 6) that becomes the Philosopher's Stone at the end of the work.

> **From the Alchemist**
>
> A serpent or dragon eating its own tail is known as an ouroboros (or uroboros). It symbolizes the union of opposing energies and is one of the primary symbols for the Philosopher's Stone. The caption "All Is One" is usually included with drawings of the ouroboros. Alchemists sometimes referred to the ouroboros as the *Agathos Daimon* ("Good Spirit"), which was another name for Thoth, the father of alchemy.

Chemically, the Red Dragon is the pure red oil of lead in its initial state and the red powder of projection in its perfected or tamed state.

A fire-breathing dragon or a dragon in flames indicates a metal melting or a substance undergoing calcination. Several dragons fighting amongst themselves depict metals undergoing the process of putrefaction. Dragons with wings represent the volatile (spirit or energetic) principle, and wingless dragons represent the fixed (soul or material) principle. The cyclic interplay of volatile and fixed, light and darkness, spirit and soul, energy and matter, creation and destruction, is rendered in drawings showing two dragons, one winged and the other with feet, each eating the other's tail.

Silent Secrets of the Rose

No symbol inspired alchemists of the Renaissance more than the rose. The flower is one of the fundamental symbols of alchemy and became the philosophical basis of the Rosicrucians, an alchemical movement that flourished in the seventeenth century. So important was it to alchemists that dozens of manuscripts are called *Rosarium*, Latin for Rose Garden, and all deal with the alchemical relationship between the King and Queen.

The rose is much more meaningful, much older, and more deeply embedded in the human subconscious than most people believe. In Europe, rose fossils 35 million years old have been found, and archeologists have unearthed petrified rose wreaths from the oldest Egyptian tombs. To understand the alchemists' fascination with the rose, let's take a deeper look into its complicated symbolism.

The rose is a paradoxical symbol of both purity and passion, heavenly perfection and earthly desire, and life and death. Originally a symbol of joy, the rose later indicated secrecy and silence but is now commonly associated with romantic love. In general, the color of the rose denotes its meaning:

◆ Red roses are symbols of passion, soulful love, deep creativity, and high personal energy.

◆ White roses symbolize purity, innocence, acceptance, and unconditional love.

◆ Black or withered roses indicate that love is gone or over, as well as impending disaster, depression, or death.

◆ Pink roses stand for gentleness, thankfulness, and loving or supportive friendship.

◆ Yellow roses signify compassion, sociability, free-flowing conversations, confidence, and security.

◆ Orange roses carry feelings of enthusiasm, fascination, and optimism.

◆ Blue or purple roses indicate spiritual longing, meditation, and the promise of a perfect world.

◆ Gilded or golden roses convey the idea of personal perfection, completion of the Great Work, or the invocation of divine powers.

In alchemical terms, the golden rose means a successful marriage of opposites to produce the Golden Child, and the rose in general is a symbol of the operation of conjunction, the mystical marriage of opposites. The rose represents the regeneration of purified essences and their resurrection in a new compound or body. The white rose is associated with the White Queen of alchemy and represents the feminine, receptive, contractive principle of lunar soul. The red rose is associated with the Red King and is regarded as a masculine, active, expansive principle of solar spirit. "The rose red color," said psychologist Carl Jung, "is related to the *aqua permanens*, eternal water or blood of the soul, which are extracted from the First Matter."

The union of white and red roses (of soul and spirit) symbolizes the birth of the Philosopher's Child. Also, white roses were linked to the White Phase of the work and the White Stone of Multiplication, while the red rose was associated with the Red Phase and the Red Stone of Projection.

> ### From the Alchemist
>
> Alchemist Daniel Maier discussed the symbolism of the rose in his *Septimana Philosophica:* "The rose is the first and most perfect of flowers. The Gardens of Philosophy are planted with many roses, both red and white, which colors are in correspondence with gold and silver. The center of the rose is green and is emblematical of the Green Lion or First Matter. Just as the natural rose turns to the sun and is refreshed by rain, so is the Philosophical Matter prepared in blood, grown in light, and in and by these made perfect."

In alchemical drawings, the rose garden is a symbol of sacred space and could mean a meditation chamber (Oratorium) in a lab, a sacred tabernacle, an altar, a sacred location in nature, or paradise itself. In all these instances, the rose garden is the mystical bridal chamber, the place of the mystic marriage. "Mystery glows in the rose bed and the secret is hidden in the rose," wrote the twelfth-century Persian alchemist Farid Attar.

In Christian alchemy, the rose and the rosary became symbols of the union between God and human beings. Scenes of Mary in a rose garden or under a rose arbor or before a tapestry of roses reinforce this idea. In the art of the Middle Ages, Mary is almost always shown holding a rose, which indicates her power comes from divine love.

In spiritual alchemy, the single rose represents the mystic center of a person, her heart of hearts. As a symbol of the mystical marriage within a person, the rose represents a special kind of love in which one melts away into the beauty of another and the old identity is surrendered for that of the beloved or a higher identity discovered within oneself. Sufi spiritual alchemist Rumi had this idea in mind when he wrote: "In the driest whitest stretch of pain's infinite desert, I lost my sanity and found this rose." In this sense, the rose is a symbol of complete surrender and permanent transmutation.

Because of its association with the deepest workings of the heart, the rose has come to symbolize inner secrets and things that cannot be spoken. The Latin phrase *sub rosa*, "under the rose," is used to indicate writings or discussions that should be kept secret. The concept originated in the medieval tradition of hanging red roses from the ceiling of meetings of Hermetic organizations (such as the Freemasons, Rosicrucians, or alchemy guilds) to indicate that the discussions were not to be shared with outsiders. For instance, in Sebastian Brant's fifteenth-century alchemical treatise *Ship of Fools*, the author warns: "What here we do say, shall under roses stay."

Ciphers of the Alchemists

Ciphers are symbolic glyphs used by alchemists to indicate chemicals, metals, and the basic principles and operations of their craft. Common ciphers used by alchemists are shown in the following figure.

Symbol	Name	Symbol	Name
△	Air	♄	Lead, Saturn
♒	Albedo (White Phase)	♆ ♀	Life Force, Health
⟂	Alembic	☿	Mercury, Quicksilver
♣	Amalgam	𝔸	Mixture, to Mix
♁	Antimony	♒	Multiplication (Aquarius)
♏	Autumn Work	⌣	Nigredo (Black Phase)
⚴	Boiling, to Ferment	∴	Oil
♀	Copper, Venus	♉	Precipitation
⊽	Combine	♓	Projection (Pisces)
⊱	Composed of	♌	Purification
♉	Conjunction (Taurus)	☆	Quintessence
▽	Crucible	♑	Receiver
◈	Crystal, Crystallization	⅁	Retort
♋	Day and Night	◐	Rubedo (Red Phase)
⊹	Decompose	⊘	Salt (General)
♌	Digestion (Leo)	♉	Salt (Magnesia, Clay)
♋	Dissolution (Cancer)	♏	Separation (Scorpio)
♍	Distillation (Virgo)	☽	Silver, Moon
▽	Earth	♀	Silver (Spirit of)
♐	Electrum, Platinum	♁+	Spirit
⚷	Essence	♉	Spring Work
⚘	Essence (Plant)	⊞ ⊕	Stone (Elemental)
♑	Fermentation (Capricorn)	◉ ✿	Stone (Philosopher's)
⚸	Filter	Ω	Sublimation (Libra)
⊕	First Matter (rectified)	♈	Sulfur
⊗ ⊜	First Matter (unrectified)	♅	Sulfuric Acid
△	Fire	♈	Summer Work
♊	Fixation (Gemini)	♃	Tin, Jupiter
♒	Fuse, Meld	⊕♋	Vitriol
☉	Gold, Sun	▽	Water
♐	Incineration (Sagittarius)	⊹	White Lead
♂	Iron, Mars	⚌	Zinc

Chart of common ciphers.

In the process of alchemical initiation, ciphers were used as coded teaching tools, and meditation on ciphers was thought to convey unspoken wisdom. The alchemists' ciphers have much to say about the hidden meanings and *archetypal* power of their materials and operations.

def•i•ni•tion

> **Archetypal** refers to the influence of archetypes, which are elementary ideas rooted permanently in our consciousness. They are the divine ideals or spiritual essences from which existing objects or situations arise. Archetypes seem to be embedded in the fabric of creation and transcend all languages and cultures. They are primordial patterns that show up on all levels of reality and are most clearly described in myths and stories.

As an exercise in deciphering ciphers, let's investigate a Renaissance drawing intended to help initiates penetrate the deeper meaning of the fundamental ciphers of alchemy. In the following figure, we see an esoteric schematic drawing imbued with archetypal influences. The sun, moon, and 15 stars look down over symbols centered on a tree trunk with a massive root system in the ground.

To the right is a five-petal flower indicating the presence of the Quintessence, and on the left is a seven-branched plant indicating the steps or operations of perfection. On top of the tree is an eagle representing the operation of distillation, which in this case is the mental operation of distilling these symbols. It is a sign that we need to reflect or meditate on this drawing.

Supporting the tree trunk are two lions, one with wings and one without, representing the union of the volatile and fixed faculties of spirit and soul, which we must use together to understand these symbols. In other words, we have to combine the masculine, logical and argumentative way of knowing of spirit with the feminine, intuitive and reflective way of knowing of soul. This is the key needed to decipher the coded material being presented. In fact, this is the key to understanding all the symbols of alchemy. Without this key, alchemy remains an obscure puzzle.

In the drawing, we see two ciphers buried in the ground at the foot of the tree. These are the basic raw materials with which the alchemist works. On the left is the symbol for salt, which represents the physical compounds and chemicals alchemists use. On the right is the cipher for the First Matter, which is the spirit matter of the work, the elusive source that exists between worlds.

The cipher for the First Matter can be shown in two orientations. Shown here as a cross "+" in a circle, it signifies the purified or rectified First Matter. If it were shown as an "x" in a circle, it would have signified the chaotic or unrefined First Matter.

Relationship of the basic ciphers.

The other ciphers in the drawing are arranged in the shape of a cross with horizontal and vertical components. In Hermetic geometry, horizontal lines and earthly orientation stand for material reality or things fixed in time and space. Vertical lines and heavenly orientation stand for energetic or spiritual forces that are not fixed in time and space.

Ciphers for the Elements

On the horizontal component of the cross are the ciphers for the Four Elements which make up our material reality. On the left side of the tree trunk, the first cipher is Fire, a triangle pointing upward. Fire seeks to ascend because of its hot and dry qualities.

On the right side of the tree trunk, the first cipher is Water, a triangle pointing downward. Water seeks to descend and condense because of its cold and moist qualities. Fire and Water are the purest Elements, and if allowed full expression of their urges, Fire would disappear into the Above, and Water would be absorbed into the Below.

Next to Fire on the left is the cipher for Earth, the downward-pointing triangle cipher of Water with a horizontal line through it. Next to Water on the right is the cipher for Air, the upward-pointing triangle of Fire with a horizontal line through it. In other words, Earth is cold and dry and seeks to descend, but its dry component blocks its full descent, and the horizontal line in the triangle of Water indicates this. Air is hot and moist and seeks to ascend, but its moist component blocks its full ascent, as is indicated by the horizontal line in the triangle of Fire.

Thus the Elements Earth and Air are suspended in time and space, caught between and connecting the extremes of Above and Below. In the Hermetic teachings, Earth and Air are considered more manifested and stable versions of the pure Elements Water and Fire (see Chapter 7).

Ciphers for the Three Essentials

The triangular shape of the ciphers for the Elements is not without significance. It indicates that the Elements of creation are made up of three primordial forces present in the First Matter and expressed in all created things. The alchemists called these three essential ingredients Sulfur, Mercury, and Salt, and for now, we are concerned only with the ciphers the alchemists chose to represent them.

In the drawing, the ciphers for the Three Essentials are arranged vertically on the trunk of the tree. This orientation indicates these are archetypal forces from Above not fixed in time and space. At the bottom of the tree nearest the ground is the cipher of heavenly Salt. This is the same cipher as the one for terrestrial or physical salt. While vertical orientation indicates spiritual processes, horizontal orientation indicates physical processes. Thus the horizontal line through the salt cipher suggests its materiality or tendency to form bodies.

Tread Carefully

The way alchemists capitalized words can sometimes be confusing. In general, a capitalized word refers to spiritual or archetypal connotations, while the uncapitalized version refers to physical or everyday connotations. For instance, "Salt" stands for the heavenly substance or universal principle of materialization, while "salt" refers to the common physical compound. Sometimes the term "sophic" was used to emphasize the spiritual or philosophical aspect of a substance. Thus, Sophic Mercury was the spiritual ideal of the common metal mercury.

The next cipher up the tree trunk is for Sulfur. It consists of the cipher for Fire with a cross attached beneath it. The cross indicates the Fire Element is being expressed along both the horizontal (material) and the vertical (spiritual) axis of reality. Common sulfur is known as brimstone (literally the "burning stone") and carries the signatures of the Fire Element.

Above the cipher for Sulfur and at the same level as the horizontal line of elements is the cipher for Mercury. Mercury's position on the cross of ciphers is significant as it is the transforming medium that exists in both material and spiritual realms. This is also indicated by the cross at the base of the cipher.

The circle in the middle of the Mercury cipher stands for the sun and is sometimes shown with a point or dot at its center, which is the cipher for the sun as well as for gold. The curved line or semicircle at the top of the cipher stands for the moon. The semicircle or crescent is the cipher for the moon as well as for silver. Thus the cipher for Mercury results from a union of the sun and moon, which in alchemy means just one thing. It is the sacred marriage, the union of the King and Queen within, the merging of masculine and feminine ways of knowing, and the creation of the Philosopher's Stone.

The cipher for the Philosopher's Stone is shown above Mercury at the top of the tree. It is a circle with a cross above it. It means that this object has power over all realms, both material and spiritual.

The Least You Need to Know

- Alchemists communicated in a secret, coded language of metaphors and symbols known as the language of the birds.

- Bird symbols in alchemy stand for spiritual principles as well as stages of the work.

- Lions in alchemy represent the properties of sulfur and the use of heat and sulfuric compounds with the metals.

- Dragons in alchemy represent the properties of mercury and the use of mercuric compounds with the metals.

- The rose is one of the most profound symbols in alchemy, and its meaning changes with the color of the flower.

- The ciphers of alchemy were deliberately designed to invoke secret or esoteric principles.

Chapter 6

The Elusive First Matter

In This Chapter

◆ The enigma of the First Matter

◆ Philosophy of the First Matter

◆ Characteristics of the First Matter

◆ How alchemists worked with the First Matter

The First Matter, *Prima Materia* in Latin, is the most confusing concept in alchemy, and even alchemists had a difficult time defining it. The 1612 edition of the *Lexicon of Alchemy* lists over 80 different definitions for the First Matter, and at least 200 different descriptions of it are found in the writings of medieval alchemists. Among the popular synonyms for the First Matter were such alchemical concepts as fire, water, air, earth, sulfur, mercury, salt, quintessence, the sun, the moon, and the stone. Also included were philosophical ideals like imagination, love, light, consciousness, thought, spirit, soul, and God. Even such terms as blood, urine, menses, manure, and dirt were considered fitting definitions by alchemists.

The reason the First Matter is so hard to pin down is that it is everything and nothing at once. It is the primal One Thing that existed before time, as well as the primordial chaos that contains all possibilities. It is said the First Matter carries the germ or seeds of all things that ever existed and ever will exist in the future. It is the infinite cornucopia from which the myriad of all created things in the universe emerge.

Yet this unbelievably elusive and potent cosmic force was the subject of the alchemists' work as they tried to accumulate it in its pristine form from natural sources and expose it in metals and other compounds through their chemical manipulations. They sought it deep in underground mines and in the black virgin soil in the middle of forests. They carefully spread out burlap bags to collect the morning dew, which they believed held traces of the First Matter. They even distilled hundreds of gallons of children's urine seeking the magical essence. They looked for it everywhere, including in their own bodies, minds, and souls.

What Is the First Matter?

The Emerald Tablet refers to the First Matter as the "One Thing," the primordial chaos of the universe fashioned into material reality by the thoughts or Word of the One Mind. This idea of a divine presence seeking expression in the material universe seems to have originated with the ancient Egyptians and has become a basic tenet of Hermetic philosophy.

The Egyptians denoted the First Matter with the hieroglyph known as *kh*, which looks like a circle with two wide horizontal black bands running through it. This cipher for the First Matter is the first hieroglyphic letter that makes up the Egyptian word *khem*, which is the root of our word alchemy. It is also the only hieroglyph that no traditional Egyptologist knows the meaning of for sure. Other hieroglyphs are associated with a common item such as a basket, stool, owl, vulture, and so on.

But this particular symbol has both tangible and intangible nuances. The easiest definition is "black matter that is alive," but what exactly is that? Most language experts have translated it as "placenta," but others feel it might mean "fertile dirt" or "living black soil." In fact, it is the holy script for the First Matter, the basic dark matter of the universe from which all things have sprung.

The ancients thought of the First Matter as a spiritual substance of which external visible nature is an expression and manifestation. This primordial matter contains the powers that form minerals and metals, vegetables and animals, and everything that breathes; all forms are hidden within its depths, and it is, therefore, the true principle or beginning of all things.

In ancient China, philosophers referred to the First Matter as the "Tao," which is an equally difficult term to describe. The Chinese spiritual alchemist Lao Tzu considered the Tao as plural in manifestation but singular in essence, totally real yet totally unknowable, a nonpersonal, amoral, primordial chaos. He described it in the *Tao te Ching:* "There is a thing confusedly formed, born between heaven and earth. Silent and void, it stands alone and does not age, goes round and does not weary. It is capable of being the mother of the world." The Tao is the unborn origin of the universe, the chaotic source of all that exists between heaven and earth.

Western alchemists depicted the First Matter as the ouroboros or uroboros, which is a serpent or dragon eating its own tail (see Chapter 5). In alchemical drawings, sometimes two serpents or dragons were shown, with a lighter, winged serpent above and a darker, walking serpent below. The interplay between these two primordial principles is the engine that drives reality—that creates the singular force behind the evolutionary perfection of the universe.

From the Alchemist

Psychologist Carl Jung commented on the psychological meaning of the uroboros in his *Mysterium Conjunctionis:* "In the age-old image of the uroboros lies the thought of devouring oneself and tuning oneself into a circulatory process, for it was clear to the more astute alchemists the Prima Materia of the art was man himself. The uroboros is a dramatic symbol for the integration and assimilation of the opposite, i.e., the shadow. This feedback process is at the same time a symbol of immortality, since it is said of the uroboros that he slays himself and brings himself to life, fertilizes himself, and gives birth to himself."

To alchemists, the First Matter is a primordial, unorganized state of energy or proto-matter that is the same for all substances and exists in an unmanifested state between energy and matter. The chaos or energy of the First Matter is organized or directed by the light of consciousness. Hermetic philosophers believe the whole universe came into being because of an image, thought, or word projected by the divine mind of God in the fabric of the universe, the First Matter.

Unfortunately, our culture has rejected the concept of the First Matter. For us, things are either real or not real. We have no room in our thinking for the gray area of reality between manifested and unmanifested where the First Matter exists. For this reason, the alchemists often referred to the First Matter as the "cornerstone the builders forgot." That is why rejected things like feces, manure, urine, and even the shadowy dark desires and beliefs we shove into our unconscious are symbols of the First Matter.

Properties of the First Matter

Down through the ages, alchemists have written about the characteristics of the First Matter in an attempt to help identify, accumulate, and transform the mysterious substance. In the following sections, I've brought together some of these descriptions.

The First Matter Is Eternal

The First Matter cannot be created or destroyed. It can only be transformed. The amount of First Matter in the universe is fixed, permanent, and unaffected by time. Modern alchemists associate it with dark matter, which the equations of physics say makes up most of the universe but cannot be detected. Physicists believe dark matter is responsible for the basic structure of the universe and have proven that billions of bits of the invisible matter stream through our bodies every second.

The First Matter Is Everywhere to Be Found

Because the First Matter is the source of all things, it is present everywhere and in all things. To find the First Matter, you must search in the twilight area between manifested and unmanifested reality. Scholars call the kind of space in which the First Matter appears a liminal location, which means anything at the edge, crossroads, or threshold where normal boundaries fade away.

Thoth's Tips

Check out J. K. Rowling's *Harry Potter* series of books for many subtle descriptions of the First Matter. For instance, the in between or liminal aspect of the First Matter is captured in the invisible train platform Nine-and-Three-Quarters located in King's Cross station between platforms Nine and Ten. Rowling is saying that even in the most common and everyday situations, the magical possibilities of the First Matter are available to us if we only break free of our Muggle-headed preconceptions and see the world as the alchemists saw it.

The First Matter Is Cyclic

Both Eastern and Western alchemists understood the cyclic nature of the First Matter and believed it changed into all things light and dark, manifested and unmanifested, in a grand pattern of transformation. In the West, the ouroboros (the dragon eating its own tail) symbolized this idea.

The Eastern symbol for this process is the Tai Chi or Yin-Yang diagram, which depicts the spinning forces of darkness (Yin/matter) and light (Yang/mind), each containing the seed of the other and constantly changing into one another. Yin is seen as feminine, passive, and satisfied in its existence, while Yang is seen as masculine, active, and hungry.

The First Matter Contains All the Elements

The First Matter contains all the components of creation, including the Four Elements and the Quintessence (see Chapter 7). The alchemists believed that the actual form the First Matter takes when it manifests into a material substance depends on the proportions of the Four Elements being expressed. The Elements can be changed into each other, and this manipulation of a substance's First Matter is what transforms it.

The First Matter Is the Source of the Philosopher's Stone

The First Matter was believed to be the only thing from which the Philosopher's Stone could be prepared, and as far back as the Alexandrian alchemist Zosimos, alchemists stated that once the First Matter was known and purified, it became the much-sought-after Stone.

The German alchemist Heinrich Khunrath described the First Matter as the true Light of nature, which guides and illuminates all seekers after divine truth. "It is in the world," he wrote, "and the whole edifice of the world is beautifully adorned and will be naturally preserved by it. But the world knows it not. Above all, it is the subject of the great Stone of the philosophers which the world has before its eyes and yet knows it not."

Working with the First Matter

No alchemical process of transformation—whether in the laboratory, in the body, or in the soul—can succeed without the participation of the elusive ingredient of the First Matter. Certainly nothing was more important to an alchemist's work than this spiritized essence. The alchemists made it clear in their writings that by applying the grades of fire with which they worked, they could extricate the First Matter from any substance and render it tangible and visible.

Alchemists, in their attempts to change base metals into gold, developed most of the laboratory methods of working with the First Matter. The idea behind their work is fairly simple. Strip a metal of the gross qualities and physical properties that identify it, and it yields the one "primitive matter" that is the same for all metals. Next, impose the appropriate new qualities upon the primitive matter, and the desired new substance is attained.

So the metals all originate from the same matrix, which is their First Matter. "The metals are similar in their essence, and differ only in their form," wrote Albertus Magnus in *Of Alchemy*. In another work, he added, "One may pass easily from one metal to another, following a circle." The modern atomic theory of matter expresses a strikingly similar conclusion.

The First Matter can be exposed and accumulated from any material if that material is completely dissolved and broken down into its most fundamental essences. The Alexandrian alchemists believed all one had to do to accomplish this was to divest a material of the gross physical properties represented by Fire, Water, Air, and Earth. However, reducing a substance to its First Matter was always a difficult task, although some materials, such as dew and fertile black earth, released their First Matter easier than other substances.

Trying to extract the First Matter from a substance represented months of hard work roasting, pulverizing, dissolving, and breaking down materials said to contain large amounts of the mysterious essence. Alchemists also referred to the First Matter as the "Mercury of the Philosophers," because they believed the essence or soul of all metals was mercury and therefore spent much effort trying to extract the First Matter from mercury.

Tread Carefully

If you attempt to find the First Matter, whether in nature, in the lab, or within yourself, beware of its awesome power. The alchemists described the First Matter as a "poisonous dragon" whose fire can instantly reduce us to ashes. Yet it is also the "Egg of Nature" and a source of tremendous transformative energy. The secret is to acknowledge the mystery and power of the First Matter and work with it slowly and reverently. But if you look this dragon in the face and attempt to take control of it, you will be destroyed.

The alchemists often referred to the hidden essence of First Matter in a substance as its inner "star," and appearances of the First Matter are often accompanied by displays of light. In this sense, the First Matter is the *Anima Mundi* (Soul of the World), and is present in all things. Alchemists believed the First Matter also existed in the human body as the eternal star which we call the soul. The spiritual work in alchemy focused on purifying or rectifying the First Matter within and, thereby, perfecting the very soul of the alchemist.

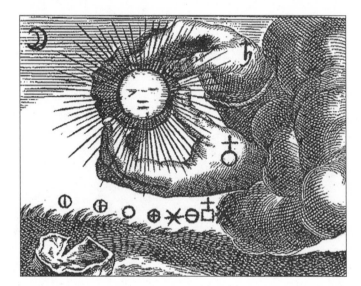

The hidden First Matter.

The Least You Need to Know

- The First Matter gave the universe its properties and existed before our concepts of time and space.

- The First Matter exists on the borderline between manifested and unmanifested reality.

- The First Matter is best understood as the spiritized essence or soul of a substance that gives it its identity, form, and function.

- The First Matter is chaotic and fluid, constantly changing into its opposite in a cosmic play of creation and destruction.

Chapter 7

The Four Elements

In This Chapter

- ◆ Four Elements in the First Matter
- ◆ Theories of the Elements
- ◆ The Four Humors
- ◆ The Square of Opposition
- ◆ The Fifth Element: the Quintessence
- ◆ The four kinds of Fire

The theory of the Four Elements arose out of early philosophers' fascination with the concept of the First Matter. While the First Matter exists in a state of utter chaos and potential, for the universe to exist at all, the First Matter at some point has to become organized. According to the Emerald Tablet, the organizing principle is the One Mind, which projects the vibration of the Word into the chaos to bring about the creation of the world.

In order for the First Matter to take on form or manifest into space, philosophers held the general feeling that it had to take on a fourfold structure. The basic forces that create this fundamental cubic structure of space have come to be called the Four Elements. Most Western alchemists used the Greek system of Elements, which consisted of Earth, Water, Air, and Fire. The

Greek word for Element, *stoicheion*, literally means "letter of the alphabet"; the idea is that the Elements are the building blocks of the words (or thoughts) of the creator.

In studying the Four Elements, keep in mind that they are not our everyday ideas of earth, water, air, and fire, which are only the specific physical expressions of their respective archetypes. The Elements are really spiritual essences and originate in the higher realm Above, where they represent perfect images or cosmic ideals. In the Hermetic teachings, the Four Elements result from the materialization of light or imagery within the divine One Mind of the universe.

The Concept of the Elements

Contrary to popular belief, several pre-Socratic Greek philosophers proposed the classical Four Elements independently and not all together at once. Thales first proposed that Water was the root of creation; then Anaximenes added Air. Xenophanes added Earth to the list, and finally Heraclitus proposed that Fire was among the fundamental building blocks of nature. Not until Empedocles (494–434 B.C.E.) proposed that they had all existed together in fixed quantities since the beginning of time did the theory came together as we know it.

In his book *Doctrine of the Four Roots*, Empedocles stated that all matter emerges from the four "roots" of Earth, Water, Air, and Fire. In his view, Fire and Air are expansive "outwardly reaching" constants of nature, reaching up and out, whereas Earth and Water are contractive and turn inward and downward.

To show their archetypal power, Empedocles associated each essence with a god. "Hera rules the fruitful Earth," he wrote, "Hades rules the central Fire, Zeus the luminescent Air, and Persephone the mollifying Water." Empedocles believed these four parts of creation were animated through the interaction of two great living energies he called Love and Strife. Love he associated with the goddess Aphrodite, and Strife with the god of war, Ares. This idea is very similar to the Eastern tradition idea of Yin and Yang, with Yin being the passive, feminine energy of Love and Yang being the aggressive, masculine energy of Strife. In alchemy, these two contrary principles became known as the King and Queen. And this simple view explained nearly every aspect of the Greek world.

Plato (427–347 B.C.E.) reiterated the archetypal nature of the Four Elements by describing them as "idea-forms" that had a separate and real existence. He also discovered that the Elements were not static, but could transform or "go over" into one another. For instance, Water freezes to ice, being like a stone or Earth, yet it evaporates to vapor or becomes Air.

> ### From the Alchemist
>
> The Four Elements in astrology describe the basic nature or temperament of each sign of the zodiac. In general, Earth is connected to the body and practical considerations; Water with feelings and emotions; Air with thoughts and imagination; and Fire with energy and activity. The signs that express the Earth Element are Taurus, Virgo, and Capricorn. The Water Element is dominant in Cancer, Scorpio, and Pisces. The Air signs are Gemini, Libra, and Aquarius. And the Fire signs are Aries, Leo, and Sagittarius.

Aristotle (384–322 B.C.E.) first used the word Element, and the Alexandrian alchemists popularized it. And Aristotle further developed the theories of Empedocles and Plato by explaining the Four Elements as combinations of two sets of opposing qualities of hot and cold, wet and dry. Water is cold and wet; Earth is cold and dry; Air is hot and wet; and Fire is hot and dry. This concept became the foundation upon which Western alchemists based their theories and practices.

Aristotle postulated that wet and dry are the primary qualities of matter. Wet, or moistness, is the quality of fluidity or flexibility, which allows a thing to adapt to its external conditions; whereas dry, or dryness, is the quality of rigidity, which allows a thing to define its own shape and bounds. As a consequence, wet things tend to be volatile and expansive, because they can fill spaces in their surroundings. Dry things are fixed and structured, because they define their own form.

> ### From the Alchemist
>
> Polish alchemist Michael Sendivogius (1566–1636) expressed the alchemical view of the Elements in his book *The Water Which Does Not Wet the Hands*. "There are four common Elements, and each has at its center another deeper heavenly Element which makes it what it is. They were each in the beginning evolved and molded out of chaos of First Matter by the hand of the Creator; and it is their contrary action which keeps up the harmony and equilibrium of the mundane machinery of the universe."

In Aristotle's view, each of the Four Elements has its natural place. He placed the Earth Element at the center of the physical universe, and then arranged Water, Air, and Fire in increasing "subtlety" around it. When an Element is out of its natural place, it has an innate tendency to return to its level. Thus bodies sink in water; air bubbles up; rain falls; and flames rise.

Aristotle added a Fifth Element to his philosophical system to explain the actions of the planets and stars. He called it the Ether Element and said it was what the heavens were made of. The alchemists refer to this Fifth Element as the Quintessence, which comes from a Latin phrase meaning "fifth essence." By adding the Fifth Element, Aristotle brought Western alchemy into agreement with Chinese and Indian versions of the Elements.

Aristotle also predicted that one substance could be transformed into another by altering the mix of its archetypal Elements and their qualities, and this made understanding the Elements and their qualities of primary importance to the alchemists. Aristotle's elegant view was the accepted philosophy of matter throughout the Middle Ages.

The Four Humors

The Greek physician and "Father of Modern Medicine" Hippocrates (460–370 B.C.E.) further developed the theory of the Four Elements. He viewed the Elements as bodily fluids he called "humors":

◆ He associated Fire with the Choleric humor of yellow bile, which is carried in cholesterol as a bi-product of digestion in the body. Choleric people tend to be energetic, enthusiastic, and constantly moving. In Aristotle's view, such people are hot and dry.

◆ He associated Water with the Phlegmatic humor of phlegm, which represents the clear fluids of the body carried by the lymphatic system and secreted by the mucus membranes. The phlegmatic person is cold and wet in Aristotle's terms and tends to be in touch with his feelings, yet can be moody and brooding. People in whom the Phlegmatic humor is dominant tend to be flowing and flexible, oriented toward emotional harmony, and let their feelings guide them.

◆ He associated Air with the Sanguine humor of the blood, which distributes oxygen throughout the tissues of the body. The word sanguine refers to a ruddy complexion in which the blood flows close to the skin. Sanguine people tend to be very changeable and even flighty, a little irritable yet basically optimistic, and full of personal integrity. According to Aristotle, such people are hot and wet in their elemental qualities, which produces a melding of intellect and emotions.

◆ He associated Earth with the Melancholic humor of black bile, which probably refers to waste products associated with digestion such as stool, from which useful energy has been removed leaving only the dregs of matter behind.

Melancholic people tend to be apathetic, passive, stubborn, sluggish, yet practical. Because Earth is the principle of structure and materialization, the Melancholic humor is dominant in the person who focuses on physical reality and tends to exhibit the qualities of perseverance, inflexibility, realism, and pragmatism. In Aristotle's terms, such people are cool and dry.

The Four Humors.

Hippocrates' theory of the Four Humors survives today in psychologist Carl Jung's theory of personality types. Jung saw the Four Elements as archetypes existing in the collective subconscious and are thus present in everyone. Like Aristotle, he considered Fire and Air the active, masculine Elements and Water and Earth the passive, feminine Elements.

Thoth's Tips _____

The Luscher Color personality profile offers a way of relating to the Elements as colors. The Fire color red invokes excitement and passion. The Water color blue encourages relaxation and tranquility. The Air color yellow brings out qualities of mind and imagination. The Earth color green elicits natural balance and practicality.

Balancing the Elements

Empedocles noted that those who had near equal expressions of the Four Elements in their personalities were more intelligent and had the truest perceptions of reality. Carl Jung noted the same thing in his patients and called the balancing of the Elements in a person "integration."

Aristotle's theory of the Elements implied a scheme of transformation in which one Element could be changed into another. Because the Four Elements came into being by impressing their opposing qualities of hot and cold and dry and wet on the First Matter, it follows that one Element can change into another by altering these basic qualities.

For instance, when we impose the qualities of wet and cold on the First Matter, the Water Element results. But if we change the quality of cold for that of hot, such as what happens when we boil Water, it transforms into Air (steam). By manipulating this simple relationship between a substance's inherent qualities, we can change one thing into another.

We can visualize this scheme of transformation in Aristotle's Square of Opposition, which depicts all the relationships between the qualities and the Elements. Opposing Elements form a cross within the square, and each Element is composed of two qualities shown in the corners of the square. Thus, Earth is dry and cold; Water is cold and wet; Air is wet and hot; and Fire is hot and dry. The qualities form a diagonal cross of opposition within the square.

Square of Opposition.

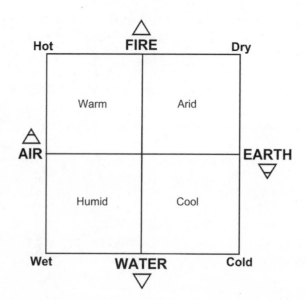

The alchemists considered the Square of Opposition a dynamic rotating machine that was in constant motion, like a video. In other words, changes in the qualities of the Elements cause movement through the square. Or we could say that the "strife between opposites" is the motor of rotation. Cold becomes hot; hot becomes cold; wet becomes dry; and dry becomes wet. We call this movement the Rotation of the Elements. "It is clear that generation of the Elements will be circular," explained Aristotle, "and this mode of change is very easy because corresponding qualities are present in adjacent Elements."

This natural circulation of the Elements in the Square of Opposition begins with the process of adaptation (Water) and continues through expansion (Air), production (Fire), and retraction (Earth). We can see the same pattern of movement through the Elements in many elemental rotations, including the seasons (winter, spring, summer, fall), the ages of man (childhood, youth, maturity, old age), and the cyclic rise and fall of nations and ideas.

Hot (or heat) in the upper left-hand corner of the Square of Opposition is the primary quality, and Fire at the top of the square is the most active Element. The alchemists saw Fire as the most important agent of transformation. So important was Fire to the alchemists that they often referred to themselves as Philosophers of Fire.

Water, at the bottom of the Square of Opposition, is the most passive Element and represents the agent of coagulation or materialization in the current situation. Air and Earth were considered secondary Elements made up of different qualities of Fire and Water. The Greeks believed Air was a combination of the hot quality of Fire and the wet quality of Water, and Earth was a combination of the cold quality of Water and the dry quality of Fire.

Four rules determine movement within the Square of Opposition:

1. Movement progresses in a clockwise rotation starting at Fire, which is where the work of transformation begins. As one moves through the square, each Element follows its dominant quality. Therefore, Fire is predominantly hot; Earth is predominantly dry; Water is predominantly cold; and Air predominantly wet (or humid). The qualities drive the Elemental rotation of the turning square: hot on the top, dry on the descending side, cold on the bottom, and wet on the rising side.

2. Because we can only move around and not across the Square of Opposition, direct transformation of opposing Elements into one another is not possible. Thus Water cannot be transformed directly into Fire because they have no common

quality; however, Water can be transformed by first changing it into one of the secondary Elements of Air or Earth. Then, Air or Earth can be transformed into Fire.

3. The qualities are inversely proportional to each other. That means that the higher the intensity of an earlier quality in the rotation, the greater the rate of increase in the following opposite quality. Or the higher the intensity of a later quality in the rotation, the more the preceding complementary quality decreases. For instance, increasing the hot quality increases dryness and decreases wetness. To illustrate this concept, let's work through one complete cycle starting at Earth. An increase in heat causes Earth to melt and take on the characteristics of Water. Further heating, however, decreases the cold of the Water component and increases its hot quality, which makes it boil and turn into steam or Air. When Air is heated, its moisture is reduced, and it rises higher into Fire. When Fire becomes cold, it loses its heat and becomes ashes or Earth again.

4. Whenever two Elements share a common quality, the Element in which the quality is not dominant is overcome by the one in which it is dominant. This property is known as the Cycle of Triumphs and was first noticed by Spanish alchemist Raymond Lully (1229–1315). For example, when Water combines with Earth, Earth is overcome because both are cold, but cold dominates in Water. Therefore, Water overcomes Earth, and the result will be predominantly cold. According to this scheme, Fire overcomes Air; Air overcomes Water; Water overcomes Earth; and Earth overcomes Fire.

Using the Square of Opposition to transform things is really quite simple when you work through it a few times. The archetypal relationships between the Elements are so plainly depicted in the Square of Opposition that it's an amazingly versatile tool for all kinds of transformation. The alchemists used these same relationships and progressed through the Square of Opposition whether they were doing laboratory experiments, producing medicines, or working on their own personal transformations.

To use the Square of Opposition in your own transformation, you must first meditate on the qualities of the Elements to know how they are expressed in your personality or temperament. To balance your dominant Element, find its opposite on the cross within the square. You want to increase the presence of this neglected Element to balance your temperament; however, because they are opposite and cannot be changed directly into one another, you must work through one of the adjacent Elements.

For example, if in your personality your dominant Element is Water and you need to balance it with more Fire, begin by working with the adjacent Element (Air or Earth) with which you are the most comfortable or which is more dominant in you. If you choose the more spiritual path of Air, you need to work to increase the quality of wetness, which means becoming more flowing and allowing emotional energy to surface. If you choose the more material path of Earth, you need to do the opposite and try to become less flowing, more grounded, and more controlling of emotional energy. The choice of which path to follow obviously requires some insight about the true nature of your inner self.

One of the dark secrets about the Square of Opposition is that it's possible to work with the reverse (counterclockwise) rotation. This is known as the Death Rotation. The Byzantine emperor and alchemist Heraclitus (600 C.E.) described the process thus: "Fire lives in the death of Earth, and Air lives the death of Fire; Water lives the death of Air, and Earth lives the death of Water."

So the Death Rotation is a process of sacrificing one Element to give life to another, and in its applications requires the use of negative imagery and negative energies. In his book *Purifications*, Empedocles used this reverse rotation as a kind of personal crucifixion to cleanse the soul of broken promises, crimes against humanity, and other bad karma. This tortuous personal alchemy demanded extreme awareness and brutal honesty and required the alchemist to direct negative energies like anger and disgust inward. Empedocles warned it was so cosmic a process that it might last through numerous rebirths and go on for "thrice ten thousand years" in the soul of the alchemist.

The Quintessence

We call the mysterious Quintessence of the alchemists the Fifth Element not because it was considered one of the Elements but because it lay beyond the Elements in both form and function. The Quintessence was viewed as something new and unexpected in creation that transcended the limitations imposed by the Four Elements. As Isaac Newton put it: "The Quintessence is a thing that is spiritual, penetrating, tingeing, and incorruptible, which emerges anew from the Four Elements when they are bound together."

The Quintessence partakes of both material and spiritual realities and is described as a luminous light that is invisible to ordinary sight. Like Pythagoras before him, the alchemical philosopher Paracelsus believed the Quintessence is what the stars are made of and that within everything there exists a hidden star that is that thing's Quintessence.

From the Alchemist

Alchemist Benedictus Figulus described the Quintessence in his book *The Golden Casket* (1608): "For the Elements are composed of a subtle substance diffused through their parts. This spirit fertilizes or brings to life all subjects natural and artificial, pouring into them those hidden properties we call the Fifth Essence or Quintessence, which the Fount of Medicine, the Elixir of life and restoration of health, and in this may be the cherished renewal of lost youth and serene health be found."

The idea of the Quintessence is part of the Perennial Philosophy and is present in every spiritual tradition. In Chinese alchemy, the Fifth Element is Wood, which is a product of the plant kingdom and associated with the life force. In Taoist alchemy, the Quintessence is known as Chi, which is an unseen energy that flows through the body and can be accumulated and directed in moving meditations such as performed in Tai Chi and Chi Kung. In Tantric alchemy, the Quintessence is the kundalini or sexual energy coiled like a sleeping serpent at the base of the spine. In Hindu alchemy, the Quintessence is the spirit of breath known in Sanskrit as *prana*. This is very similar to the Western concepts of the spirit of air known as *pneuma* in Greek and *rauch* in Hebrew.

Philosophers of Fire

To the alchemists, Fire was the most important Element, and they considered it the universal agent of transformation that made alchemy possible. "Alchemy is only that which makes the impure pure by means of Fire," said Paracelsus. "Though not all fires do burn, it is however only Fire and continues to be Fire that interests us."

Alchemists recognize four grades or types of fire with which they perform their transformations. Let's take a closer look at each.

Elementary Fire

The lowest grade of fire is known as the Elementary Fire, which is the common fire we are all familiar with. "The Elementary Fire, which is the fire of our stoves," wrote the French philosopher-alchemist Antoine Joseph Pernety in 1758, "is impure, thick and burning. This fire is sharp and corrosive, often ill-smelling, and is known through the senses. It has for its abode the surface of the earth and our atmosphere and is destructive; it wounds the senses, it burns, it digests, concocts, and produces nothing other than heat. It is external to the alchemist and separating."

Celestial Fire

The highest grade of fire is the Celestial Fire, which is the brilliant white fire that issues forth from the One Mind of God and represents the power of divine will. "The Celestial Fire is very pure, simple and not burning in itself," said Pernety, "It has for its sphere the ethereal region, whence it makes itself known even to us. Celestial Fire shines without burning and is without color and odor. It is gentle and known only by its operations."

Central Fire

Between the lowest and highest grades of fire are two more kinds. One is the Central Fire hidden within matter at its very center. Central Fire is the fire of creation, the embedded Word of God in all manifested objects. According to Pernety: "The Celestial Fire passes into the nature of the Central Fire; it becomes internal, engendering in matter. It is invisible and therefore known only by its qualities. The Central Fire is lodged in the center of matter; it is tenacious and innate in matter; it is digesting, maturing, neither warm nor burning to the touch."

Secret Fire

Alchemists rarely speak of the fourth grade of fire even though they consider it the primary fire with which the true alchemist works. They refer to it only as their Secret Fire. "The fire of the sun could not be this Secret Fire," hints Pernety. "It is unequal and does not penetrate. The fire of our stoves, which consumes the constituent parts of matter, could not be the one. The Central Fire, which is innate in matter, cannot be that Secret Fire so much praised, because this heat is very different within the three kingdoms; the animal possesses it in a much higher degree than the plant."

The true nature of the Secret Fire has been concealed in myths and legends down through the ages. "In allegories and fables," Pernety confirms, "the philosophers have given to this Secret Fire the names sword, lance, arrows, javelin, etc. It is the fire which Prometheus stole from heaven, which Vulcan employed to form the thunderbolts of Jupiter and the golden throne of Zeus."

From Pernety's clues, maybe we can figure out the truth about the Secret Fire. It seems the Secret Fire has a direction or evolution and behaves with purpose like a sword or arrow. We also know that animals possess more of it than plants and that it is an ancient secret passed down from alchemist to alchemist in myths and legends.

Let's look for more clues. Franz Hartmann, a nineteenth-century German physician, was another alchemist who wrote openly about the Secret Fire. In his book *Alchemy*, he admitted: "The Secret Fire of the alchemists is sometimes described as a serpentine working power in the body of the acetic. It is an electric, fiery, hidden power, an electro-spiritual force and creative power."

Any alchemist worth his salt knows what the code word "serpentine" means. Since the days of Thoth and Hermes, the serpent has symbolized the life force, the basic animating energy that finds expression in our sexuality and state of health. The life force is the Quintessence of matter, the hidden Fifth Element, the inner divine spark that makes all things come alive. We have just cracked one of the greatest secrets of alchemy—the Secret Fire of the alchemists is the life force itself, and it is an important ingredient in their work. It is something the alchemist tries to accumulate, control, and add to his experiments.

The Least You Need to Know

- The Four Elements are archetypes or idealized essences expressed in the manifested world as common earth, water, air, and fire.

- Aristotle was responsible for bringing earlier concepts of the Elements together into one cohesive theory that allowed for the transformation of one Element into one another.

- The Square of Opposition is a diagram of the relationships of the Elements and how they can be transformed.

- The Fifth Element (or the Quintessence) is equated with the life force in most traditions.

- The Four Grades of Fire in alchemy are Elementary Fire, Celestial Fire, Central Fire, and Secret Fire.

Chapter 8

The Three Essentials

In This Chapter

- The three-headed dragon of the First Matter
- Doctrine of the Two Contraries
- The three philosophical substances
- The Three Essentials within all of us
- The three treasures of Taoist alchemy

The Three Essentials are the trinity of forces that make up creation, and the alchemists named them Sulfur, Mercury, and Salt. Sulfur and Mercury are the primordial opposites that are part of the inherent duality of the universe. We have only to observe nature to see this fundamental duality, which can be expressed as masculine and feminine, positive and negative, light and dark, expanding and contracting, energy and matter, Yang and Yin, and many other names depending on our perspective.

Salt, on the other hand, is the static result or resolving force created by the union of Sulfur and Mercury. In alchemy, Salt is associated with the Philosopher's Child and considered the principle of form or structure. The alchemists saw Salt at work in the formation of fetuses and the growth of plants, as well as in the formation of chemical compounds and in processes like precipitation and crystallization. Salt is active anywhere a new body forms.

All created things consist of Sulfur, Mercury, and Salt, and alchemical procedures can break everything down into these three principles. To differentiate them from the mundane substances of the same name, the alchemists always capitalized the names of the Three Essentials in their writings. Sometimes they clearly designated them philosophical or sophic substances and called them Sophic Sulfur, Sophic Mercury, and Sophic Salt.

Three Children of the First Matter

According to alchemical philosophy, the Three Essentials emerge into creation from a common source—the First Matter (see Chapter 6). The three-headed serpent or dragon, which is a symbol of the First Matter, captured this idea. In a scenario that mirrors our modern concept of the Big Bang, alchemists believed the Three Essentials were born from the chaotic darkness of the First Matter into our universe in a tremendous burst of energy and light.

Thoth's Tips

The Three Essentials are so important in alchemy that, generally, any grouping of three things in drawings or discussions refers to these three universal principles. They were also known as the Three Supernals; the Supreme Trinity; the Three Principia; the Three Universals; the Three Treasures; the Three Magisteriums; and the *Tria Prima*, Latin for the First Three.

Once created, the Three Essentials are indistinguishable from the First Matter in their powers of transformation, and their primal interaction is responsible for myriad manifested things in our world. At the end of the Great Work, the Three Essentials are reunited and integrally fused into the Philosopher's Stone.

The alchemists' motto conveyed this idea: "The Stone is single in essence, but triple in form." Not surprisingly, the three-headed serpent or dragon is also a symbol for the Philosopher's Stone, although there are distinct differences in attitude and coloring when compared to the beast of the First Matter. Somehow, the First Matter itself has been transformed.

We are beginning to get a glimpse of the Big Picture in alchemy. The Great Work begins with the emergence of the First Matter and ends with the creation of the Philosopher's Stone. Furthermore, the First Matter and the Philosopher's Stone are composed of the same three essential ingredients. The Great Work is nothing more than the *rectification* of the First Matter into the Philosopher's Stone.

def•i•ni•tion

> Rectification is an alchemical term that literally means "to set right" and implies that the original substance was corrupt or imperfect. Chemical rectification is a process of refining by repeated distillations or purification using filters or membranes that separate out impurities. To rectify a system means to set all energy currents working in the same direction. Rectification of light results in an intense, coherent, tightly focused, single-frequency beam. These are all fitting descriptions of the creation of the Stone.

The Two Contraries

The roots of the alchemists' theory of Sulfur and Mercury lie in an ancient doctrine known as the Two Contraries. The Two Contraries were seen as reciprocal principles of nature, usually described as male and female or active and passive. Symbolized by the sun and moon, they were an expression of the fundamental natural law of reproduction.

Originating in Egypt in the myths of Isis and Osiris, the doctrine of the Two Contraries eventually spread to Babylonia and China. Although the two opposing principles took on a variety of names, they always shared the same characteristics of the original myth. Isis was the moon goddess—the feminine, receptive, reflective, productive principle of nature. Osiris was the sun god—the masculine, aggressive, penetrating source of energy and identity. Their child was Horus, who became the symbol for all new birth, growth, the green earth, and transformation in general.

Among Alexandrian alchemists, the principle of the sun or Osiris became linked with Sulfur, and the principle of the moon or Isis became linked with Mercury. Their child Horus would eventually become associated with the alchemical substance of Salt. The archetypal principles of the sun and moon represented by Osiris and Isis were thought to give rise to all things, and the concept that all things are engendered through the union of these two opposing forces took root among alchemists around the world.

Alchemists in ancient India believed the metals were born of the union of the gods Hara and Parvati through the powers of Agni, the god of Fire. Sulfur was Agni; Mercury was the semen of Hara; and the crucible of earth in which their union occurred was Parvati.

In China, the doctrine of the Two Contraries arose from the Taoist concept of the Tao (First Matter). Around 300 B.C.E., the concept of the Tao changed to include the two opposing qualities of Yang and Yin. Yang was masculine, positive, expansive, solar, and fiery; and Yin was feminine, negative, contractive, lunar, and watery. Yang was light and tended to rise into the sky; Yin was heavy and tended to descend into the earth. Yin was the unperfected soul and the only thing that could quench the yearnings of Yang, which was the perfect spirit. The interaction between these two contrary principles was what created the material universe.

The Arabian alchemist Jabir expanded the doctrine of the Two Contraries by combining his philosophical readings with his experimental observations. As you learned in Chapter 3, Jabir believed the First Matter deep at the heart of the earth gave off two opposing "exhalations" or spirits that became Sulfur and Mercury.

According to Jabir, metals were formed by differing impurities and concentrations of Sulfur and Mercury. Gold was the purest and most balanced or perfect combination of this primal pair. To transform base metals into gold, it was necessary to purify and balance their Sulfur and Mercury. Jabir also believed there existed a Philosopher's Stone that would instantly transform base metals into gold by permanently joining the Two Contraries of Sulfur and Mercury.

Sulfur, Mercury, and Salt

For nearly 700 years, Jabir's version of the Two Contraries dominated alchemy. Then the great Swiss alchemist Paracelsus reorganized the Sulfur-Mercury theory to include a third component called "Salt." He also clarified and corrected what other alchemists had been saying about these very basic ideas for so many years.

The result was the theory of the Three Essentials, which turned Sulfur, Mercury, and Salt into powerful universal tools that gave alchemists greater insight into the nature of reality. Philosophically, the Three Essentials were viewed as universal forces present on all levels of reality. Their relationship and interaction determine how substances come into being and are transformed.

Paracelsus defined the Three Essentials by how they behave in fire. Sulfur is seen as what fuels the fire or what is changed in the fire. Thus oil, fat, wood, and coal are all forms of Sulfur. Mercury is the volatile watery essence of the fire that Paracelsus called the "phlegma" and is represented by the flames, light, heat, and smoke issuing from the fire. The new principle of Salt exhibits the fixed essence of the substance burning that resists the fire and is found in the ashes. "The three principles from which all things are born and generated," said Paracelsus, "are phlegma, fat, and ash."

In the burning of wood, for example, Sulfur is the wood fuel which is consumed in the fire; Mercury is the smoke, heat, and light that come from the fire; and Salt is the wood ashes created by the fire. As Paracelsus put it: "The fire is Mercury; what is burnt is Sulfur; and all ash is Salt."

Sulfur is the fiery, solar, active, masculine principle that gives a substance its active properties and identity in relationship to other substances. In alchemy, it is usually associated with the sun and King. In the laboratory, Sulfur is the flammable oily material extracted from substances, such as the essential oils of plants. For alchemists, Sulfur embodied all those characteristics that we now associate with the idea of active energy.

Mercury is the watery, lunar, passive, feminine principle that represents the hidden essence and creative source of life within things and is usually associated with the moon and Queen in alchemy. In the laboratory, Mercury is usually extracted from substances by the process of distillation, such as the alcohol distilled from fermented grains and fruits. The alchemists referred to Mercury as the "Mother of the Stone" and felt it was the mediator between Sulfur and Salt in the creation of new compounds.

In Hermetic philosophy, Mercury is like the basic blueprint of a thing, the carrier of its image or ideal form that comes into being through the interaction of Sulfur and Salt. Mercury embodied those characteristics that we now associate with the concept of light and mind.

Salt represents fixity, materialization, and the formation of bodies and embodies those characteristics that we associate with the idea of mass or matter. In their writings, the alchemists sometimes referred to Salt as "Magnesia," which was actually a mystical term referring to the transformative principle concealed in Salt.

Like the First Matter, Salt shows up at both the beginning and the end of the work. It is the imperfect and corrupted matter at the beginning of the experiment that must be destroyed and dissolved to release its essences, so they can be purified and reconstituted into the perfected new Salt at the end of the experiment.

The Four Elements, the fundamental principles of matter, have their origin in the Three Essentials. The archetypal force of Sulfur gives rise to the Fire Element. Mercury, in keeping with its dual nature, produces both the Air and Water Elements. And finally, the Salt principle is the source of the Earth Element.

In this drawing from Splendor Solis, the Three Essentials are depicted as three dragons sharing one body inside a glass retort. At the end of the work, the Three Essentials are united.

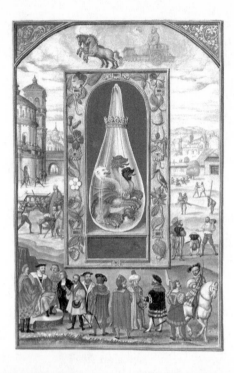

From the Alchemist

Although alchemists and modern physicists use different terminology, they agree about the three fundamental forces of nature. In fact, Einstein's equation of the universe ($E = mc2$) is as valid in alchemy as it is in modern science. Sulfur is energy (E); Salt is matter (m); and Mercury is light (c). For both alchemists and physicists, energy and matter are really the same thing, whose final expression is determined by the intermediary of light. In alchemical philosophy, matter is like condensed energy whose form is projected by the light of mind. So, if that little "c" in Einstein's equation stood for consciousness instead of the speed of light, there would be no difference between alchemy and modern physics.

The Dance of Sulfur and Mercury

A surprising thing about the Three Essentials is usually revealed only at the later stages of initiation. The Three Essentials are not really as identifiable and set in their properties as you might suppose. They are not the static laws or immutable universal constants you assume them to be. I've already noted that Salt can exist in two forms—one at the beginning and the other at the end of the work. Well, Sulfur and Mercury have a much more dynamic relationship.

Sulfur and Mercury are like two dancers who change into one another as they spin around the dance floor. These two volatile principles are sometimes so hard to distinguish from one another that alchemists believed they were actually two faces of the same thing. They named it the *Rebis* (Latin for "double thing") and pictured it as a two-headed hermaphrodite. The strange love affair between Sulfur and Mercury is what makes alchemical transformation possible.

This unique relationship of Sulfur and Mercury is also suggested in drawings of the ouroboros showing two dragons or serpents eating each other's tails. One is dark and one is light, or one has wings and the other has feet. As the ouroboros spins through time and space, the two parts change into one another. The alchemists viewed this as the engine that drives reality.

The Sulfur-Mercury dynamic is most clearly depicted in the Taoist symbol of Yang and Yin known as the Taijitu. The opposing forces of Yang and Yin are shown inside a circle that is divided into a white Yang section with a small black circle within it and a black Yin section with a small white circle within it. The smaller circles represent the seeds of their opposites that both Yang and Yin carry. In other words, each carries the seed of its opposite and eventually transforms into it.

Psychologist Carl Jung called this mysterious process of one thing changing into its opposite by the unwieldy name of "inandromedria." Whatever you call it, it requires a fluid mind and a little dedication to fully absorb its power. "If your meditation prolongs itself," promised the Persian mystic Zoroaster, "you can unite all these Symbols."

The kindred affair between Sulfur and Mercury explains a conundrum faced by most students of alchemy in their reading of alchemy texts. In some descriptions, Mercury is associated with spirit and Sulfur with soul. In other texts, however, Sulfur is spirit, and Mercury is soul. We can now understand that both views are correct. The identities of Sulfur and Mercury depend on the situation or the context of the discussion. It all depends on where we stop them in their whirling dance.

In general, Sulfur deals with the energy aspects of a substance or situation, while Mercury deals with the aspects of inner life and awareness. If the subject is any kind of active energy or fire, then Sulfur is spirit.

Tread Carefully

Don't let the dance of Sulfur and Mercury confuse you. Their blurred identities are part of the mystery of creation. Unfortunately, every author seems to have an opinion as to what they represent. That is why Paracelsus set the standard definitions that most alchemists after him have followed: Mercury is spirit and Sulfur is soul.

If the subject is any kind of potential or unexpressed energy, then Sulfur is soul. On the other hand, if the topic is an indwelling life or active intelligence, then Mercury is spirit. And if the subject is an unborn identity or unconscious force, then Mercury is soul.

Salt is the resultant force that gives expression and purpose to the dance of Sulfur and Mercury. Salt is the child of their marriage. It freezes the dance of opposites, grounds them, and condenses their light and energy form and matter.

The Three Essentials in People

Psychologically, the principles of Sulfur, Mercury, and Salt form a triad of transformative powers that are available to us if we can learn to purify and control them. "In the Body," says the *Book of Lambsprinck*, "there is Soul and Spirit. He that knows how to tame and master them by Art, to couple them together and to lead them, may justly be called a Master, for we rightly judge that he has attained the golden flesh."

In people, the Three Essentials are represented by the three concepts of body, mind (or spirit), and soul. Salt is the body, Mercury is spirit, and Sulfur is soul. "Know then," declared Paracelsus, "that all the seven metals are born from a threefold matter, namely, Mercury, Sulfur, and Salt, although each metal has its own distinct and peculiar colorings. Mercury is the spirit, Sulfur is the soul, and Salt is the body. The soul, which indeed is Sulfur, unites those two contraries, the body and the spirit, and changes them into one essence."

In general, when talking about people, the easily ignited Sulfur of soul stands for our inner passion and willpower, while the fluid force of the Mercury in spirit represents our ever-changing thoughts and powers of visualization and imagination. The hermaphroditic Salt of their union is the Philosopher's Stone, a perfected state of consciousness that combines passion and feeling with thought and imagination.

From the Alchemist

In the Golden Dawn and other magical traditions, Mercury is associated with spirit and the mental faculty of imagination. Sulfur is associated with willpower and its connection to the deep reservoir of transformative energy in the soul. "Both the Imagination of Mercury and the Will of Sulfur must be called into action," said a nineteenth-century Golden Dawn member. "They are co-equal in the Work. When the two are conjoined and the Imagination creates an image and the Will directs and uses that image, then marvelous magical effects can be obtained."

The Three Treasures of Taoist Alchemy

In Taoist alchemy, the Three Essentials are known as the Three Treasures and are called Shen, Chi, and Ching. These concepts translate roughly as Spirit, Vitality, and Essence. In general, Shen represents Mercury; Chi represents Sulfur; and Ching is Salt. However, because Taoist alchemy focuses so much on working in the body, subtle differences exist between the Eastern and Western viewpoints.

In Taoist teachings, the characteristics of the Three Treasures can be found in the burning of a candle. Shen (Mercury) is the radiant light given off by the flame. Chi (Sulfur) is the heat given off by the candle, and Ching (Salt) is the wax and wick of the candle, which are both its structure and the condensed energy of its fuel.

Shen (Mercury) is considered the guiding spirit or mind that directs the energy of Chi (Sulfur). Like Mercury in the Western tradition, Shen is the most important of the Three Treasures in the alchemy of transformation.

Shen is experienced as a presence or spirit within that produces an "all-embracing sense of compassion that resides in the heart." It gives people their spiritual radiance and is the source of our innate knowledge that everything is one. Shen resides in both heaven and Earth and gives us the ability to rise above the mundane world.

Chi (Sulfur) is the energy that moves in our bodies and gives us our vitality. It is the universal energy created by the constant interaction of Yin and Yang, the two "moving powers" in the world. Chi embodies these Two Contraries of Yang and Yin. Fast-moving Chi is considered to be Yang, while slow-moving Chi is Yin. All movement and all functioning are the result of Chi, and the nature of Chi is to keep moving.

In esoteric anatomy, Chi is carried in the blood and in the air we constantly breathe in and out. Blood is produced from the fires of metabolism, and Chi is extracted from ingested food through the action of the spleen. Red blood cells are nourishing and are considered Yin, while white blood cells are protective and are considered Yang. Chi also enters through the lungs, where it circulates through energetic pathways, called "meridians," throughout the body.

Ching (Salt) is a mysterious substance called the "superior ultimate" of the Three Treasures. The word Ching means "regenerative essence" and is considered to be a concentrated energy that manifests physically in the body. Ching is seen as a perfect blend of Yang and Yin energy, and it is, therefore, not moving energy but static or heavy energy. It is the source of our sexuality and the life force that operates the body's cells and organs.

Ching exists before the body comes into being and becomes the "root" of our body when we are born. We cannot live without Ching. It's a fundamental heavy essence that accumulates in the body. If we can learn to conserve Ching, we can live vigorous and long lives. Ching is burned up by chronic stress and excessive behavior such as overwork, overeating, sexual excess, emotionalism, and substance abuse.

Shen is intimately related to Chi and Ching, and only when all Three Treasures are in balance does the whole system thrive. Chi condenses into Ching, and when we develop and accumulate Ching, we also increase Chi automatically. And when Chi is accumulated and purified, it strengthens Shen. "When the Three become One," said the alchemist Lu in his treatise *Complete Reality*, "the Great Elixir is made."

The Least You Need to Know

◆ The Three Essentials originated from the First Matter at the beginning of creation.

◆ The Two Contraries are Mercury and Sulfur in the Western tradition or Yin and Yang in the Eastern tradition.

◆ The Three Essentials are the philosophical substances known as Sulfur, Mercury, and Salt.

◆ The Three Essentials are present everywhere in the universe and are expressed in every substance, including people.

◆ The Three Treasures of Taoist alchemy are Shen (Mercury), Chi (Sulfur), and Ching (Salt).

Chapter 9

The Philosopher's Stone

In This Chapter

- ◆ Origins of the concept of a Philosopher's Stone
- ◆ The powers of the Philosopher's Stone
- ◆ The appearance and preparation of the Stone
- ◆ The genius of Dr. John Dee
- ◆ The magical cipher of the Stone

The idea of the Philosopher's Stone originated with Alexandrian alchemists and soon captured the imagination of people around the world. By the Middle Ages, the Philosopher's Stone became the Holy Grail of alchemy. It became not only the key to transforming base metals into gold, but also held the secret to eternal life and spiritual perfection. Because the Stone could turn a corruptible base metal into incorruptible gold, it would similarly transform human beings from mortal (corruptible) beings into immortal (incorruptible) beings.

The origins of the concept of the Philosopher's Stone can be seen in the theory of the Four Elements and the possibility of transforming one Element into another. There was also an ancient belief that metals could be transformed into one another. This belief probably originated with the observation that some precious metals could be obtained from the ores of base metals. For instance, silver is often obtained from galena, the mineral ore of lead. The preparation of metal tinctures and alloys that imparted the characteristics of gold suggested a single agent might exist that would transmute the metals.

The spiritual significance of the Philosopher's Stone originated in the Egyptian belief in the perfection of the soul and the creation of an immortal golden body. The mystical doctrine of the regeneration of mankind was part of the spiritual traditions of many early civilizations, and the Philosopher's Stone was the physical manifestation of that fundamental desire for perfection.

The Magical Touchstone

In Latin, the Philosopher's Stone was called the *Lapis Philosophorum* or Stone of the Philosophers, but the Greeks knew it as the *Chrysopoeia* or Heart of Gold. It was also referred to as the Magisterium, the Magistry, *Spiritus Mundi* or Spirit of the World, Stone of the Wise, Diamond of Perfection, Universal Medicine, and the Elixir.

The eighth-century Arabian alchemist Jabir did much to popularize the notion of the Philosopher's Stone among alchemists. He reasoned that one could accomplish the transmutation of one metal into another by the rearrangement of its basic qualities, and that a magical substance would expedite the transformation. The Arabs called this agent *Al-Iksir*, from which our word elixir derived.

Many religious scholars believe the Philosopher's Stone is synonymous with the symbol of the stone found in many spiritual traditions, such as the Old Testament stone Jacob rested his head upon, the New Testament rock Christ laid as the foundation of the temple, the Holy Grail or cup of Christ, the Yesodic foundation stone of the Kabbalah, and the Cubic Stone of Freemasonry. In some ways, the Philosopher's Stone also resembles the forbidden fruit of Genesis and symbolizes knowledge that human beings are not meant to possess.

No doubt the Philosopher's Stone was the key to success in alchemy. Not only could it instantly transmute any metal into gold, but it was also the alkahest or universal solvent, which dissolved every substance immersed in it and immediately extracted its Quintessence or active essence. The Stone was used in the preparation of the *aurum potabile*, drinkable gold, a remedy that would perfect the human body. It was also used to restore a plant or animal from its ashes in a process called palingenesis. Because the Philosopher's Stone carried the Quintessence or life force, it could even be used to create artificial living beings called *homonculi*.

Thoth's Tips _____

Did you know that the first book in the *Harry Potter* series deals with the Philosopher's Stone? However, publishers felt the British title (*Harry Potter and the Philosopher's Stone*) was, well, too philosophical for American audiences, so they changed it to the more fetching *Harry Potter and the Sorcerer's Stone*. The book acknowledges that alchemist Nicolas Flamel successfully created the Stone, although he ultimately destroyed the wondrous object because he feared human beings would never learn to use it wisely. "The Stone," Dumbledore explains to Harry, "was really not such a wonderful thing. As much money and life as you could want—the two things most human beings would choose above all. The trouble is humans do have a knack of choosing precisely those things that are worst for them."

What the Philosopher's Stone Looked Like

Much has been written about the Philosopher's Stone, and there are scores of recipes for its preparation. In fact, whole books have been devoted to its creation. One example is the seventeenth-century *Mutus Liber* (*Silent Book*), which is a symbolic instruction manual of 15 illustrations showing how to concoct the Stone.

Surprisingly, we know quite a bit about what the Philosopher's Stone looked like. It was dark red in color and resembled a common irregular stone. The material of which the Stone was made was the same red powder of projection so prized by the alchemists.

The Philosopher's Stone had the peculiar property of exhibiting a variable weight. Sometimes it was as heavy as a piece of gold and other times light as a feather. Its primary ingredient was an equally mysterious element known as carmot. Carmot may have been a mythological substance, because no mention of it exists outside alchemy, nor does it appear in any list of modern chemical compounds.

Although many reports of the creation of the Philosopher's Stone exist among Arabian and European alchemists, one of the most credible is from the revered alchemist Albertus Magnus, who reported he had successfully created gold by transmutation in the later years of his life. When Magnus died in 1280, he passed the miraculous object on to his student Thomas Aquinas, who is also said to have made many successful transmutations using it.

Another credible report of the creation of the Philosopher's Stone comes from the sixteenth-century Swiss alchemist Paracelsus. He discovered what he called the "Alkahest," a single substance from which all the Elements (Fire, Water, Air, and Earth) derived. He used this substance as the chief ingredient in creating his Philosopher's Stone.

> **From the Alchemist**
>
> The power of the Philosopher's Stone to transform anything lies in its connection to all realms, light and dark. Like the First Matter, it exists suspended in the twilight world between energy and matter. The Philosopher's Stone heals all rifts and unites all opposites. "Receive this stone which is not a stone," said the Alexandrian alchemist Zosimos, "a precious thing that has no value, a thing of many shapes that has no shape, this unknown which is known by all."

Preparation of the Philosopher's Stone

According to alchemical literature, there were two ways to create the Philosopher's Stone: the Wet Way and the Dry Way. The Wet Way, or Humid Way, used natural processes and was more gradual and safer than the Dry Way, which relied on intense heat and powerful chemicals to achieve the Stone in a shorter time.

Even in spiritual alchemy, there was a Wet Way, in which natural inspiration built gradually in the initiate to reach the fervor necessary for personal transformation; and a Dry Way, in which the initiate attempted to ascend on a direct path to divine knowledge. The Wet Way worked with the "slow fires of nature," while the Dry Way worked with the "raging fires of our lower nature."

The rapid spiritual ascent of the Dry Way was very dangerous for unprepared initiates and could result in a loss of personal identity or even madness. Tantric alchemists of India followed the direct path by trying to release and control sexual energies, while the path of shamanic alchemy consisted of the use of powerful plant allies and psychoactive drugs. There is no doubt some medieval alchemists made use of such preparations. Alchemists, the first chemists, were very much aware of the psychological and spiritual effects of the compounds they created.

In the laboratory, the Wet Way began with slow digestion and putrefaction of the matter that could go on for many months. The Dry Way began with roasting and heating in an intense fire that might only last a few hours. In both methods, this process was known as the Black Phase, in which the matter blackened as it was reduced to its basic essences.

The Black Phase gave way to the White Phase, in which a purification of the matter took place and the essences were separated out from any contamination. In the Dry Way, this appeared as a white crust formed by dried matter carried by gases bursting in bubbles on the surface of the material. Sometimes the crust puffed up and released a cloud of white vapor into the flask, which was called the White Eagle. In the Wet Way, a white layer of digesting bacteria formed on top of the putrefied material, which was called the White Swan.

During the final Red Phase, the energies released in the previous operations were captured in a solution or powder. In the Dry Way, this was the appearance of a red coloring on the surface of the molten material or in the ashes, which was caused by high temperature oxidation-reduction reactions and was symbolized by the Phoenix rising from the fire. In the Wet Way, the final phase was sometimes signaled by the appearance of a reddish swirl of oil or pink globules on the surface of the matter. This was associated with the Pelican, which sometimes regurgitated a meal of freshly killed fish for its young and stained its white breast plumage with red blood.

The Mysterious Dr. Dee

The most powerful cipher in all of alchemy is a rather odd-looking glyph (see the following illustration). This is the symbol of the Philosopher's Stone, and it's said to incorporate some of the powers of the Stone whenever it is drawn. In other words, the cipher is believed to carry its own spirit or intelligence, which is evoked every time it is written down or constructed.

The name of this cipher is the Hieroglyphic Monad, and it was created by Dr. John Dee (1527–1608), a British alchemist who revealed the Hieroglyphic Monad to the world. Dee was a true Renaissance man who achieved world renown as a mathematician, mapmaker, cryptographer, magician, philosopher, and astrologer. His library was once the largest in England with over 4,000 rare texts and manuscripts, and his alchemical laboratory rivaled any in the world at the time.

Having entered Cambridge College at the age of 15, Dee began a five-year regimen of sleeping only four hours a day so he could devote more time to studying Hermetic philosophy and alchemy books. "I was so vehemently bent to study," said Dee of his time at Cambridge, "that for those years I did inviolably keep this order: only to sleep four hours every night; to allow to meet, eat, and drink two hours every day; and of the other eighteen hours all was spent in my studies and learning."

Dee grew into an imposing figure with a commanding presence. John Aubrey described him in his book *Brief Lives:* "He had a very fair, clear, rosey complexion and a long beard as white as milk. He was tall and slender, a very handsome man. He wore a gown like an artist's frock, with hanging sleeves, and a slit. A mighty good man was he."

Dee was a close confidant of Queen Elizabeth, who gave him a license to practice alchemy and "make gold." As a favor to the Queen, it is said, he "controlled the Elements" and cast a spell on the Spanish Armada by causing bad weather to thwart the invasion of England. Shakespeare used him as the model for Prospero in *The Tempest*, and he is also said to have been the inspiration for Goethe's *Faust*.

With an intense purity of intention and motive, Dee embarked on a systematic plan to discover the Philosopher's Stone. He viewed it as much a philosophy as a physical object. In his view, the Stone was "the force behind the evolution of life and the universal binding power which unites minds and souls in a human oneness." While most alchemists of his time sought the Stone for its ability to transmute base metals into gold, Dee wanted to possess it as a source for spiritual transmutation as well.

The Hieroglyphic Monad

Before long, Dr. Dee realized that he could represent all the powers and characteristics of the Philosopher's Stone in one magical symbol. After seven years of intense study of alchemical symbols, he found what he was looking for. In just 13 days in January 1564, Dee entered a state of deep concentration and completed a step-by-step mathematical proof called the *Monas Hieroglyphica* (*Hieroglyphic Monad*).

The frontispiece for John Dee's Monas Hieroglyphica *(Hieroglyphic Monad) shows his magical cipher for the Philosopher's Stone.*

According to the Greek philosopher Pythagoras, the Monad was the first thing that came into existence in the universe. It can be described as the spiritual atom or egg that gave birth to the whole cosmos. To the Gnostic philosophers, the Monad was the single higher spiritual being (the One Mind) that created all the lesser gods and elemental powers. In Jungian terms, it is the first archetype that contains all the other archetypes. Today we might look at it as a mega microchip that contains all the software of the universe.

When the alchemists depicted the Monad, they often added the Latin caption *In Hoc Signo Vinces* (In this sign you will conquer). All the coded ciphers of the alchemists were thought to be pieces of the Hieroglyphic Monad, and as we shall see, this is geometrically quite true.

From the Alchemist

In describing the power of Dr. Dee's cipher, Hermetic researcher Tobias Churton wrote in *The Gnostics:* "If one can imagine a great ocean of First Matter, then we are seeing the beginning of the universe. If a hand were to, as it were, drop the cipher of the Hieroglyphic Monad into that ocean of infinite potentials, the First Matter would immediately start forming itself into the universe we imagine we know today."

In his proof, Dee used the ancient ciphers of alchemy as geometric figures and applied Euclidean geometry to show their deeper meaning and relationships. Dee believed his proof would "revolutionize astronomy, alchemy, mathematics, linguistics, mechanics, music, optics, magic, and adeptship." He even urged astronomers to stop peering through their telescopes trying to understand the heavens and instead spend their time meditating on his Monad.

The Cipher of the Stone

Dee believed his cipher was the true Philosopher's Stone. The frontispiece of his *Hieroglyphic Monad* is a succinct explanation of the cipher itself, and the frontispiece was considered so important in Elizabethan times that it became known around the world as the Greater Seal of London.

At the center of the frontispiece is the Monad cipher within an inverted egg filled with embryonic fluid and known as the Hermetic Egg. The fluid represented the First Matter; the yolk is represented as a circle and point at the center of the figure. The circle with a center point is the cipher for gold and the sun.

The lunar crescent symbol of the moon intersects the upper part of the yellow yolk of the sun. Thus the sun and moon are united in gold at this level, which represents perfection or the end of the Great Work. Within the frame surrounding the Monad are found the Four Elements and the Three Essentials of Sulfur (the sun on the left pillar), Salt (the moon on the right pillar), and Mercury (the center symbol).

Two rounded lunar crescents or waves representing the Water Element are at the bottom of the Monad. They come together to form the ram horns of the sign of Aries, which signifies Fire. Aries, the first sign of the zodiac, is associated with the burst of life force in the Spring, at which time the Great Work begins. "To begin the Work of this Monad," wrote Dee, "the aid of Fire is required."

A cross, known as the Cross of the Elements, connects the bottom and the top of the cipher. Here the workings of manifested reality play out. In this section of the Monad, all the glyphs of the five visible planets along with the symbols for the sun and moon intersect. The metals are also indicated, because in alchemy, the ciphers for the planet and its metal are the same (Saturn/lead, Jupiter/tin, Mars/iron, Venus/copper, Mercury/quicksilver, moon/silver, and the sun/gold; see Chapter 10). By tracing the connecting lines and arcs in different ways, one can locate all the symbols of the planets and their metals and thereby reveal the invisible forces behind Nature.

The merged planetary ciphers are arranged left to right and top to bottom around the Cross of the Elements. According to Dee, by placing the planetary ciphers in their proper relationship, the astronomical symbols are imbued with an "immortal life," allowing their coded meaning to be expressed "most eloquently in any tongue and to any nation." In this arrangement, the sun is the only symbol that is always the same, and in that sense, incorruptible like gold. No matter which way the Monad is turned—upside down, left to right, right to left, or its mirror image—the cipher of the sun and gold is always exactly the same.

Thoth's Tips

The Monad is a powerful symbol, and alchemists believe it should be treated with the greatest reverence. Starting with the cipher of Saturn/tin, see if you can identify all the planetary ciphers. Then recreate the Monad on a sheet of paper by constructing the ciphers one on top of the other. Drawing the Monad in this way is a meditative exercise that invokes the symbol's transformative power if done properly.

The heart of the Monad and the one cipher that encompasses all the others is Mercury. In alchemy, Mercury stands for the principle of transformation itself. Just as depicted in the Monad, Mercury is part of all the metals and Elements of alchemy and melds them together as one. Dee embedded the spirit of Mercury at the heart of his master symbol and believed he had successfully captured the essences of all the archetypal Elements and metals.

The Lost Key to the Monad

Dee believed his Monad carried the secret of transformation of anything in the universe, but he never spoke of its meaning publicly because he felt the Monad was much too powerful to share with the uninitiated. He privately told other alchemists that his symbol not only described the precise interrelationship of the planetary energies, but also showed the way to transmutation of the metals, as well as the spiritual transformation of the alchemist.

Dee wrote a private unpublished book explaining in detail the workings of the Monad. In the inventory of his massive library was a description of that book, which he intended only for his fellow alchemists. But Dee's secret key was destroyed when a mob of Anglican fundamentalists broke into his home and burned his entire library.

Dee had the final say, however. "He who devotes himself sincerely to these mysteries," he said, "will see clearly that nothing is able to exist without the virtue of our Hieroglyphic Monad." And he gave this advice to anyone who would read his proof: "Whoever does not understand should either learn or be silent."

The Least You Need to Know

- The idea of the Philosopher's Stone originated with Alexandrian and Arabian alchemists.

- The Philosopher's Stone was like a magical touchstone that could instantly perfect or cure anything.

- Dr. John Dee created a cipher that embodied both the formula to create the Philosopher's Stone and its magical powers.

- Dr. Dee's mathematical proof for his cipher of the Philosopher's Stone is called the Hieroglyphic Monad.

Part 3

The Operations of Alchemy

The secret processes by which alchemists achieved their transformations were organized in an ancient pattern known as the Ladder of the Planets. Following the Emerald Tablet's dictum of "As Above, so Below," the operations corresponded to the order and characteristics of the visible planets. The archetypal energies of the planets were reflected on Earth in the evolution of the metals, as well as in the planetary archetypes found in plants, minerals, animals, and human beings. The overall work in alchemy progressed through specific operations that occurred in three phases. The initial work of purification took place in the Black Phase; the separation of purified essences that resulted in the empowerment of the substance took place during the White Phase; and the final manifestation of the perfected substance took place at the end of the Red Phase.

Chapter 10

The Ladder of the Planets

In This Chapter

- ◆ Climbing the Ladder of the Planets
- ◆ Influences of the celestial powers
- ◆ The planetary metals and other correspondences
- ◆ Appreciating the music of the spheres

The idea that heavenly bodies influence our daily lives originated in ancient Egypt and Babylonia. This concept was part of the basic philosophy that believed humans contained within themselves all the parts of the universe. The Doctrine of Correspondences expressed in the Emerald Tablet's dictum of "As Above, so Below" echoed this concept.

Similarly, the ancients believed a corresponding link existed between the slowly moving planets seen in the sky and the metals found buried in the earth. All the luminous planetary bodies exhibit colors that resemble the hue and brilliance of the corresponding metals, and there were many other similarities that led people to believe the metals were associated with the planets. At one time, it was believed that as the planets revolved around the earth, they spun off their corresponding metals into the earth where they could be extracted by the operations of alchemy.

Eventually, each of the planets and its corresponding metal became associated with an operation in alchemy. Each metal had its own characteristics that required specific processes to transform it, and these operations seemed to be a progression of steps. These practical observations were coupled with the Egyptian stages of initiation in a scheme known as the Ladder of the Planets, which consisted of seven steps corresponding to the five visible planets with the sun and the moon. The basic tenet of this system holds that the planets represent powerful primordial forces that express themselves on all levels of reality. These powers are arranged in a pattern of transformation that ranges from the most material and base level (Saturn) to the most spiritual and noble level (the sun).

Correspondences of the Planets

The Great Work of alchemy is to climb the Ladder of the Planets and reach material and spiritual perfection. Our spiritual return to the stars, or the gaining of cosmic consciousness, is accomplished by climbing the philosophical ladder of the visible planets from Saturn through Jupiter, Mars, Venus, Mercury, and finally the moon and sun.

> **From the Alchemist**
>
> Each planet and its metal are associated with a day of the week: Saturn rules Saturday, Jupiter rules Thursday, Mars rules Tuesday, Venus rules Friday, Mercury rules Wednesday, the moon rules Monday, and the sun rules Sunday.

The sun makes the same journey through the Ladder of the Planets that alchemists try to duplicate in their work. In the sky, the sun appears to travel through the planetary ladder depending on the time of year. For instance, in winter in the Northern hemisphere, the sun is in the signs of Saturn (Aquarius and Capricorn), while in summer the sun is in the signs of the sun and moon (Leo and Cancer). Between these two extremes, the sun makes its journey through the remaining planets and their corresponding astrological signs. The time it takes the sun to travel between signs is approximately one lunar month (28 days).

An interesting correspondence exists between the Ladder of the Planets and the human body. Each of the planets rules an energy center in the body and the corresponding organs. These seven centers and their relationships to the planetary ladder were known by Pythagorean philosophers, and there is some evidence that the energy centers were also known to the ancient Egyptians.

In Indian alchemy, the planetary energy centers in the body are called "chakras" ("spinning wheels"). In this system, Saturn corresponds to the root chakra at the base of the spine; Jupiter is associated with the sex chakra at the genitals; Mars is connected with the raw power of the solar plexus chakra; Venus rules the heart chakra; Mercury is expressed at the throat chakra; the moon is reflected in the third eye charkra at the forehead; and the sun shines through the crown chakra at the top of the head.

In the remainder of this chapter, we steadily climb up each rung of the Ladder of the Planets to help us understand the universal pattern of transformation. The following table summarizes this process and reviews some of the major correspondences of the planets with which we will be working.

The table lists the planet and its corresponding metal, the planet's archetypal characteristics, and the alchemical operation to be performed at that stage. The astrological cipher associated with each operation is also given. These are the operations and astrological energies that transform or "cure" the deficiencies of each planet. The traditional signs of the zodiac associated with the journey of the sun through the planetary ladder are also listed.

Correspondences of the Planets

Planet	Metal	Operation	Cipher	Archetype	Zodiac
Saturn	Lead	Calcination (Incineration)	Aries (Calcination) Sagittarius (Incineration)	Contraction, discipline, potential	Capricorn, Aquarius
Jupiter	Tin	Dissolution (Solution)	Cancer (Solution)	Expansion, freedom, sociability	Sagittarius, Pisces
Mars	Iron	Separation	Scorpio (Separation)	Assertiveness, masculinity	Aries, Scorpio
Venus	Copper	Conjunction (Congelation)	Taurus (Congelation)	Receptiveness, femininity, intuition	Taurus, Libra
Mercury	Quicksilver	Fermentation (Digestion)	Capricorn (Fermentation) Leo (Digestion)	Transformation, androgyny, light, mind	Gemini, Virgo
Moon	Silver	Distillation (Sublimation)	Virgo (Distillation) Libra (Sublimation)	Purification, subconscious powers, body, soul	Cancer

continues

Correspondences of the Planets (continued)

Planet	Metal	Operation	Cipher	Archetype	Zodiac
Sun	Gold	Coagulation (Fixation) Multiplication (Projection)	Gemini (Fixation) Aquarius (Multiplication) Pisces (Projection)	Empowerment, creativity, true self, energy, spirit	Leo

The Dark Powers of Saturn

Saturn, the farthest planet from the sun, is the first rung on the Ladder of the Planets, and in esoteric terms represents the galactic starting point on our journey in from the stars. To the observer on Earth, distant Saturn looks like a grayish yellow star and is most easily spotted during the twilight hours when the sky takes on a deep blue color. Saturn reaches its peak visibility high in the northern sky in the dead of winter.

Saturn is the coldest planet and also the slowest moving. While the other planets dance merrily around the warm sun, lumbering Saturn takes 30 years to complete its orbit. Saturn is the largest planet in terms of mass and the second largest (after Jupiter) in terms of size.

The shimmering triple ring of rocks and 10 moons circling Saturn are remnants of its greedy attempt to attract more mass with its powerful gravity. Its largest moon is bigger than our planet Earth. Had Saturn been able to attract more mass, it would have transformed into a star, and our galaxy would have had two suns. But now ancient Saturn sleeps in darkness, having lost its bid to become a shining star.

The Babylonians considered Saturn the ghost of a dead sun and the oldest spirit in the heavens. Saturn was considered the place where created matter first manifested and represented its most primitive state, and it stands for the cosmic law that limits or defines manifestation. Therefore Saturn and its metal, lead, represent the principles of contraction, stability, structure, and materialism.

The symbol for Saturn is Father Time with his distinctive hourglass and sickle, who personifies the forces of age, death, and transformation. Sometimes Saturn is shown with a peg leg to indicate his infirmity and incompleteness. The black crow is the messenger of Saturn and also symbolizes the beginning of the Black Phase of alchemical transformation, a period of darkness over light and matter over spirit.

From the Alchemist

From at least 1500 B.C.E., the Egyptians were using the circle and dot to denote both the sun and its metal gold and the crescent to denote both the moon and its metal silver. Then Alexandrian alchemists associated a metal with each of the five visible planets: Saturn with lead, Jupiter with electrum, Mars with iron, Venus with copper, and Mercury with tin. Later they omitted electrum, which is an alloy of silver and gold, and Jupiter became associated with tin. The planet Mercury was then connected with the metal mercury (or quicksilver).

In myth, Saturn was imprisoned by his father in a deep cave while still a child. The child conspired with his mother to overthrow his father and ended up castrating him with a sickle. Saturn then became king and ruled just as ruthlessly as his father had. When he heard a prophecy that his own children would dethrone him, Saturn ate them at birth. But his wife saved one child and fed it to Saturn in the form of a stone, which he later vomited out to become Jupiter. Jupiter eventually overthrew his father and banished him to the darkness of the underworld.

The darkness of Saturn is also the fertile soil of new birth. In fact, the word Saturn comes from the Latin *serere* meaning to sow or plant. Also, on the Ladder of Planets, Saturn marks the boundary between the personal and transpersonal (or cosmic) powers. For those reasons, Saturn acquired a dual reputation as both a stubborn protector of the status quo and the initiator of profound transformation.

Astrologically, Saturn is represented by two signs of the zodiac. Capricorn is the tenacious mountain goat that patiently moves toward its goal to reach great heights by remaining firmly grounded. Aquarius is the herald of a new age and represents the potential of transformation that is part of Saturn's makeup.

Because of its transformative potential, Saturn was the most important planet to the alchemists. They equated it with the First Matter and considered it both the beginning and the end of the Great Work. Within the darkness of saturnine energies, the alchemists saw all the possibilities for change and healing. An early cipher for Saturn was Rx, which medieval alchemists wrote on a slip of paper and prescribed as a cure. Their patients actually ate the piece of paper with the sigil of Saturn, which the alchemists had animated with magical intent. Today, the sigil of Saturn ("Rx") is still written on nearly every prescription issued by medical doctors.

The Exuberant Powers of Jupiter

Jupiter, the second rung on the Ladder of the Planets, is the largest and most impressive planet in our solar system, but it is mostly gas. It has four moons, all of which are more active and larger than our moon.

Jupiter and Saturn have a similar chemical makeup and are dozens of times larger than any of the other planets. Their cores are thought by scientists to be made of pure hydrogen metal, and they are the true Olympian gods of our solar system.

Jupiter's light and expansive presence balances the heavy and contractive influence of Saturn, and Jupiter is considered the great "benefactor" of the solar system and thus represents the principle of divine grace. Esoterically, Jupiter and its metal tin represent the light and energy of spirit without which the soul would remain imprisoned within the saturnic darkness of matter.

Astrologically, Jupiter is primarily linked with Sagittarius, the centaur with his bow and arrow. The half-man, half-horse centaur symbolizes the person who has grown above his instinctive nature and gained social values and wisdom. Jupiter is also linked with the compassionate sign of Pisces. In direct opposition to the signatures of Saturn, it produces a state of spirit over matter in which creativity, music, science, and prosperity prevail.

The planet's name is the root of the word jovial, which means cheerful, and the energies of Jupiter are expansive, optimistic, and joyful. With the combination of growth and a positive attitude, it is not surprising that Jupiter represents the power of healing and regeneration.

Thoth's Tips

For a complete list of books on the planetary powers, go to www.Astrology.co.uk/Books/Subjects/bs.ThePlanets.html. For more information on the operations of alchemy and their relationships to the planetary powers, go to www.AlchemyLab.com/directory.htm.

In mythology, the biggest planet in our solar system is the rightful home for the heavenly father who was known as Jupiter to the Romans and Zeus to the Greeks. In India, Jupiter takes the form of Indra, the god of fire and lightning, who in Scandinavian tradition is represented by the thunder god Thor.

In all these traditions, Jupiter was the great god of thunderstorms and was worshipped as a rain god. In Rome, he was commonly known as *Jupiter Pluvius*, Heavenly Father Who Rains, and his function was to fertilize the mother god with his seminal moisture.

The Masculine Powers of Mars

The third rung on the Ladder of the Planets is Mars, which is considered the brother of Earth, and the two planets share many characteristics. They have the exact same tilt on their axis of rotation, and they rotate in the same direction at about the same speed. That means they experience nearly identical daily cycles and seasons, although temperature extremes are much more severe on Mars.

In alchemy, the red planet Mars represents energy and raw power. The metal associated with Mars is iron, which actually gives the planet its red color. Mars, the warrior, is aggressive and masculine and governs our animal passions and survival instincts. Martian qualities reinforce the ego, strengthen will, and help us surpass previous limitations. Mars provides us with the energy to act, to begin new projects, or to transform any situation.

In the zodiac, the month of Mars (March) is the period when the sun enters the sign of Aries. In fact, the word Aries is derived from the Greek word for Mars, *Ares*. This is the time of year when spring begins and a new solar cycle of the Zodiac starts. Astrologers believe that wherever Mars is located in your natal chart is the astrological sign that will be your source of energy for the rest of your life. This is also when the Great Work of alchemy begins, and it is believed that the energy generated during this period is what propels us through the next twelve months of transformation. Mars is also linked with the astrological sign of Scorpio, which carries the signature of masculine consciousness and discernment.

In mythology, Mars is the God of War and is considered an overexuberant cosmic troublemaker. None of the other Roman gods liked Mars, and in Greek myth, Venus was always getting her consort Mars out of trouble.

The Feminine Powers of Venus

The next rung on the Ladder of the Planets is Venus, which is known as the veiled planet and has a dense and sultry atmosphere. Thick sulfurous clouds constantly hide the face of Venus, which has an average surface temperature of around 450°F. Venus has the slowest rotation about its axis of any planet and is twice as close to the sun as Mars. It is the brightest planet in the sky and appears as both the evening star and the morning star.

Esoterically, Venus represents refinement of the senses, the passion of the arts, mystical love, romantic relationships, and physical desire. The feminine energy of the planet is passive, receptive, magnetic, relating, adapting, nurturing, and gentle.

Venus is associated with the astrological signs of Taurus and Libra. Taurus represents the sensual part of Venus, while Libra is focused on relating and connecting with others. In terms of the Earth sign Taurus, the attracting power of Venus is expressed more in possessions and money, while in Libra the energetic trend is more toward art and harmony in all things.

In mythology, Venus is the Great Goddess of the Romans who was known as Aphrodite to the Greeks. Both Greeks and Romans emphasized her sexual energy, and temples to Venus were actually schools of instruction in ecstatic sexual techniques taught by harlot-priestesses.

The religion of Venus, as well as the Hermetic teachings of alchemy, promised a "sacred marriage" through which the initiate could escape the cycle of rebirth and be reborn on a whole new level. Death was seen as a transformative event that mimicked *le petit mort*, the little death of sexual orgasm.

The romantic city of Venice was named for the goddess, and our word veneration literally means to pay homage to Venus. Known as the Lady of the Animals, Venus was often shown naked in the forest with animals, especially deer. Several myths tell of hunters encountering Venus and falling in love with her. In fact, our word venison literally means son or follower of Venus.

Venus is a very meaningful symbol in alchemy. Married to Vulcan, the god of alchemy, she could not resist the virile powers of Mars with whom she shared many romantic trysts. To alchemists, Venus was the goddess of generation, and sexual imagery in alchemy almost always refers to the deeply transformative energies of Venus, her metal copper, and the mysteries of the operation of conjunction.

Tread Carefully

Be careful in working with the Ladder of the Planets on the personal level. It is very tempting to view it as a strictly linear process or checklist of where you stand in your personal work. Such an attitude elicits what the alchemists called "Monk's Pride," which is a smug feeling of being further along the spiritual path than others. The truth is the Ladder of the Planets is a dynamic, living process. Often the stages are not in any set order, since we tend to return to previous phases at different levels in an ever-spiraling process of transformation.

The Transformative Powers of Mercury

The next rung on the Ladder of the Planets is Mercury, the closest planet to the sun and the fastest moving planet in our solar system. Most of the time Mercury is absorbed into the bright light of the sun, but when it is visible in the twilight of the early morning or late evening, the tiny planet is one of the brightest objects in the sky. Mercury has a very irregular and eccentric orbit and sometimes even appears to go backward in the heavens. The surface of Mercury looks just like the moon, and the two bodies have the most reflective surfaces of any of the planets, each reflecting exactly the same amount of sunlight, 7 percent.

Esoterically, the swiftest planet is known as the Messenger of the gods and governs communication, intellect, writing, speech, and any kind of conversing or commerce. The urge of Mercury is to know and to communicate that knowledge. In the body, Mercury is associated with the brain and nervous system, as well as breathing and the organs of sense. The god Mercury is usually depicted with winged sandals and a winged helmet to connote the ability to move and deliver information quickly.

Mercury rules the astrological signs of Gemini and Virgo. Gemini, the third sign in the Zodiac, is associated with discrimination and awareness of duality. Virgo is associated with purified consciousness and the alchemical operation of distillation.

In mythology, Mercury is depicted as a hermaphrodite because Mercury derives its light or consciousness from the union of the left and right brain or, in alchemical terms, from the marriage of the masculine, rational sun and feminine, intuitive moon.

The Greeks knew the Roman Mercury as Hermes, who was the founder of alchemy. Hermes was the twilight god of boundaries, and one of his duties was to conduct souls to the underworld. Hermes was believed to have magical powers over sleep, dreaming, and altered states of consciousness.

The Soulful Powers of the Moon

The sixth rung on the Ladder of the Planets is the moon. It seems the ancients were correct in their assumption that the moon was a planet. Because it has a completely different mineral composition than Earth and other considerations, most modern astronomers believe the moon is a small planet captured by Earth's gravity.

Because of the moon's synchronous captured orbit, it always shows the same face to Earth. However, since the moon shines only by the reflected light of the sun, Earth casts shadows on its face that make it appear to change shape in a 28-day cycle. The moon's varying distance from Earth controls the ebb and flow of tides, human hormones, and the female menstrual cycle. Our words for menstruation and menopause are based on the Greek word *meno*, meaning moonpower.

The esoteric meaning of the moon is receptivity, reflection, fertility, and nurturing. In many areas of the world, the 13-month lunar calendar governs the cycle of planting and harvesting. The moon is said to control the subconscious and is the source of magnetic and astral powers. The moon is the archetypal Queen of alchemy, and its metal is silver.

In mythology, the moon is associated with the virgin goddess Diana and the multi-breasted symbol of fertility Artemis. Egyptians referred to the moon as the "Mother of the Universe," and in several traditions the moon is where our souls go when we die. The moon is associated with the astrological Water sign of Cancer, whose traits are deep emotions and moodiness, genuineness, loyalty, and a strong sense of family.

The Spiritual Powers of the Sun

The sun is the seventh and last rung on the Ladder of the Planets. The alchemists saw the sun as the King and husband to the moon Queen. In an amazing synchronicity, the sun and moon appear to be exactly the same size in the sky. Because the moon's image is 400 times smaller but also 400 times closer than the sun's, they seem to be the same size to an observer on Earth. When a total solar eclipse (or alchemical conjunction) occurs, the lunar disc exactly and completely covers that of the sun.

The sun is our own personal star at the center of the solar system, which emits energy in every conceivable wavelength from x-rays to visible light to radio waves, and this energy is what makes life on Earth possible.

The sun is the fundamental metaphor of the whole alchemical process. Composed of over 90 percent hydrogen atoms, it is the simplest form of matter known. It also represents a process of constant purification in which cooler and darker impurities, known as sunspots, rise to the surface and are ejected or burned off.

Esoterically, the sun is an image of wholeness, health, wealth, and happiness. Its metal gold has the same associations. The blazing sun corresponds to ambition, courage, vitality, creative energies, and electric or masculine energy.

In mythology, the sun is associated with the Egyptian god Osiris, as well as the Greek Hercules in his aspect of monumental strength. In astrology the sun as Leo presides over selfless will, beneficent governing, and shared energy and power. On the personal level, the sun represents our deepest identity, the true self and inner authority, the source of our dignity and integrity.

The Music of the Spheres

To the ancients, the Ladder of the Planets represented individual melodies in the Music of the Spheres, which are archetypal vibrations of energy that influence every part of our lives.

The Ladder of the Planets is an example of the Law of Octaves. The musical octave is a seven-stepped process that raises the vibration of the first note on the scale to a higher vibration, and so on through the remaining notes. The eighth note repeats the cycle on a higher level. In chemistry, the Law of the Octave is expressed in the Periodic Table, where every eighth element repeats the characteristics of the first on a more complex level.

In alchemy, the Law of Octaves is the overall pattern of harmony in the universe expressed as a seven-stepped formula embedded in our solar system. The first seven notes of the musical scale represent our progress through the planets, while the eighth note of the octave is a return to the first note at a higher level of vibration.

> **From the Alchemist**
>
> Pythagoras explained the Music of the Spheres in 550 B.C.E. "Each celestial body produces a particular sound on account of its movement, rhythm, or vibration. All the sounds and vibrations together form a universal harmony in which each part, while having its own function and character, contributes to the whole."

In our solar system, that eighth note is Saturn, the one planet the alchemists considered both beginning and end, the alpha and omega of our transformation. They considered Saturn and our return to Saturn the most important part of the Great Work, because it represented the beginning of a whole new octave of creation that represents our leaving behind the grosser materiality of the planets and experiencing the more subtle matter of the spiritual universe.

The Least You Need to Know

◆ The Ladder of the Planets is an ancient system based on the archetypal influences of the planetary bodies.

◆ Saturn and Jupiter represent the universal powers of darkness and light, matter and energy.

◆ Mars and Venus represent the complementary powers of aggression and passivity, the masculine and feminine archetypes.

◆ The moon and the sun represent the universal principles of soul and spirit.

◆ The planet Mercury represents the principle of transformation that connects all the planetary powers.

◆ The Music of the Spheres is an ancient doctrine that treats the planetary powers as increasing vibrations of energy or tones.

Chapter 11

The Black Phase

In This Chapter

◆ The three phases of the Great Work

◆ The calcination operation

◆ The dissolution operation

◆ Personal calcination and dissolution

The exact sequence of operations alchemists used to accomplish their transformations was one of their greatest secrets, and the actual order was often deliberately scrambled to mislead the uninitiated. Instead of specifics, the alchemists spoke of three overall phases of their work, and each phase contained several different operations.

This color-coded process of transformation went from an initial Black Phase to an intermediary White Phase and culminated in a Red Phase. This same sequence of colors occurs in working with the metals. If the four base metals (lead, tin, iron, and copper) are melted and fused into a new alloy, the resulting surface color is black. If this black alloy is heated with the noble metal silver and then heated in mercury, it turns white. If all has gone well, the final iridescent red-violet color appears in the metal, which indicates a small amount of genuine gold was formed.

While we can often find detailed descriptions of the operations leading to the appearance of these color markers in the writings of alchemists, the processes are veiled in mystical and allegorical language that makes them very difficult to understand unless one is an adept. That suggests the alchemists were also talking about spiritual or psychological exercises they performed along with their laboratory work. These were the actual colors that appeared in the laboratory work, as well as the same colors that dominated the images and visions of the corresponding spiritual work.

Alchemists referred to the three general phases of the Great Work by their Latin names, so if you plan to do any further reading in alchemy, it's very helpful to know these Latin terms. They called the work of blackening the *Nigredo*, pronounced *nee-gray-doe*; the work of whitening the *Albedo*, *al-bay-doe*; and the work of reddening the *Rubedo*, *ruh-bay-doe*.

Jungian psychologists use these same Latin terms to refer to the stages of psychological transformation. The Nigredo refers to the depression accompanying the dark night of the soul that underscores the need for deep change on the personal level. The Albedo represents the spiritual purification that results from the suffering of the Nigredo. And the Rubedo is the sense of empowerment and confidence that results from psychological integration in the final phase of personal transformation.

The Blackening

The work of "blackening" was the longest and most difficult phase in alchemy. The alchemists said that by comparison, the White and Red stages seemed like child's play. They considered the Black Phase of Nigredo a tortuous stage of the work in which the substance at hand suffered and was forced to surrender many superfluous characteristics in order to reveal its true nature.

The goal at this initial phase of transformation is to reduce the subject to its bare essence or most fundamental ingredients. All the *dross*, impure, and extraneous material must be removed, or they will contaminate and destroy the later stages of the work.

The alchemists called the overall process that occurred during the Nigredo as mortification, which meant to them "facing the dead part." In the lab, mortification results in a powder or ashes in which

def•i•ni•tion

Dross is an alchemical term that refers to the scum of solid impurities that float on top of molten metal. It usually consists of dirt, nonmetallic contaminants, metal oxides, and other chemical waste, which can easily be skimmed off the surface and discarded. Dross is always solid material, as opposed to slag, which is liquid or oily impurities that surface in melted metals.

the characteristics of the former substance can no longer be recognized. In personal alchemy, mortification is characterized by feelings of shame, embarrassment, guilt, and worthlessness as one confronts the base, repugnant material he has hidden away inside himself.

The operations which take place during the Black Phase are two processes that involve applying the Elements of Fire and Water. After these operations are completed, the purified essences of the matter at hand are separated out and saved for further work in the next phases.

From the Alchemist

The symbol for the Nigredo is the black crow. If you see one in an alchemical drawing, it means the process shown is taking place during the Black Phase of the work. In Greek mythology, the black crow came into being because the white crow maiden Coronis, who was pregnant from the god Apollo, had an affair with another young man. When Apollo heard of her infidelity, he transformed the crow from white to black and then killed Coronis and her lover. Her child was born on her funeral pyre and became the great healer Asclepius. The myth shows how both death and life arise from the darkness of suffering and that the blackness carries the seeds of light and healing.

The Calcination Process

The initial fire operation in alchemy is called calcination, which means literally "reduced to bone by burning." Bone is essentially calcium oxide, and the word comes from an ancient method of obtaining calcium oxide (or lime) by heating limestone. The word calcination and related words like calcify and calcium come from the Latin root *calx*, which means limestone or bone. After calcination, the substance becomes dry and hard and is no longer affected by common fire.

The cipher the alchemists assigned to the process of calcination was the ram horns of the astrological sign for Aries. Aries is the most fiery of all the signs, and the Great Work of alchemy begins in the spring when the sun is in the house of Aries. Skulls and skeletons are also used as symbols in the drawings of calcination and represent both pure white calcium oxide and the hidden structure of materials revealed by fire. Other images of calcination include funeral pyres, scenes of hell, torture by fire, crucifixion, birds rising from flames, and frightening confrontations with dragons or demons.

Another popular symbol for calcination is the salamander. Because salamanders were observed scurrying in and out from under bonfires as the cold-blooded creatures sought warmth beneath the burning logs, the idea took hold that salamanders were born in the fire and frolicked in its flames.

The alchemists referred to this process of dehydration by fire as the "dragon who drinks the water," and the fire-breathing dragon is another symbol. Calcination, also referred to as calcining, drives off water and other volatile compounds and brings about a decomposition of the material.

Heating ores directly in a fire was also an ancient way of obtaining metals. This open-flame heating or roasting is a kind of calcination in which material is heated in an open flame with plenty of free-flowing air, which also helps oxidize impurities.

Generally, any process that involves the heating and breaking up of a solid to drive off water and other volatile compounds can be classified as calcination. In the lab, it usually meant heating a substance in an oven, crucible, or over an open flame until it was reduced to ashes.

In their laboratory work, alchemists recognized two kinds of calcination, which they called actual and potential. Actual is typical heating in a fire produced by a fuel such as wood, coal, oil, or gas. Potential calcination used acids and corrosive chemicals, which the alchemists felt were a kind of liquid fire that carried the potential of flaming fire within them.

From the Alchemist

All metals can be calcined and reduced to ashes by adding a potential calcining agent or combination of chemicals and then applying heat. Lead is calcined by adding sulfur; tin requires the addition of antimony. Iron needs vinegar and sal ammoniac. Copper uses sulfur and salt. Mercury needs to be mixed with nitric acid (*aqua fortis*). Silver requires a mixture of table salt and alkali salt. And gold can be calcined with the help of mercury and sal ammoniac.

Beyond chemical calcination, alchemists recognized philosophical calcination, which is the reduction of living things to their material basis by application of heat. They associated this phenomenon with a loss of the life force carried in bodily fluids and gave examples that featured the dehydration of living tissue.

One example of philosophical calcination is human cremation, which results in a dehydration of bodily fluids and tissue that leaves only bone fragments and ashes behind. Another example occurs when animal horns or hooves are suspended over boiling water for a long period. Thick liquid called musilage drips out of the horns or hooves, leaving a dried mass, which is easily reduced to powder by grinding. In both cases, the powdery material resulting from philosophical calcination was considered quite different from the ashes left over from common chemical calcination. The ashes of once-living things were sacred, and it was felt that they still contained the ultimate essence of the living person or thing.

Personal Calcination

At the same time alchemists worked in their laboratories on the calcination of the metals or other compounds, they were also working to accomplish corresponding calcinations on the personal level and suffered through the same transformations as the substances with which they worked.

By applying the operations of alchemy to the human mind, alchemists became the first psychologists. For them, personal calcination was similar to what happened in the laboratory, except on the personal level the heat was generated by the fire of their own consciousness and life experiences. The resulting drying up of one's "inner moisture and volatility" represented the loss of his emotional and psychic energy as he matured. In other words, as we mature and are heated by the natural forces of existence, we tend to lose contact with our own life force.

The truth is that personal calcination takes place whether we want it or not. This natural humbling process takes place as we grow older and are assaulted and overcome by the trials and tribulations of life. Decline of self-esteem, loss of standing in families and at work, personal embarrassments, failure to be loved, loss of material possessions, and all the other harsh realities of life gradually crucify our pampered egos. By the time people reach middle age, many feel they have lost a precious part of themselves and are leading inauthentic lives.

Tread Carefully

Never try to apply the operations of alchemy to just one level of the work. Remember that the alchemists believed their operations were universal and applied to all levels of reality—the physical level of chemicals and the body, the level of mind and personality, and the unseen spiritual level. For a transformation to be complete and lasting, it had to be successful on all three levels of reality.

The alchemists saw personal calcination as a loss of spirit in a person, although modern psychologists view it as a loss of ego or personal identity. The result is the same: diminished mental energy and an increase of darkness or depression in one's life. It's as if our souls finally despair trying to survive in a world of spiritual drought.

What fuels the fires of personal calcination? Our ego. In psychological terms, calcination is the destruction of the false ego we have built up in response to pressures from our parents, friends, schools, church, and government. We have built up the impurities within ourselves, the blackness that veils the true light of our being. Personal calcination begins when we realize that the things we have accepted as true and important may not, in fact, have any relevance to what is real in our lives.

One of the fundamental ideas in alchemy is that anything superfluous or impure must eventually be removed or destroyed to reveal the true essence of something. The basic problem in human psychology is that we identify with our superficial personalities and not our true essences. We invest all our energy in our egos, which are artificial constructs that often don't reflect who we really are. So the first step in personal transformation is for us to turn up the fire of consciousness in the inner laboratory and focus it on our thoughts, habits, assumptions, judgments, and relationships to see what is real and true in our lives.

In alchemy, the symbol of the King referred to what we now call ego or personality, and alchemical drawings of personal calcination show the King being boiled alive, cremated, or sitting inside a sweat box or sealed vessel. The idea here is that the ego King must be sacrificed for the good of the whole person. As in the Grail legends, the kingdom of one's personality will wither and decay until the rightful King is restored to power.

From the Alchemist

The sacrifice of the King is an important motif in alchemy. In the Middle Ages, there were many festivals in which an effigy of the King was burnt, so his spirit could be reborn and multiply for the good of the whole community. The tradition continues today with the popular Burning Man festival in northern Nevada's Black Rock desert, in which New Age enthusiasts burn a giant wooden effigy of modern man.

In describing the suffering of the King, the seventeenth-century German alchemist Daniel Stolicus wrote: "The fiery man will sweat and become hot in the fire. Also will he resolve his body and carry it far through moisture." Stolicus was referring to the conclusion of the fire operation and the promise of healing and cleansing in the next operation, which is an application of the Water Element in the work.

Calcination of the King.

The Process of Dissolution

The next operation which alchemists used in the Black Phase was dissolution, some-times referred to simply as solution. Dissolution is the transformation of a substance by immersing it in water or other liquid. In the lab, it is the liquefaction of a solid or the absorption of a solid into a liquid. It usually involved dissolving the ashes from calcination in water or liquid chemicals. The water in which the ashes were dissolved took on magical properties, and the term elixir from the Arabic *Al-iksir* literally means "from the ashes."

Fascination with the powers of the Water Element dates back at least as far as the female alchemists of Alexandria, who developed equipment for performing dissolution and distillation. To the astonishment of ancient experimenters, solids disappeared into solvents as if they had been returned to their original, undifferentiated state. They saw this as reduction to the First Matter, a purification they likened to a return to the womb for rebirth.

The astrological sign associated with the dissolution process was the Water sign of Cancer, which the Egyptians called the sign of the Scarab. Symbols of dissolution include lakes, floods, underground streams, quicksand, reflecting pools, tears, melting, menstruation, washing in tubs, fish swimming on the surface of water, and other allu-sions to the Water Element. Glass vessels, clay pots, cauldrons, and other womblike vessels of transformation also refer to this process.

Drawings of women riding great fish, taming wild animals or dragons, or naked women walking quietly in the forest are images of dissolution that emphasize the deep connection between nature and the darker feminine side of our being. While the King derives his powers of light and active energy from the sun, or solar archetype, the Queen's source of power resides in the darkness and potential energy of the moon, or lunar archetype. Psychologically, therefore, the King represents the conscious mind and thoughts while the Queen represents the subconscious mind and feelings.

Thoth's Tips

Understanding the differences between the King and Queen will enable you to more readily recognize these opposing forces in yourself. The King is the aggressive masculine ego and powers of reasoning, and the Queen represents the forces of passive acceptance and feminine ways of knowing, like feelings and intuition. While the King and Queen represent opposing qualities of our personalities, they are really two aspects or faces of the same thing, which is our true self.

Personal Dissolution

Just as the King was the primary icon of personal calcination, the Queen is the primary icon of personal dissolution. Images of dissolution may feature the King sitting in a boiling cauldron, swimming naked, or drowning in a lake. The Queen may be shown sitting with the King together in a bath or relaxing by herself in a tub of water.

Dissolution of the King.

Personal dissolution further breaks down the corrupted and artificial structures of the personality by immersion in the dark waters of the unconscious. This is a forbidding realm with slumbering dragons or other monsters guarding great treasures. Other symbols of the unconscious realm in alchemy include depictions of poisonous toads, basilisks (winged serpents), menacing fish, great whales, and confrontations with stags or scenes of rabbits diving down into holes in the earth.

Alchemists sometimes referred to the energies found in this forbidding psychic realm as "the water which does not wet the hands." These dissolving waters can take the form of inner voices, visions, dreams, or just odd feelings that reveal a world of shadowy energies existing simultaneously with us in our everyday life. This buried material and rejected energy surfaces during dissolution because the conscious mind of the King relinquishes control after suffering through the fires of calcination. Direct confrontation with the primordial energies of the unconscious during dissolution further humbles the beleaguered ego King and results in a surrendering of stubborn beliefs and *projections*.

During the early stages of personal alchemy, projection is a dangerous thing. When we are angered or revolted by things we see in the world, it is because that same negative quality lives subconsciously within us. We end up expending tremendous psychic energy projecting these rejected qualities into the external world while keeping them hidden from view within ourselves.

def•i•ni•tion

Projection in alchemy is the mixing or casting of the transmuting agent (or Philosopher's Stone) into molten base metal to instantly transform it into gold. Psychological projection is the extension of our thoughts or emotional energy into the world at large.

The blackening caused by dissolution was often expressed as the darkness of depression and melancholia. However, alchemists considered personal dissolution a completely natural process. Instead of running for Prozac, the true alchemist must work with the darkness and suffer through it in order to emerge transformed. By bringing this threatening material to light in therapy or personal work, the alchemist rises above the "poisonous vapors" of the subconscious and learns to integrate the dark side into a reborn self.

This may seem like a scary process, but it's a necessary step in personal transformation. We all have built up a personal trash heap of rejected material that is incompatible with our chosen conscious attitude. Psychologists call this part of our personality the "shadow," which is the inferior or rejected part of our personality. Slowing down and paying attention to feelings allows this material to surface and come to light, where we can examine it and transmute its dark energy in positive ways.

How exactly do you transform the threatening darkness of a negative experience? First, you need to stop thinking about the individual incident behind the negative emotion and try to work only with its pure energy—what the alchemists would call its vital principle. If you can dissolve the connection between the emotion and the shadow material that fuels it, the energy will be free to use for healing or further transformation.

One way of doing this is a method of dissolution called cibation. Cibation is the addition of water or other fluids to dried-out substances at precisely the right moment in the experiment. Psychologically, this involves coldly and deliberately reviewing painful, hardened memories without letting them upset you, and then holding the memories in your mind until the emotions behind them finally break to the surface.

If you let yourself fully re-experience these emotions, sometimes a lump will form in your throat or tears will well up in your eyes. The idea is to let yourself go and cry as long and as hard as you can. Crying therapy is a valid technique used by therapists to overcome eating disorders, sex problems, drug abuse, insomnia, anger, and many other problems, but the uncontrolled crying must take place at precisely the right time to work. Medieval alchemists were the first to understand this process and actually believed that the salt in tears was the remnants of crystallized thoughts and memories broken down by crying.

Other effective methods of personal dissolution include paying attention to dream symbolism, mental images, slips of the tongue, and other meaningful coincidences. Keeping journals of thoughts and feelings also helps bring the shadowy material to light.

If successful, the initial operations of Fire and Water have eliminated the dross of the substance, whether it is of a chemical or psychological nature. The goal of calcination and dissolution is to eliminate contaminating materials and reveal the most basic constituents or essences of a substance. The job of the next phase in alchemy, the Albedo, is to separate out these essences and recombine them at a higher level of purity and power.

The Least You Need to Know

♦ The work of alchemy is divided into three phases of transformation: the Black Phase (*Nigredo*), the White Phase (*Albedo*), and the Red Phase (*Rubedo*).

♦ Calcination, an operation of the Black Phase, involves heating a substance in an open flame.

◆ Dissolution is an operation of the Black Phase that involves dissolving the substance in water or other liquid.

◆ Because the operations of alchemy also apply to psychological transformation, many modern psychologists use the same terms in their therapy as the alchemists used in their lab work.

◆ Personal calcination involves burning up artificial psychic structures and ego complexes using introspective techniques.

◆ Personal dissolution frees subconscious energy trapped in mental habits, rejected material, rigid beliefs, and projections.

Chapter 12

The White Phase

In This Chapter

◆ Reclaiming the essences of mortification

◆ The White Light of the Albedo

◆ The operation of separation

◆ The operation of conjunction

◆ Personal separation and conjunction

In the previous chapter, our matter suffered through the mortifications of the Black Phase of alchemy. However, the blackness is now slowly giving way to light, and a new day is dawning. The matter has died and is being reborn. Psychologically, we have experienced the death of old habits, beliefs, judgments, projections, and dependencies, and a new person is emerging.

We have entered the second phase of alchemy, the White Phase or *Albedo*, which is a purification of the matter that survived the *Nigredo*. It results from a washing or cleansing of the products and their reunion on a new level of purity.

Spiritually, the whiteness of the *Albedo* is the brilliant white light at the end of the dark tunnel between death and the afterlife. The alchemists believed our souls, which are the immortal essences of our being, follow the same progression through the phases of alchemical transformation as do substances in the lab or the facets of our personalities.

The Whitening

The *Albedo* phase of alchemy grows out of the blackness of the *Nigredo* in a gradual process of cooking and purification. This stage is extremely important in the overall progress of transformation, because any remaining contamination or impurities that make it through to the third and final phase can ruin the whole experiment.

def•i•ni•tion

Albification is a chemical term for the process of whitening. The word comes from the Latin words *albus*, meaning "white," and *ficare*, "to make." Albification is accomplished by washing, scrubbing, grinding, or bleaching with chemical agents.

Albification releases the purified essences of the matter, and the goal is to separate these essences from the dross and waste materials of *Nigredo*. One of the biggest difficulties during *Albedo* is keeping these pure essences from recombining with each other or picking up contaminants until the alchemist has isolated them. The final operation of the *Albedo* is to combine the pure essences into a new incarnation or body.

Another characteristic of the work during *Albedo* is that the alchemist discovers the underlying duality of the substance she is attempting to transform. The level of purification is so great that the fundamental duality of nature is observed in the experiment. In other words, the essences revealed turn out to have opposing positive and negative qualities. In personal transformation, the opposing essences are the masculine and feminine characteristics of the personality, which the alchemists referred to as the King and the Queen.

Symbols of the White Phase of alchemy include the naked King and Queen standing next to one another, as well as more abstract images such as baptismal fonts, silver chalices, fountains from which two streams of water flow into a single basin, or two lions sharing one head vomiting forth a stream of liquid.

Other symbols include a white dove, white swan, white dragon, white Queen, white rose, white stone, and white mercury. The full moon and the morning star, Venus, are also symbols. In mythology, Aurora, the Roman goddess of the dawn, is often used by alchemists to refer to *Albedo*.

The alchemists believed they could only accomplish the *Albedo* with divine grace through a merging of the powers Above and the powers Below. The actual mechanism of whitening was regarded a mystery that could not be explained, and during this phase, the alchemist spent much time in prayer and meditation. The Benedictine alchemist Anthony-Joseph Pernety (1716–1796) said of this stage: "When the alchemist sees the perfect whiteness, the philosophers say that one has to destroy his books, because they have become superfluous."

The operations that take place during the White Phase are two processes that involve applying the Elements of Air and Earth. After these two operations are completed, the essences of the matter at hand will be fused inseparably together to create an exalted matter at a new level of strength and integrity the alchemists called the Stone.

The Separation Process

Separation is the alchemical operation of disuniting, dividing, cutting, or breaking down substances to retrieve their basic constituents or essences.

Chemically, it is the isolation of the components of dissolution by filtration and then the discarding of any ungenuine or unworthy material. To ancient Egyptian alchemists, separation was represented by the compound sodium carbonate, which separated out of water and appeared as white soda ash on dry lakebeds. The oldest known deposits are in Egypt. The alchemists sometimes referred to this compound as Natron, which meant the common tendency in all salts to form solid bodies or precipitates.

In the laboratory, the components of the polluted results from calcination and dissolution are usually separated out by a process the alchemists called "inhibition" or holding back. The most common method of inhibition is filtration, in which material is separated out by passing it through a screen or porous paper.

Other methods of separation include settling, decomposing, skimming, sifting, or agitation with air. Sometimes more sophisticated methods such as layered (or fractional) melting or distillation are used. The result is that any ungenuine or unworthy material is discarded, and the essences are isolated in separate containers.

The alchemical cipher for separation is the astrological sign of Scorpio. The Egyptians associated Scorpio with a descent into the underworld to bring back knowledge of universal truths, which is a perfect metaphor for the separation process. Other ciphers for separation were stylized filters and funnels, as well as piles of sand used for filtering liquids.

Images of separation include double-edged axes, swords hanging down from above, knights wielding swords, and scenes of dismemberment. The splitting of the Red Sea is sometimes used as a metaphor of separation, as are scenes from the Apocalypse. Alchemical engravings show white birds flying over a burning or blackened country-side. The destruction symbolizes the results of the earlier operations of *Nigredo*, while the white bird represents the essences saved by the separation process.

Personal Separation

Separation on the psychological level is the rediscovery and isolation of your essence or true self. During personal separation, you lift yourself out of the quagmire of your broken personality and recognize your true self. The operations of *Nigredo* have broken down your personality into your most basic traits and desires, and during the first stage of *Albedo*, you become aware of the pure essences within and isolate them from ego complexes and unwanted subconscious elements.

A typical alchemical drawing of the separation operation is shown in the following illustration. Separation requires decisive action, as suggested by the armored male figure with the sword. The process involves cutting into the heart of the subject of the work at this stage to reveal the deepest essences of soul and spirit. The great egg about to be cut open represents the sealed Hermetic vessel that contains these essences. That vessel can be a retort in the lab that contains a solution from which the essences must be saved, or it could represent the deeper aspects of your own personality or subconscious that must be exposed to the light of consciousness to succeed at personal transformation.

Separation of the essences.

Personal separation requires a certain amount of objectivity and honesty about your strengths and faults and what is worth salvaging from your old personality. Dissecting and discarding what is no longer relevant or useful is an important role of the separation process. The goal of separation is to preserve what is genuine by removing it from contaminating influences and keeping it safe for further alchemical transformation. This stage is about getting beyond the restraints to your true nature, so the real you can shine through.

From the Alchemist

The alchemists saw separation as the introduction of the Air Element into their work. Air is associated with spiritual energy, divine will, and energies from Above, and the Air Element purifies by increasing vibrations, spiritizing, and elevating the matter. Within your personality, the Air Element is simply taking the higher road of an enlightened attitude and maintaining an optimistic view of the possibilities open to you. The only way to really refine yourself is to raise the noble parts of your personality and bring them into the light.

The Conjunction Process

If the preceding operations were successful, only the most genuine and essential parts of the matter are left to work with. The next step in the alchemy of transformation is the conjunction, which is the recombination of those saved elements into a new compound or purer substance. In terms of the Four Elements, conjunction is the union of the Elements of Fire, Water, and Air to produce a purified or reborn Earth Element.

The process begins with commixtion, which is a mixing or commingling of the saved essences from separation. Vessels of conjunction have two glass globes or sections joined by a middle chamber in which the mixing or commingling occurs.

However, just bringing these essences together in the same vessel is not enough to accomplish this important operation. The essences must create a new compound, which the alchemists called the child of the conjunction. If the recombination of essences does not produce a new compound, the alchemists felt that material impurities or negative spiritual energies had polluted the process and the whole experiment had failed.

The alchemists saw the coming together of essences during conjunction as a sexual union or mating of chemicals to conceive a child, which was the new compound or alloy. For this reason, many of the drawings of this stage of the work show the King and Queen embracing or making love. Not surprisingly, the bird of conjunction is the cockerel—the young and virile rooster.

The alchemical cipher that stands for conjunction is the astrological Earth sign of Taurus, the virile bull. The bull was sacred to ancient Egyptians, who used it to symbolize fertility and growth. They even timed the plowing of their fields and mating of cattle with the rising of Taurus in the heavens.

Other images of conjunction include rams and satyrs, double-chambered furnaces, rope or chains binding opposing entities, birds chained to earthbound animals, and two streams coming together in one stream. Often engravings show the King and Queen in reconciliation at this stage, with Hermes or Mercury in between or joining them with an embrace or handshake.

Personal Conjunction

Psychologically, conjunction is the union of the opposing parts of our personality, the masculine King and the feminine Queen. The alchemists referred to this initial reconciliation as the fetus or Lesser Stone, and after it is accomplished, the initiate should be able to clearly discern what needs to be done to achieve permanent enlightenment, which would become the Greater Stone or Philosopher's Stone.

Drawings of conjunction usually show two animals, vessels, or other objects being mixed or joined in some way. In the following illustration, we see the alchemist patiently waiting for the conjunction process to begin. He has successfully separated and isolated the purified essences of soul and spirit, which are depicted by the two birds facing opposite directions in the retorts. The bird in the inverted vessel on top is spirit and the bird in the vessel below is soul. Once these opposing essences are mixed together, nature takes over. This is indicated by the alchemist pointing with his right hand to a plant on the ground. The stone cube that holds the vessels suggests this is a process of physical manifestation that takes place in real time and space. The whole process is like breeding animals, in that you can only bring the living essences together and hope for the best.

In spiritual terms, the essences of conjunction were the very soul and spirit of the alchemist, and their union was known as the Sacred Marriage (see Chapter 20). Alchemical images of this blessed event include the sun and the moon uniting in the sky, two white birds raising a crown into the heavens, red and white lions or dragons sharing one body, or elaborate outdoor wedding celebrations.

The conjunction of opposing spirits.

Because the marriage partners in the Sacred Marriage of conjunction were essences of soul and spirit within the alchemist, many alchemical texts described the marriage as an act of incest. To church officials, who took such metaphors literally, this was one more example of the immorality of alchemists.

Many people confuse the terms soul and spirit; however, the ancients saw these as two distinct entities. Spirit, the inner King, is constantly striving for change and betterment, while soul, the inner Queen, is happy with things as they are and wants only to settle down.

Spirit is associated with energy, aggression, expansion, and intellectual pursuits, while soul is associated with matter, passivity, contraction, bodily sensations, and emotions. Spirit craves action and adventure, feeds on abstract concepts, and seeks objective unifying principles. Spirit is responsible for business, science, technology, and the patriarchal world in which we live. The soul, on the other hand, craves memories and reflection and prefers storytelling over theorizing. Her language is art and music, and food for the soul comes from subjective feelings about everyday objects and relationships. Spirit is focused on the future but requires the passion of the soul to succeed, and for that reason, spirit must always seek out soul and court her favors.

The union of spirit and soul within an individual produces a third kind of consciousness that combines masculine and feminine ways of knowing into a deeper awareness. The Egyptians called it "Intelligence of the Heart," while medieval alchemists referred to this blossoming of wisdom as the "Philosopher's Child." It is the merging of thought and feeling to produce a highly intuitive state that was considered a direct experience of reality.

What does conjunction feel like on the personal level? Many adepts through the ages have compared it with the development of a spiritual fetus within, something new and unexpected, a wonderfully refreshing presence that emerges from the suffering and darkness of the *Nigredo*.

In the later stages of alchemy, this golden presence becomes an incorruptible "stone" in the sense that it survives untainted no matter what happens. No matter how confusing things get in your life, no matter what emotions swell up within you, no matter where your thoughts take you, no matter how cruel or inconsiderate others are toward you, you will have this solid refuge inside that is very much like a personal stone. This stone in your personality creates a feeling of deep integrity and confidence in everything you do.

Thoth's Tips

Conjunction is the doorway to a new level of empowerment, whose secrets are revealed only at the highest levels of initiation. You must progress a little further in your apprenticeship before you can appreciate this powerful Hermetic mystery. We will return to conjunction to take a look at its deeper significance in Chapter 20. In the meantime, two books by psychologist Edward Edinger that explore this topic in depth are *The Mystery of the Coniunctio* (Inner City Books, 1994) and *The Mysterium Lectures* (Inner City Books, 1995).

Conjunction is a prerequisite to progressing further in alchemy. It is the culmination of the work Below in the realm of matter, habits, and thoughts, and the beginning of the work Above in the realm of energy and spirit.

But conjunction is the operation where most failures occur both in the lab and on the personal level. The child of the conjunction is often stillborn and the work must be abandoned. That is, if the child is the product of an experiment, it might fail to create a new compound. If it is tincture, the plant essences may die or lose their life force when mixed in alcohol. On the psychological level, the child could be a new mental attitude of confidence and optimism that cannot survive in the everyday world of family, co-workers, and stressful responsibilities. For those reasons, conjunction is often called the turning point or pivotal operation in alchemy. If the child of the conjunction survives, it will be nurtured and grow into something entirely new and empowered during the operations of the Red Phase of alchemy.

The Least You Need to Know

◆ The White Phase of transformation is known as *Albedo* and begins at the darkest moment of the Black Phase.

◆ Separation is an operation of the White Phase that involves removing or isolating the surviving components of the Black Phase from their contaminated and impure environment.

◆ Conjunction is an operation of the White Phase that works to recombine the purified essences of the Black Phase into a new compound or higher manifestation.

◆ Personal separation involves finding the essences of the true self within and protecting them from any contaminating influences.

◆ Personal conjunction is about recognizing the essences of soul and spirit within and uniting them in a new level of consciousness and spiritual awareness.

Chapter 3

The Red Phase

In This Chapter

- ◆ The peacock spreads its tail
- ◆ The union of the White Queen and the Red King
- ◆ The operation of fermentation
- ◆ The operation of distillation
- ◆ The operation of coagulation
- ◆ Personal operations of the Red Phase

The third and final phase of alchemy, known as the Red Phase, or *Rubedo*, is a natural continuation of the White Phase. The alchemists believed the deep purification of essences begun during the White Phase was what released the powerful energies experienced during the Red Phase.

That these phases complement one another is reflected in the symbols alchemists chose to represent them. The symbol of *Albedo* is the White Queen; the symbol of *Rubedo* is the Red King. Often the White Queen and Red King are shown holding hands together or holding onto a small vessel or container. This was the alchemists' way of saying they work together. In the laboratory, the white becomes united with red through increasing the heat in the furnace.

Early European alchemists originally separated the *Rubedo* into two short stages or moments that indicated they were on the right path. The first moment was the appearance of a yellow or golden color in the matter. They called it the Yellow Stage and used the Latin word for yellow, *Citrinatis,* to refer to it. This short-lived phenomenon was a sign that the golden stage of transformation was coming. If they were working with a metal, it meant that transmutation into gold was a real possibility.

The second moment was signaled by the appearance of a deep purple color in the work. This Purple Stage was also known by the Latin word for purple, *Iosis.* Purple is actually the color of gold in solution and is an indicator of pure gold atoms in chemistry. To alchemists, it meant the minute quantity of gold revealed by the Yellow Stage was being seeded in the experiment and would eventually grow to transform the entire matter. Alchemists also referred to this stage as the "Transmutation of the Venom," and they believed it meant that any contamination or poisons left over from the *Nigredo* were now completely purified and assimilated.

With the successful completion of the Red Phase, the Philosopher's Stone was produced and the base metals transmuted into pure gold. Psychologically, this meant the integration of opposing and rejected elements in the personality and the experience of one's true self.

The Peacock's Tail

A curious thing happened during the transition from the *Albedo* phase to the *Rubedo.* The work entered another dark phase as the child of the conjunction neared birth. The alchemists called this short stage putrefaction, and it occurred both in the laboratory work and during the work on the psychological level.

The alchemists believed putrefaction was a final cleansing of impurities in the work and sometimes referred to it as the "Purgation of the Stone." Putrefaction was considered a final death to any contaminants or remnants of ego in the matter, and it was a necessary prelude to the resurrection or rebirth of the matter on a more perfect or spiritual level.

At the darkest moment of putrefaction, often a sudden and glorious display of many brilliant colors occurred. The alchemists named this the Peacock's Tail, or *Cauda Pavonis* in Latin. Again, it was observed in both the laboratory and on the personal level of transformation.

> **From the Alchemist**
>
> In mythology, the peacock was considered sacred to Juno, the Roman goddess and protector of childbirth. In the Middle Ages, peacocks were thought to fight snakes and consume or neutralize their poisons. Eating peacock meat became synonymous with integrating the many colors of the work to medieval alchemists.

The rainbow of colors seen in the Peacock's Tail gradually merged together into pure whiteness. Because black is the absence of color, the sudden appearance of colors in the Peacock's Tail during putrefaction signaled a fundamental change in the matter. And it's only natural that the Peacock's Tail eventually turned white because white contains all colors together.

Symbolism of the Peacock's Tail includes a rainbow appearing in the dark clouds of a thunderstorm, the bursting forth of the colors of spring after the darkness of winter, and the colors of the Aurora Borealis (Northern Lights) gleaming against the night sky.

In the lab, the Peacock's Tail was observed in iridescent oil that floated on the surface of the blackened matter and gradually turned into a white fatty substance. This milky liquid was composed of digesting bacteria that accumulated on the rotting material. Psychologist Carl Jung compared this phenomenon to daybreak, a period of peace and tranquility before the next and final phase, which is the full sunrise of *Rubedo*.

The Reddening

After suffering through the *Nigredo*, undergoing the intense purifications of *Albedo*, and experiencing the death of putrefaction, the matter of the work was depleted of energy and life force. It was pure but sterile Earth, which the alchemists compared to the bleak face of the moon. To make the work come alive again, the alchemists felt it must have fresh blood and undergo reddening in the fire.

The infusion of life into the dead matter was accomplished by the loving union of the White Queen with the Red King, who work together during *Rubedo* in a cosmic process sometimes referred to as the "Marriage of the sun and the moon." Obviously, these are profound symbols with universal meanings.

If you have been a good apprentice and have paid attention to the symbolism presented thus far, you should know what spiritual forces are represented by the White Queen and Red King. According to Hermetic philosophy, these spiritual forces are the basic essences of every created thing in the universe. Do you know what they are?

The White Queen represents the universal feminine essence of soul; the Red King represents the universal masculine essence of spirit. If you missed the answer to this question, go back to the last chapter and make sure you understand the meaning of the symbolism described under the conjunction process before you proceed further in your apprenticeship.

From the Alchemist

German alchemist Franciscus Kieser described the work of the White Queen and Red King during *Rubedo* in his 1606 book *Cabalistic Chemistry:* "As the body used to be slow, rough, impure, dark and destructible because it lacked power and energy, so the reddened rebirth unifies soul with spirit, vivified and volatile, light and penetrating, pure, refined and clear, overflowing with energy, indestructible and full of energy. And it is able to maintain this."

Among the operations alchemists used to complete the Red Phase of transformation are two dynamic processes known as fermentation and distillation, which combine opposing energies in the work. The third and final operation during *Rubedo* is known as coagulation, which is the final crystallization of energy and matter that becomes the Philosopher's Stone.

The Fermentation Process

To the ancients, fermentation was a miracle of nature. As early as 7000 B.C.E., the Egyptians used their knowledge of fermentation to make mead, wine, and beer. By 4500 B.C.E., the Egyptians and Chinese had learned to ferment milk to make yogurt and cheese. Fermentation requires living cells, such as bacteria or yeast, and is considered a kind of cellular respiration that usually takes place in the absence of oxygen.

In chemical terms, fermentation is the conversion of organic substances into new compounds in the presence of fermenting bacteria. The most common fermentation is the conversion of sugars into alcohol, which held special meaning for alchemists. They felt alcohol was the actual spiritual essence of a substance, and thus we refer to liquors and other alcoholic beverages as "spirits."

Some examples of fermentation will make this process clear. Beer is made by germinating grain and then drying and crushing it into pulp. This mash, as it is called, is mixed with warm water. Wine is made by crushing grapes and separating out the juice. In both cases, fermentation begins naturally if the material is allowed to decay, though yeast is usually added to get the process started. After proper aging to allow the alcohol to accumulate, the beer or wine is filtered and bottled.

The putrefaction, whose end was signaled by the appearance of the Peacock's Tail, is actually a natural part of the fermentation process. Putrefaction is the first step in fermentation, when the matter is allowed to rot and decompose. Medieval alchemists sometimes added manure to help get the process going. Unlike the hopeless blackness of *Nigredo,* the alchemists considered the blackness of putrefaction to be a pregnant darkness that would lead to the birth of the Philosopher's Child.

The cipher alchemists used to designate putrefaction was the astrological Fire sign of Leo, which the Egyptians associated with the lion-headed sun god Sekhmet. Images of putrefaction include corpses, graves, coffins, massacres, mutilation, worms, dung beetles, and rotting flesh. Alchemical drawings at this stage depict birds descending from a pitch black sky, skeletons standing over coffins or black boxes, or a snake crucified on a cross.

From the Alchemist

The life of dung beetles is a metaphor of the processes of putrefaction and fermentation. The huge beetle makes a ball of animal feces into which it deposits its eggs. Then it rolls the ball back to its underground den, where the natural heat of putrefaction warms the eggs. As the larvae mature, the beetle rolls its ball toward the heat of the rising sun, where the newborn beetles emerge and take wing into the light of a new day. Egyptians worshipped the dung beetle as the sacred Scarab, whose esoteric meaning is "secret enclosed fire." This is the heat generated in decomposing material, as well as the secret fire that must be generated within alchemists to accomplish their work.

When true fermentation begins, the dead material seems to come to life again as movement and bubbling gases emerge from the influx of digesting bacteria. Drawings of fermentation sometimes show a bird descending into water where a black toad waits, two birds nesting in a tree, an alchemist waiting patiently for changes to take place in a darkened vessel, or a farmer sowing gold coins in a field.

Other scenes of fermentation feature grapevines, sowing, germination, greenness, and rebirth. The color green is often associated with successful fermentation, and other green symbols include the Emerald Tablet, green gemstones, lush gardens, and the Green Lion stretching up toward the sky. Images capturing the energies of the fermentation process include dark clouds and thunderstorms, lightning, sexual activity in caves or darkened vessels, and angels coming down from heaven.

Alchemists assigned the astrological cipher for Capricorn to stand for the process of fermentation. Capricorn is an Earth sign whose symbols are both the goat and the unicorn, representing the most basic and the highest natural instincts. Alchemists believed that Capricorn encompassed the entire work from beginning to end. Capricorn is the first sign of the year, and movement from Capricorn to Capricorn encompassed the one symbolic alchemical year in which the Great Work could be accomplished.

The primary symbol of successful fermentation is a curious two-headed human figure known as the *Rebis*, which is from the Latin phrase *res bina*, meaning "a double thing." The Rebis is usually depicted as a winged hermaphrodite with a male head on its right and a female head on its left and represents the Philosopher's Child resulting from the union of the King and Queen that took place during the conjunction phase.

The naked and purified Rebis is shown being heated by the fires of fermentation in the following figure. This fire is not the direct consuming flames of calcination, but a controlled heat that has been likened to birds sitting on eggs to hatch them. The Rebis is like an embryonic being or intermediate stage in transformation that requires more toil in the final stages of the work.

This new being emerges from the dark womb of putrefaction and takes its first breath during fermentation. The Rebis is a hermaphroditic melding of the masculine and feminine characteristics of its parents, the King and Queen. In mythological terms, the hermaphrodite results from the sacred marriage of our Hermes with the Greek goddess of love, Aphrodite.

Fermentation of the Rebis.

Personal Fermentation

Just as chemical fermentation is the introduction of new life into the matter, so is psychological fermentation the introduction of new life into the inner presence created during personal conjunction. Any problems starting the fermentation process giving birth to the child of the conjunction stem from impurities carried over from the White Phase. These hidden impurities in our character are finally destroyed during the psychological death of putrefaction.

Fermentation on the personal level starts with the inspiration of spiritual power that reanimates, energizes, and enlightens the blackened ego. Personal fermentation can be achieved using a wide variety of tools that include intense prayer, desire for mystical union, transpersonal therapy, visualization, and deep meditation. In simplest terms, fermentation is a living, loving inspiration from something totally beyond and outside us in the spiritual realm. "Separate the Earth from Fire, the Subtle from the Gross," the Emerald Tablet instructs us at this stage.

Like the colorful Peacock's Tail of its chemical counterpart, psychological fermentation is often initiated by colorful visions that involve a higher form of imagination the alchemists called the "True Imagination." They felt the mental images experienced during fermentation were true representations of a higher spiritual reality and not mere fantasy.

The Distillation Process

Distillation is the boiling and condensation of a solution to increase its concentration and purity. The alchemists believed that distillation released the pure essence or spirit of a substance in the evaporating vapors. For example, one can obtain the pure alcohol spirit of wine by distilling a solution of fermented grapes. The essence could be concentrated using a process known as *rectification*.

def•i•ni•tion

Rectification is the process of refining or purifying a substance by repeated distillation. The evaporated distillate is returned to the boiling vessel to be distilled again. Continued cycles of distillation eventually produce a thick and extremely concentrated solution the alchemists called the "Mother of the Stone."

The typical distillation apparatus consists of a lower boiling vessel (the cucurbit) and an upper stillhead (the alembic), which is a hooded vessel that collects the rising vapors. The hot vapors are cooled in a long condenser, and the purified condensed liquid (the distillate) is directed by a tube or funnel into a receiving vessel.

A popular medieval distillation device was nicknamed the Pelican. It was a glass retort (a type of container) with two tubes connecting the neck of the vessel with the lower body (see Chapter 14). The result was a reflux or rectification still, in which the mixture was boiled and vapors condensed in the neck and then flowed back into the boiling liquid through the tubes. This inner circulatory process produced a very pure essence from the original mixture. In alchemical drawings of this operation, the pelican is shown pecking herself in her chest in order to feed her young, which are usually gathered at her feet lapping up her fresh blood or life essence.

Another kind of distillation is cohobation, in which solid matter is repeatedly soaked in liquid and distilled to capture its purified essences. In a kind of distillation known as sublimation, no liquid is used at all. The solid material gives off vapors that condense directly into an extremely pure powder at the top of the distilling apparatus. The solidified material remains stuck to the sides of the alembic until collected by the alchemist. The alchemists considered sublimation a superior form of distillation that led directly to their treasured Philosopher's Stone. "He who knows how to sublime the Stone," said the Greek alchemist Eudoxus (400–350 B.C.E.), "justly deserves the name of a philosopher, since he knows the Fire of the Wise, which is the only instrument which can work this sublimation."

Distillation is the most important operation in practical alchemy, and some alchemists spent months distilling the same solution over and over. Distillation is described in the Emerald Tablet in these words: "It rises from Earth to Heaven and descends again to Earth, thereby combining within Itself the powers of both the Above and the Below."

The alchemists chose the astrological Earth sign of Virgo as the cipher to signify distillation. The Egyptians associated the alchemical goddess Isis with this sign. The cipher for the operation of sublimation was Libra, an astrological Air sign the Egyptians associated with the divine child, as well as Maat, the goddess of truth.

Two-headed creatures are shown rising into the air on wings and then returning to Earth in drawings depicting the distillation process. This repeated circulation between the spiritual forces Above and the material forces Below eventually lead to a concentration and purification of the essences of the substance at hand.

In the following figure, we see the distillation of the Rebis as it nears the final stages. The Rebis stands on a winged stone or globe that is the new Salt or permanent body that forms after distillation is complete. Above we see the seven planetary operations that the Rebis will go through before the transformation is complete. The square and compass and octagon figure indicate that distillation is an objective process of rectification and gradual enlightenment.

Distillation of the Rebis.

Other images of distillation include flowers in bloom, such as the rose, the lotus, jasmine, and the Edelweiss, as well as scenes of fountains, waterwheels, dew, rain, and snow. Animal images include the unicorn, white doves, soaring birds, owls, pelicans, winged serpents, the Green Lion eating the sun, and a dragon in flames eating its own tail.

Personal Distillation

In psychological terms, distillation is a process of spiritization that involves repeated separation and recombination of the subtle or spiritual aspects of the personality with the unrefined thoughts and emotions or gross aspects of the personality. This is actually a very natural process that we can observe simply by paying attention to our everyday thoughts. We are always recycling thoughts and regurgitating emotions in a never-ending struggle to organize our lives and find direction and meaning. This chaotic process goes on unchecked and unnoticed until a distilled idea breaks through in the form of a new insight or revised judgment.

Personal distillation, however, requires being conscious of this process and deliberately pursuing it to its conclusion. The deliberate agitation and sublimation of psychic forces is necessary to ensure that no impurities from the inflated ego or submerged shadow are incorporated into the new self manifesting in the final stages of transformation.

Tools used in personal distillation include introspective meditations that raise the content of the psyche to the highest or most objective level possible, free from the emotional energy that often controls our behavior. Almost all types of psychological therapy are methods of personal distillation that seek a reconciliation of subjective and objective realities.

Many meditations used by Taoist alchemists are also methods of personal distillation. For instance, in the meditation called "Circulation of the Light," one is taught to focus the light of consciousness on the lower cauldron of energy in the abdomen below the navel. Following the natural rhythm of the breath, this base energy is heated by the powers of intention and attention and rises up the back to the upper cauldron in the head. There the purified light is condensed and accumulated, and any unconverted energy returns to the navel area along the front of the chest. The distillation of the light is repeated daily for months or even years, until enough of the liquid light collects to crystallize in the brain. According to Taoist alchemists, the subtle matter distilled through this process congeals into a Golden Pill, which is the adept's passage to perfect health and even immortality.

The Coagulation Process

The final rung on the ladder of transformation is the operation of coagulation, in which the body is made spiritual and the spirit is made corporeal. Coagulation produces a new incarnation that can survive in all realms.

Chemical coagulation is the physical manifestation of the essence created during conjunction, born during fermentation, and purified in distillation. It is accomplished by the congealing, precipitating, or sublimating of the solidified essence or child of the conjunction. This fixation of spiritual forces is what creates the Philosopher's Stone, which embodies the principle of transmutation itself.

With the creation of the Philosopher's Stone, two more operations are now available to alchemists. The first is projection, which is the process of transmuting the base metals into gold. It is said that just a tiny piece of the Stone or a pinch of the red powder of projection made from it is enough to perfect the metals and transmute lead into gold. The second operation of the Stone is multiplication, which is the act or process of multiplying or increasing the quantity or volume of something. Just a touch of the Stone or a grain of the red powder will cause plants to grow to perfection or cells to be healed and multiply perfectly. Even the Stone itself and its powers can be magically multiplied. Multiplication provides the raw material for the elixir of life, drinkable gold, and other panaceas that the alchemists promised would cure all diseases.

The cipher for coagulation is the astrological Air sign of Gemini, the Divine Twins that to alchemists represented their Rebis. The cipher for projection is the Water sign of Pisces. From at least 2300 B.C.E., the Egyptians used two fish to denote this constellation. The cipher used for the multiplication operation is the Water sign of Aquarius, whom the Egyptians associated with Osiris, their god of grain, seeds, and semen.

Coagulation images include brilliantly shining new gold, a balanced set of scales, an egg-shaped stone, the Holy Grail, and a naked androgynous youth. Scenes of coagulation include such things as wingless creatures being carried away by winged creatures, a lone eagle soaring high in the sky, the serpent and lion united, the King and Queen breaking free of their chains, or the sun and moon beaming down proudly over a naked child.

The most common symbol of coagulation is the Phoenix, a mythical bird that built its nest in a fire and then rose from the ashes completely reborn as a new creature. Alchemists sometimes called the Phoenix the "Ortus," the rectified one. They described it as a four-legged bird with black eyes, a white face, white forepaws, black hind paws, and a red head with streaks of pure gold reaching to its neck.

From the Alchemist

The Phoenix and the Emerald Tablet are closely related. Both are said to have originated in the ancient land of Phoenicia, and in some traditions, the Emerald Tablet was written in Phoenician characters. Some Egyptian writings even refer to the Emerald Tablet as the Phoenix. "I am the Great Phoenix," reads an ancient Egyptian stele, "which is in Heliopolis. I am the rendering of all that is and will exist." The Egyptians also equated the Phoenician bird with their own sacred Bennu Bird, which symbolized the completely spiritized self that rises up from the lower nature of the soul.

Personal Coagulation

Psychologically, the Phoenix is the resurrected personality that is fully manifested during coagulation. The alchemists viewed it as the divine child of the King and Queen who embodies a new state of awareness beyond either masculine or feminine ways of knowing. Paracelsus named this cosmic essence the *Iliaster*, which literally means "the star in man." He described it as the "completely healed human being who has burned away all the dross of his lower being and is free to fly as the Phoenix."

On the spiritual level, coagulation produces an entirely new body for the alchemist. This second body is often described as a body of light, which is the *Ultima Materia* (Ultimate Matter) of the soul. Many experience it as a projected golden body of coalesced light that Paracelsus named the Astral Body, literally the Star Body. As one Renaissance alchemist described it: "You break through space, fly to heaven in broad daylight, and shed the flesh-and-bone bag, which is now as useless as the alchemical workshop and vessels once the elixir has been perfected."

In Christian alchemy, the ultimate matter of the soul is the resurrected body. In the Gospel of John, the coagulated body is described as the seamless garment that Jesus wore when he said, "I and my Father are one." In the same gospel, Jesus warned that unless a man be born of both Fire and Water, he cannot enter into the kingdom of God. In Eastern religions, the culmination of the Red Phase corresponds with the formation of the Diamond Body, the resplendent body of crystallized light that began its transformation as a lump of black coal.

"Its inherent strength is perfected if it is turned into Earth," the Emerald Tablet says of the coagulation process. "Thus will you obtain the Glory of the Whole Universe," it continues. "All Obscurity will be clear to you. This is the greatest Force of all powers, because it overcomes every Subtle thing and penetrates every Solid thing."

The Least You Need to Know

- The Red Phase of transformation is a continuation of the purification of the White Phase, and the symbols of this cooperative effort are the Red King and the White Queen.

- The transition from the putrefaction stage of fermentation is marked by a beautiful display of colors known as the Peacock's Tail.

- Fermentation is an operation of the Red Phase that seeks to revive the dead material left over from putrefaction.

- Distillation is a Red Phase operation that works to purify and concentrate the essences retrieved from fermentation.

- Coagulation is an operation in which the Philosopher's Stone is produced.

- Personal fermentation, distillation, and coagulation are operations of the Red Phase of alchemy applied to the psychological and spiritual components of individuals.

Part 4 Practical Alchemy

The primary goal of medieval alchemists was the creation of the Philosopher's Stone that would instantly perfect or cure anything. Their work involved spending many hours in the laboratory, heating materials at high temperatures for long periods and carefully distilling essences from fermented solutions. The laboratory work of the alchemists gave rise to modern chemistry and also created a new healing modality known as spagyrics. In spagyric alchemy, plant material is "opened up" by heating, cutting, and grinding, and the essences that are released are preserved in oils, tinctures, and elixirs. Unlike chemistry, however, the methods of alchemy always involve the simultaneous purification and transformation of the alchemist himself, whose conscious participation and symbiotic connection to the substance was considered a necessary ingredient.

Chapter 14

Inside an Alchemist's Laboratory

In This Chapter

- ◆ Step inside a medieval laboratory
- ◆ The heart of the laboratory: the athanor
- ◆ Chemicals and tools used by alchemists
- ◆ Sacred space of the oratorium
- ◆ Differences between chemists and alchemists
- ◆ The role of women in alchemy

The popular image of the crazed and disheveled old alchemist working late at night away from prying eyes in his cluttered laboratory is not really very accurate. For one thing, alchemical laboratories during the Middle Ages and Renaissance were actually very organized. As we can see from alchemists' workplaces that have survived, there was a place for everything and everything had its place. Equipment and chemicals were kept on shelves or bins where they could be easily accessed, and the vast variety of glassware alchemists used were usually sorted by size and conveniently hung on the walls.

As for alchemists themselves, they were mostly serious experimenters—not eccentric crackpots. They were usually highly educated, intelligent people with a keen interest in discovering the secrets of nature. During most of the history of alchemy in Europe, it was necessary to know Latin and Greek to even begin learning the subject, and alchemists were known for their dedication to scholarly pursuits. They studied alchemy manuscripts religiously, kept careful records of their own work, and traveled extensively to compare their findings with other alchemists.

Alchemists were among the leading philosophers and scientists of their times. Even many government rulers and religious authorities were alchemists. In Europe, scores of monks, bishops, and even a few popes practiced alchemy. Nearly every physician in the late Middle Ages used alchemical remedies and was familiar with the theories of alchemy. At one time, Hermetic philosophy and alchemy were taught at universities in Europe, and nearly every major university had a practicing alchemist hidden among its faculty members.

Historical researcher Mircea Eliade described the traits needed by an alchemist: "He must be healthy, humble, patient, chaste; his mind must be free and in harmony with his work; he must be intelligent and scholarly, he must work, meditate, and pray."

A Tour of a Medieval Laboratory

Perhaps the best way to get to know the alchemists and how they worked is to take an imaginary tour of where they spent so much of their time. Our alchemy laboratory is a composite of several actual labs used by alchemists, and I have incorporated features that were customary in several different time periods and countries.

From the Alchemist

A lot of the alchemists' laboratory work was done outdoors, especially in the warmer climates of Asia and the Arab lands. Alchemical experiments often produced thick smoke and fumes, which were more readily dissipated outdoors. Also, the heavy brick furnaces used by alchemists were easier to build and maintain outside.

Let's begin our virtual tour of an idealized alchemical laboratory by politely knocking on the thick wooden door of the lab. While a few alchemists were willing to talk about their theories, almost none allowed outsiders actual access to their laboratories, so this is a rare opportunity. Why did alchemists not encourage visitors? The need for secrecy in their work was the most important reason, though safety was also a factor. Often several experiments were in progress that took weeks to complete, plus potent chemicals and fragile glassware were usually involved.

Beyond that, many alchemists believed that other people's impure thoughts and emotions could actually ruin their delicate experiments, so they were very careful about whom they let in.

But the door to this lab opens, and we are invited into the alchemist's sanctuary. He respectfully greets us with a bow of his head and then cautions us about a few experiments he has going on. Before he even finishes his sentence, however, we are distracted by a powerful odor carried by a draft of air going out the door. It smells like a combination of rotten eggs and strong vinegar. The alchemist explains the repugnant odor is coming from the large digesting tub full of rotting material in the corner behind the door. He uses this digester in the operations of putrefaction and fermentation.

The Athanor

We glance over into the foul, black, gurgling liquid in the digesting tub and wonder if this might be a good time for a quick exit. But before we can turn toward the door, we notice a tall cylindrical brick furnace at the center of the room. Gentle warmth emanates from the furnace, and we move closer.

Called the athanor, this brick or clay oven is where most of the alchemist's transformations take place. The word comes from the Arabic word *at-tannaur*, meaning "oven." It is also called the "Philosophical Furnace," the "Furnace of Arcana," or the "Furnace of Secrets." In popular parlance, it is known simply as the tower furnace because it usually stands over 5 feet tall.

The alchemists nicknamed the athanor *Piger Henricus* (Slow Henry) because of its steady, slow-burning fire. Designed to maintain a constant, even heat over long periods, it had several different compartments suitable for the different stages of the work. Its primary function was to incubate an egg-shaped Hermetic vessel used for the preparation of the elixir.

Philosophically, the athanor was like a womb or fertilized egg, and many experiments required the alchemists to keep it burning for 40 weeks, which was considered sufficient maturation time for the human fetus.

On the spiritual level, the athanor was a metaphor of the inner fire in the alchemist's mind and body, and corresponding changes were expected to occur in the alchemist himself as the transformations took place in the athanor. Just as the athanor was the heart of the laboratory with everything built around it, so was the alchemist's life centered around his sacred furnace.

Alchemical Glassware

On the wall to the right of the athanor hangs a bewildering array of glass vessels on wooden pegs. The opening of each vessel is inserted over an appropriate-sized peg, and the vessel is hung there to dry or for safe storage. It is easy to discern which ones are seldom used, because they are covered in dust.

Many alchemists were skilled glassblowers and potters, and the glass or earthenware vessels they designed each had a specific function. Alchemists used these vessels to carry out the operations of alchemy, and making or finding strong and durable vessels was an important part of their work.

From the Alchemist

Alchemists viewed their vessels as containers of spiritual energies, and each had esoteric as well as practical uses. "Although an instrument, the alchemical vessel nevertheless has peculiar connections with the First Matter and Philosopher's Stone," noted Carl Jung, "so it is no mere piece of apparatus. For the alchemists, the vessel is something truly marvelous and miraculous. It is more a mystical idea, a true symbol like all the central ideas of alchemy."

The most popular vessel among alchemists was the retort, a glass sphere with a long neck or spout. It could be tightly sealed with a stopper, and the long spout was handy for pouring or connecting to another vessel. The retort was a versatile vessel that could be used to mix, separate, decompose, heat, or distill solutions.

A vessel of distillation had three parts, one of which was the alembic, which was a kind of retort that fit on the upper part of a still to collect and direct the distilled vapors into a condenser. The lower part of the still containing the boiling liquid was called the cucurbit. Alchemists sometimes called it the gourd because of its shape. The final part of this apparatus was the receiver, which was the flask attached to the outlet of the condenser that collected the distilled product or distillate.

Other vessels used by alchemists included the matrass, which was a round-bottomed flask with a very long neck that was also known as a bolt-head. The aludel was a pear-shaped glass open at both ends. Used in the process of sublimation, it was also called the Hermetic Vase. Other glassware included a wide assortment of different-sized beakers, cylinders, bottles, flasks, and jars.

Crucibles and cupels were used in melting and other high-temperature operations. Crucibles are small clay or porcelain cups made to withstand high temperatures in the oven. When the alchemists made these, they added graphite to increase the heat resistance of native clays. Cupels are porous pots made of bone ash and clay. They were used primarily in a process known as cupellation, a form of fire assaying in which noble metals were separated from base metals. Lead and other impurities were absorbed into the bone ash of the cupel or released as fumes, leaving behind pure silver and gold.

Each operation of alchemy had its own special vessel designed to contain the transforming matter as well as preserve the energies at that stage. Many of these were patterned after nature and named for animals. One of the most popular was a circulatory distillation vessel called the Pelican. This impressive glass vessel had two side-arms that fed condensed vapors back into the body and resembled a pelican pecking at its breast. It was a common belief in the Middle Ages that pelicans wounded themselves in order to feed their hatchlings with their own blood (see Chapter 13).

Other names the alchemists gave their vessels reflected the spiritual and psychological processes associated with them. Among these intriguing names were Philosopher's Egg, Skull Cup, Brain Pan, Angel Tube, Spirit Holder, Moon Vessel, Mother of the Stone Container, Matrix Vase, Hermes Cup, Cup of Babylon, and Tomb of the Dead.

The Chemicals Used by Alchemists

On the opposite wall of the laboratory are several shelves full of alchemical treasures. The lower shelf holds assorted vials, crocks, and burlap bags containing the salts, powders, colored liquids, and other compounds used by the alchemist. Each container is carefully marked with a unique alchemical cipher that signifies its contents. Alchemists had hundreds of compounds, powerful acids, metals, and other chemicals at their disposal.

The colorful names alchemists gave to their compounds were full of hidden meaning. For example, sal ammoniac (ammonium chloride) was so named because it was first made with camel dung from the Temple of Ammon in Egypt. Ammonia was also known as Spirit of Hartshorn because it was distilled from an ancient substitute for yeast and baking soda known as hartshorn (ammonium bicarbonate). Another name for ammonia was Salt of Urine because—you guessed it—it was distilled from urine.

Many of the compounds used by alchemists in the Middle Ages dated back to ancient Egypt, and among the ones the Egyptians discovered were four important chemicals that became known as the "arcana" to later alchemists. *Arcana* is Latin for "great secrets," and medieval alchemists held these chemicals in the highest esteem. They called them vitriol, natron, liquor hepatis, and pulvis solaris.

Vitriol

The earliest alchemists secured both sulfuric acid and iron from an oily substance that appeared naturally from the weathering of sulfur-bearing gravel. This substance was known as green vitriol and, in its natural state, was a powerful disinfectant. When heated, it broke down into a mixture of iron sulfate and sulfuric acid.

The Egyptians used iron sulfate to heal wounds and prepared a therapeutic tonic from it. A relaxing powder known as the Narcotic Salt of Vitriol was also made from it. Iron sulfate had many other uses in alchemy and was known as the Green Lion in the Middle Ages.

> **Tread Carefully**
>
> Do not attempt to handle or work with chemicals unless you have been properly trained in laboratory procedures. Labs are dangerous places for people who don't know what they are doing. Many compounds used by alchemists are toxic, especially metals such as antimony, lead, and mercury.

The sulfuric acid distilled from green vitriol is brown and stinks like rotten eggs. It is an extremely powerful and corrosive acid that reacts with most metals but not gold. Further distillation produces a heavy, nearly odorless, yellow liquid known as Oil of Vitriol, which has a tremendous thirst for water. If a flask of Oil of Vitriol is allowed to stand opened for some time, it absorbs water vapor from the air and overflows its container. Alchemists considered sulfuric acid to be liquid fire and the agent of change in most alchemical experiments. It remains an indispensable agent in many modern industries.

Natron

The word natron is from the Arabian name for the white salts that accumulate on dry lake beds. Philosophically, natron symbolized the common principle in all salts to form bodies out of solutions. Chemically, the word refers to either of two sodium compounds. The first of these is natron carbonicum (sodium carbonate), which appears on dried lakebeds or is mined out of the earth. The world's oldest known deposits are in Egypt. It can also be prepared by pouring sulfuric acid over common table salt.

The second natron was natron nitricum (sodium nitrate). It occurs naturally as cubic-saltpeter and needs only to be filtered to be used medicinally. It can also be obtained by pouring nitric acid over common table salt. The alchemists who made nitric acid by pouring sulfuric acid over common saltpeter (potassium nitrate) called it *aqua fortis* (strong water) and used it to dissolve silver out of gold.

Liquor Hepatis

Ancient alchemists prepared liquor hepatis, or liquid of the soul, by distilling a solution of sulfur, lime, and sal ammoniac. They considered it a permanent solution because they had no methods of breaking it down once it was prepared. Because of its deep reddish-brown color, liquor hepatis was associated with the liver, and the name comes from the Greek word *hepar*, meaning "liver." The alchemists also referred to it as Oil of Sulfur.

The Egyptians were fascinated by the pungent odor of liquor hepatis. They believed it originated from a presence hidden in sulfur that was purified by lime and brought to life by ammonia. The Egyptians equated this hidden presence with soul, which they believed resided in the liver. Soul was the ultimate universal essence and, like liquor hepatis, could not be broken down into parts. Not only did liquor hepatis contain soul, but it suggested the idea of the soul's possible resurrection.

The Egyptians made a balm of liquor hepatis by mixing it with wax and fat. This sacred balm, said to incorporate the powers of rejuvenation and healing, became known as the Balsam of the Soul or the Balsam of the Alchemists.

Pulvis Solaris

If liquor hepatis represented soul to the ancients, then pulvis solaris, or powder of the sun, represented spirit. Pulvis solaris was actually a mixture of two compounds known as red pulvis solaris and black pulvis solaris. These red and black powders were created separately by combining highly purified sulfur with either red mercuric oxide or black antimony.

Red mercuric oxide was made by heating mercury in a long-necked flask. The mercury oxidized into a white powder and red crystals. This white powder was a deadly poison, but the red crystals had healing properties. When the red crystals were mixed with pure sulfur, they combined immediately to form the red powder of the sun.

Black antimony is a naturally occurring mineral known as stibnite, which is a sulfide of antimony. The mineral was smelted and ground fine. It also had healing properties and was made into a tonic by mixing the fine powder in distilled water. When the black powder was mixed with pure sulfur, they combined immediately to form the black powder of the sun.

Mixing the red and black powders together created pulvis solaris, which the alchemists believed had tremendous healing power on all levels of body, mind, and spirit. The way the original two powders immediately clumped together with sulfur to form new compounds demonstrated the natural longing or love of these ingredients for one another.

By combining the two red and black powders of the sun together, the alchemists felt they had created a mystical third incarnation in which the sum was greater than its parts. The esoteric chemistry here also underscores a fundamental principle. Namely, soul is an indivisible, eternal thing, while spirit is a kind of energy that originates from the tension of two polarized forces.

Thoth's Tips

There are still alchemists' workshops you can visit. An alchemist's lab from the sixteenth century was recently discovered hidden in a chapel in Oberstockstall Castle in Austria. Now a museum, it is located 55 kilometers from Vienna in Kirchberg am Wagram. The Technical Museum in Vienna features a reconstruction of a medieval lab. The Alchemy Museum in Kutna Hora, Czech Republic, has a complete alchemist's workshop, and another medieval lab is in Mihulka Tower in Prague. In Germany, there are alchemists' labs in the castle in Heidelberg, the Museum of Science and Technology in Munich, and Weikersheim Castle in Baden-Württemberg. Other exhibits can be found in the Pharmacy Historical Museum in Basel, Switzerland; and the Golden Eagle Museum in Budapest, Hungary.

Hidden Energies in the Lab

As we continue our tour of the laboratory, we move our attention from the chemical supply shelf to a middle shelf that contains haphazard piles of tools and utensils which the alchemist uses. We notice assorted tongs, scoops, pincers, stirrers, spoons, ladles, and other items. Most of these are made of brass or copper, although a few are cast iron. Stainless steel was unknown in Europe in the Middle Ages. We also see a set of balance scales and a small herb press on this shelf. Small and large leather bellows are stacked at the end of the shelf.

But the items on the upper shelf make our jaws drop. The dried carcasses of assorted frogs, birds, rats, rabbits, and other less identifiable creatures adorn this shelf, and a few preservative-filled jars appear to contain large insects. The alchemists were fascinated by all aspects of nature and often had large collections of preserved animals—especially rare or unusual creatures.

Alchemists believed the life force was like a substance that they could separate from living things and preserve in special tinctures. They could then use these living alchemical solutions to impart health to sick people or even give life to inanimate objects. Many famous alchemists claimed to have created little artificial beings (homunculi) by infusing the life force into flasks of chemical compounds.

The life force was the Quintessence the alchemists sought in plants and fermented organic matter, and one of the pieces of equipment they used in this endeavor stands next to a cluttered workbench at the back of our laboratory. Known as a serpent condenser, the giant air-cooled apparatus was used for distilling the foul-smelling solution poured off from the digester. Towering over the height of man, it is composed of a shaky array of copper tubing that zigzagged upward from a thick, pear-shaped clay vessel on the floor.

Using the serpent condenser, the alchemist hoped to purify and isolate the living essences of substances. The gentle, low-temperature distillation performed by the serpent condenser was thought to safely remove and preserve the purified essences from even the foulest liquid.

The Oratorium

Next to the serpent condenser, a large dark curtain hangs suspended from the ceiling. It is carefully draped completely around a small altar on the floor. This tabernacle forms a private meditation space known as the oratorium, and as much work is done within this sacred space as is carried out in the laboratory. One of the mottos of alchemy is *Ora et Labora:* Pray and Work. Alchemists spent many hours in solitary contemplation, attempting to purify and focus their minds, so they could connect with the divine powers.

The following illustration, which is an engraving of an alchemical laboratory called the "Amphitheater of Eternal Wisdom," shows the typical oratorium. The German spiritual alchemist Heinrich Khunrath designed it in 1609. In it, we see the work of the alchemist divided into the oratorium on the left, where the spiritual work was done, and the laboratorium on the right, where he performed the practical work.

The doorway at the center of the engraving is the completion of the work, when the alchemist leaves the laboratory behind and enters a whole new level of being in the world.

The alchemical laboratory.

Hidden somewhere in the oratorium could usually be found the alchemist's incubator. This insulated, copper-clad wooden box was the most sacred spot in the lab. The sealed container, kept warm by the fermenting matter within, was where the alchemist directed his thoughts and visualizations.

During the process of fermentation, the First Matter was most exposed and most open to the influence of the alchemist. However, it was a delicate operation. At the beginning of fermentation, the resurrected life was easily corrupted by another's impure thoughts, which is why the alchemist always kept the incubator hidden—even from other alchemists. He believed that if anyone other than himself touched or even looked upon this box, all would be lost.

This attitude may seem superstitious to us, but we should not judge the alchemists too quickly. They were acting completely in accord with the ancient principles of Hermetic philosophy. To alchemists, consciousness was a force of nature that could be purified and directed through prayer and meditation. This esoteric part of the experiment was absolutely necessary for its success.

As we come to the end of our tour, we thank the alchemist for allowing us to visit his private workshop and sharing his work with us. We have learned much about the fundamental tools of alchemy.

As we pass by the digester on the way out of the lab, the odors are not nearly so repugnant as when we first encountered them. To our surprise, it now seems like the fragrance of magic is in the air.

Alchemists and Chemists

The alchemical principle that the consciousness of the experimenter influenced the outcome of the experiment just may explain why many alchemical experiments cannot be duplicated in a chemical laboratory. It is not that the experiments never worked but just that chemists do not know how to perform them.

Chemists, who fully believe their experiments take place only on the mundane physical level, see no need to purify themselves or meditate prior to beginning work in the lab. Their mindset is that chemistry operates by rearranging atoms like so many billiard balls—a methodology much too crude for the alchemist. From the alchemist's viewpoint, chemistry is a superficial and artificial science that deals only with the external forms in which substances manifest while ignoring the essences of energy and light that created them.

In our tour of an alchemist's lab, we have seen the fundamental tools of medieval laboratories that made alchemy such a unique blend of science and spirit. Still, from our modern viewpoint, it's hard to imagine how much a part of their experiments were the alchemists themselves. All matter was alive to them, and they sympathized with the subject of their work every time they exposed it to fire, submerged it in acid, or bathed it in cooling waters.

The uncanny identification with the processes in the laboratory was absolutely necessary, because the alchemist and his work fed on each other. The alchemist suffered with his work, felt its same temperament, and changed with it. For, if the experiment was truly a success, the alchemist, too, was transformed. The key to this whole magical process was the conscious connection or correspondence the alchemist was able to forge between his own mind and the "mind of nature" as expressed in the experiment.

Women in Alchemy

The role of women in alchemy was often in the shadows. During the witch hunts of the Middle Ages, it was extremely dangerous to be a female alchemist, and generally, the woman's work was out of the limelight. However, nearly every alchemist had his "Moon Sister" who worked by his side in experiments and meditations. Flamel's work could not have been accomplished without the aid of his wife, Pernelle; Rebecca Vaughn, wife of the seventeenth-century English alchemist Thomas Vaughn, is another example. Female alchemists from Alexandria, such as Maria Prophetissa, Kleopatra, Hypatia, and Theosebeia, laid the foundations of much experimental work. Other famous female alchemists include French physicist Marie Curie, German author Leonia Constantia, and the English women Anne Conway and Tomazine Scarlet.

The Least You Need to Know

- The athanor was the tall brick furnace alchemists used in their transformations.

- The shape of alchemical glassware had both practical and spiritual purposes.

- The arcana of alchemy are powerful chemicals that date back to ancient Egypt.

- Most alchemical labs were divided into an oratorium, where spiritual work was done; and the laboratorium, where the practical work was done.

- Most true alchemists were intimately connected to their work and expected corresponding transformations in their own minds, bodies, and souls.

- Although early female alchemists did their work largely out of the limelight, nearly every male alchemist had a "Moon Sister" who worked by his side.

The Spagyric Process

In This Chapter

- The hidden signatures in everything
- The kinds of medical cures
- The inner star or true identity of a substance
- The Three Essentials in spagyrics
- The times of planetary magic
- The genius of Paracelsus

Spagyrics (pronounced spa-jeer-icks) is the applied alchemy of isolating the essences of plants and herbs. The Swiss alchemist Paracelsus invented the word by combining the Greek words *spao*, "tear apart," and *ageiro*, "gather together." So the term spagyrics literally means to tear apart and bring back together again.

In spagyrics, the plant is dried, ground up, or pressed to concentrate its essences, which are then separated and brought back together in a more purified and potent form. The object of spagyrics is to isolate the living essences of the plant and preserve them for later use while at the same time getting rid of the useless or impure parts. "Spagyria," said Paracelsus, "teaches you to separate the false from the true."

Alchemists use the spagyric process to make all true alchemical tinctures and elixirs, and they must meet very specific conditions to say that a compound is spagyric. In general, spagyric compounds take much longer to make than normal chemical compounds, because spagyric preparations must be made during certain alignments of the planets that are determined by the signatures of the plant itself.

The Doctrine of Signatures

The doctrine of signatures originated in ancient Egypt with the idea that divine correspondences can be found in the manifested world. This concept was inspired by the Emerald Tablet's dictum of "As Above, so Below." According to the ancient text *Archidoxies*, signatures are the hidden archetypal patterns in things that "have the power of transmuting, altering, and restoring us."

Alexandrian alchemists started categorizing plants by their signatures. They defined signatures as the characteristics plants and other objects shared with the planetary powers and astrological events in the heavens.

In Eastern philosophy, Chinese alchemist Lao Tzu was the first to clearly elucidate the doctrine of signatures. He stressed the fundamental relationship and corresponding signatures between heavenly powers and earthly manifestation, an idea that pervades modern Taoist thought. He also stressed working only with the true signature of a thing, what he called a substance's inner virtue.

In the West, the alchemist Paracelsus expanded the doctrine of signatures into every aspect of human life. He taught that man should carefully consider the inner essence of a plant for what it tells us from its properties, structure, color, odor, and habitat. These signatures reveal the resonating correlations between plants and human beings. Paracelsus created a whole new system of planetary and astrological correspondences between plants and human organs that allowed physicians to prescribe herbal remedies according to the symptoms of their patients.

Types of Medicines

The art of spagyrics is very different from modern pharmacology, primarily because modern druggists ignore the spiritual or esoteric properties of plants and herbs. In the view of spagyricists, modern physicians rely entirely on the gross or chemical properties of drugs to treat disease and forget they are really dealing with the life force of a person.

Allopathic Medicine

Contemporary medicine relies on the allopathic approach, which means it uses medicine designed to evoke the opposite symptoms from the disease it treats. One example would be the use of the powerful laboratory chemical phenolphthalein to treat constipation. The chemical provides very fast relief by leaching water from the intestines, and was the ingredient in most popular laxatives for over 50 years. Unfortunately, it was later found to be carcinogenic and toxic with continued use and was quietly withdrawn from the market.

This physically aggressive, overkill approach to fighting disease focuses more on acute symptoms and less on preventive care. The guiding principle in allopathy is that the more powerful the medicine and faster the cure the better. As a result, physicians are caught in a never-ending spiral of developing new drugs as the life force adapts to the gross effects of the previous wonder drug.

Homeopathic Medicine

While allopathic medicine uses compounds that elicit symptoms directly opposite to those produced by the disease, homeopathic medicine uses minuscule doses of a compound to treat a disease in which large doses of the same compound would produce similar symptoms. This is done in the hopes of eliciting a healing response from the body. The German physician Samuel Hahnemann, whose motto was "like cures like," developed the homeopathic approach in the early nineteenth century.

For example, the homeopathic preparation *Nux vomica* is given for constipation. This nut from the strychnine tree contains a powerful poison that causes dehydration, constipation, and binding of the bowels. In extremely small doses, however, it relieves constipation.

Spagyric Medicine

In spagyrics, the key is to learn to increase or redirect the life force itself by using living essences with the relevant signatures or properties to cure the disease. Spagyrics is careful not to use allopathic chemicals, which are considered gross or dead remedies.

Spagyrics is also different from homeopathy, though both systems make use of the essences of plants and treat disease as disturbances of the life force. The primary difference is that plant essences are not diluted but concentrated in spagyric preparations.

So in practice, spagyric medicine is a middle approach between the extremes of allopathy and homeopathy. For example, to relieve constipation, a spagyricist might prescribe a few drops a day of a tincture of Oregon grape, *Mahonia aquifolium*. Oregon grape is ruled by Mars and stimulates the liver and gall bladder to increase acid production in the stomach to cure chronic constipation. In other words, the tincture slowly induces the body to cure itself.

> **Tread Carefully** _____
>
> In general, spagyric compounds work on very subtle levels, and using them either allopathically or homeopathically can have unpredictable results. Unlike nearly every other type of medicine, true spagyrics are living essences that grow stronger with age and maintain a characteristic ability to adapt to changing conditions. More importantly, they are considered reactive spirits (that is, they possess a kind of primitive intelligence) and can be influenced by the conscious intent of both the patient and therapist.

There are also differences between spagyrics and general alchemy. Alchemy is a unique melding of philosophy, religion, and science the goal of which is to gain knowledge of matter and perfect it on all levels. Spagyrics, on the other hand, is much more practical as it addresses the present human condition and the problems of everyday life with minimum philosophizing.

The Planetary Signatures

The spagyric remedy works by healing people of systemic blockages or imbalances in their life force. The spagyricist seeks to produce a specific medicine based on its signatures that he can use to cause the body to cure particular ailments. Here are the signatures of the planets:

◆ The signatures of Saturn are associated with fate, structure, and the passage of time. Saturn rules the bones, teeth, spleen, and slow chronic processes such as aging. The therapeutic effects of Saturn are drying, coagulation, and mineralization of tissues.

◆ The signatures of Jupiter are associated with general well-being and overall health. Jupiter rules growth, the metabolic system, the liver, and the enrichment of the blood from food. Jupiter's therapeutic effects preserve the body and promote healthy growth and organ function.

◆ The signatures of Mars are associated with stimulation and action. Mars rules the blood, adrenal glands, genitals, and the immune system. Mars's therapeutic effects are toning the blood and stimulating the immune system.

◆ The signatures of Venus have to do with refinement of energy in the body and mind. Venus rules the face, skin, and kidneys. Its therapeutic properties are detoxification, improvement of sense organs, and reversing impotency and sexual dysfunction.

◆ The signatures of Mercury are associated with mental clarity and creative energy. Mercury rules the vocal organs, throat, lungs, and lymph glands. Its therapeutic effects are physical and mental adaptability and improved regulation of bodily rhythms.

◆ The signatures of the moon are growth and fertility. The moon rules the stomach, womb, and fluids of the body. The therapeutic effects are sedative, cooling, moisturizing, balancing, and breaking of bad habits and physical addictions.

◆ The signatures of the sun are general vitality and improved overall systemic function. The sun rules the heart and circulation, metabolism, and the distribution of bodily heat. Its therapeutic effects are balancing, heating, and energizing in a steady and controlled way.

The Star in Plants

In spagyrics, the opposing operations of "tearing apart" and "bringing together" are the main processes of working with herbs, flowers, and other plants to make medicinal elixirs, tinctures, balsams, and powders. First, the plant is reduced to its most basic essences, which are further purified and recombined to make the new exalted compound.

The inner essences or strengths carry the signatures of the plant—what Paracelsus called its "inner star." By the doctrine of signatures, "As Above, So Below," a plant's inner star or essence is closely related to the stars in the heavens. Heavenly bodies rule plants because a plant's inner, microcosmic star corresponds to a universal, macrocosmic star, and the star of a plant is what gives it its signatures.

In general terms, then, the "star" is the truest part of anything, the divine thought or image that gives a thing its form and being. By opening up a plant and revealing its star, the spagyricist hopes to use its incorruptible power to affect other things in predictable ways. "One must understand," elaborated Paracelsus, "that the medicine must be prepared in the stars and that the stars become the medicine."

From the Alchemist

To make a spagyric compound, one must not only perform the mundane laboratory operations, but also have the proper mental attitude and be aware of unseen spiritual influences. The spagyric product is prepared in a sacred space that Paracelsus referred to as "in the stars," and every effort is made to protect that space from profane or materialistic influences.

The Three Essentials in Plants

A spagyric medicine is made by deliberately opening up the plant and separating it into all three of its component essences of Sulfur, Mercury, and Salt—the Three Essentials (see Chapter 8). The work of the spagyricist is to separate and recombine these three basic principles as often as necessary until they are in perfect proportion and harmony with each other.

In plants, Sulfur resides in the essential oils, the most concentrated essences of a plant's chemistry and properties and the carrier of scent, the most soulful attribute of the plant. Essential oils burn slowly, like a fuel, and are the plant's Sulfur or energetic essence. Sulfur carries the properties that differentiate one object's chemical reaction or behavior from another.

In spagyrics, Mercury is the spirit, mind, light, or animating life force of a plant. Mercury is found in the "spirit" or alcohol of a plant, its volatile juice derived by fermentation or added as part of the processes of extraction. In labwork, Mercury is the intermediary life force that animates Salt and Sulfur, acting from the middle to connect the two principles of body and soul.

Salt is the form that locks the other two principles of Sulfur (soul) and Mercury (spirit) into a body, allowing the plant to exist and function in the physical world. In plants, the Salt level resides in the mineral components and hard structural tissues (stalks, roots, leaves) that fire reduces to ashes.

The spagyric operation, which begins with the destruction and breaking up of the plant, is not complete until all three basic parts of Sulfur, Mercury, and Salt are reunited in a purer form that is actually closer to the true signature or inner star of the original plant. In order to accomplish this, the spagyric work, like the Great Work of alchemy, takes place simultaneously on all three levels (the physical, the mental, and the spiritual) and requires the purified consciousness of the alchemist to succeed.

Planetary Influences in Spagyrics

Paracelsus taught that the star (or astral) energies of each visible planet affect plants on Earth in predictable ways. Each planet influences some plants more than others, depending on the inherent astrological and planetary signatures within the individual plant. He described this active connection between plant and planet with the term "sympathy."

Spagyrics advocates that sympathy governs most of the basic characteristics of the living things on our planet, and each of the seven visible planets affects plants, animals, and humans in specific ways because of this underlying sympathy. For instance, as each planet rules an organ or organ system in the human body—and by extension, its diseases—similarly, each planet rules the plants that support the organ or are able to balance it with the corresponding planetary energies.

According to this theory, all aspects of spagyric processing, including harvesting the plant, cutting and sifting it, drying it, wetting of the plant material with alcohol for extraction or distilling it, and adding its salts and other separately extracted materials, should take place during the times ruled by its corresponding planet.

Planetary Hours

The planetary powers are greatest when the planet is visible in the sky, which is called the planetary hour. Traditionally, the planetary hours are determined by using charts originally developed by Trithemius, Paracelsus's teacher. Three types of planetary charts are used to determine the proper time to work with a spagyric compound.

The simplest planetary chart is the Mercury Level Chart, in which a single planet rules each day all day. A Mercury level preparation is directed toward disturbances and depletions of the life force, such as chronic fatigue or lethargy.

To attune a spagyric to the Mercury level, a highly refined alcohol is used for extraction, which is elevated before use in a process called animation. Animation of the Mercury is a method of spiritizing the material worked on, making it volatile so it can open up and receive the universal life force and then close again and hold that life force.

Thoth's Tips

You can download the charts of planetary hours from www.crucible.org/PDF_Files/Planetary_Charts.pdf.

To attune a spagyric preparation to the Sulfur level, the essential oils are extracted separately using steam distillation and other alchemical methods. The Sulfur Level Chart changes each hour, beginning at sunrise, and each planet rules several periods in a single day. A Sulfur level preparation is directed toward physical or mental aberrations and deep-seated disturbances of the soul.

To attune a spagyric medicine to the physical or Salt level, a concentrated extract is made with all the mineral components extracted and included in the remedy. To accomplish this, all the plant matter that would have normally been discarded is burned to an ash. From that ash, the Salt essences are extracted in alcohol. These operations must be performed at the time of day indicated in the Salt Level Chart, which divides the day into seven equal planetary periods. A Salt level preparation is directed toward specific bodily injuries and ailments.

Paracelsus the Great

Paracelsus was a vigorous and unyielding proponent of a new order in both alchemy and medicine. As such, he aroused vigorous opposition from the physicians of his time. Some evidence even indicates that a group of physicians from Vienna murdered him in his home in Salzburg. Paracelsus's provocative actions certainly did nothing to calm his detractors.

For instance, in 1525, he publicly burned the works of the revered physicians Galen and Avicenna before the assembled citizens and physicians of Basel in Switzerland. Such actions were typical of this stubborn genius. He expounded his ideas with great vigor and seasoned his words with biting sarcasm.

Paracelsus.

Paracelsus even upset the alchemists of his time with his frequent criticism that they should give up trying to make gold and instead should assist physicians by finding new cures. His determined efforts to liberate the incipient science of alchemy from the "narrow and sordid domination by the multipliers and bellows-blowers" gave alchemy a new and nobler direction.

Paracelsus's contributions to the development of alchemy in the late Middle Ages were immense. Besides developing the theory of the Three Essentials and applying it to all levels of the Great Work, he invented the art of spagyrics and gave the world a powerful new healing modality. His spagyric methods would gradually develop into what he called "iatrochemistry," (literally healing chemistry), which gave birth to our modern practice of medicine. Today, Paracelsus is recognized as the father of modern medicine for his revolutionary practical advances in medicine.

The Least You Need to Know

- Spagyrics is the art of breaking open a plant to release its fundamental living essence and preserving that essence for purposes of healing.

- Signatures are the archetypal correspondences between the manifested object and its divine image or origin.

- Remedies fall into the three general categories of allopathic, homeopathic, and spagyric.

- Planetary hours are the times of the day and week when the powers of a certain planet are at their peak.

- Paracelsus completely reorganized the theoretical and practical basis of alchemy and changed its emphasis from making gold to making cures.

Chapter 16

The Kitchen Alchemist

In This Chapter

- ◆ Setting up the kitchen laboratory
- ◆ Making alchemical compounds
- ◆ Creating custom tinctures at home
- ◆ Making the magical elixir

An old Sufi saying goes: "All the qualities of a good alchemist can be found in the person who can cook an egg perfectly." In other words, fancy glassware and exotic chemicals do not make an alchemist. The true characteristics of a good alchemist are patience, attention to detail, striving for perfection, and knowledge of how to use fire in the work.

So cooking and alchemy actually have much in common. Instead of beakers, flasks, and formulae, the cook works with pots, pans, and recipes. Alchemists and cooks work with the Four Elements—Fire, Water, Air, and Earth—and both transform materials through the application of fire. The cook dissolves, emulsifies, chars, boils, aerates, separates, macerates, blends, combines, ferments, distills, coagulates, and works through the same operations as an alchemist.

And like alchemists, good cooks add a part of themselves to their work. This hidden Fifth Element in food is its spiritual essence or level of vital wholesomeness, projected into food through the attitude and intent of the preparer. This is the real secret of gourmet cooks—and why your mother's cooking tastes so good. The alchemical cook imbues food with positive psychic energy, the true Quintessence of a meal.

In this chapter, we take alchemical cooking up a notch and demonstrate the very little difference between a medieval alchemist's laboratory and your kitchen at home. Now that you are familiar with the basic principles of alchemy, there's no reason you can't begin using them right now in your own home or apartment. Remember, you don't need a big fancy laboratory to do alchemy. In fact, you probably have everything you need to make infusions, tinctures, elixirs, and essential oils right in your own kitchen.

Setting Up Your Kitchen Lab

The first step in setting up any alchemical laboratory is to find a safe and uncontaminated space in which to work. This can be as simple as a table or countertop, as long as it's clean and uncluttered and you can work there uninterrupted. What sets an alchemical laboratory apart from other workplaces is that it is sacred space, and pollution in such an environment comes from disrespectful behavior, negative attitudes, upset emotions, and mundane thoughts.

Tread Carefully

Don't use aluminum pots and pans or utensils when making alchemical products. Modern alchemists feel that aluminum metal acts as a kind of "energy sponge" that depletes spiritual energy. Several scientific studies seem to support the alchemists' suspicions and have linked aluminum to mental retardation and Alzheimer's disease.

Most kitchens are well supplied with the necessary tools and vessels to do alchemy. Knives, spoons, ladles, brushes, tongs, basters, funnels, a set of measuring cups and spoons, thermometers, and other common utensils can all be used. However, a small scale and a mortar and pestle are required, and you may have to purchase these. Your pots and pans, baking sheets, mixing bowls, strainers, and colanders will all come in handy. You may want to keep your alchemical tools separate from your cooking utensils to avoid possible contamination. It is also advisable to have some wooden or plastic spoons and glass or plastic bowls available, because you cannot use metal containers or utensils of any kind in making tinctures.

Common ingredients you use in alchemical work include baking powder, baking soda, yeast, salt, cooking oil, lard, vinegar, and herbs. Alcoholic spirits are required to make tinctures, and the higher the proof the better. I recommend odorless vodka or pure ethyl alcohol, such as Everclear. Although it is expensive and difficult to make, absolute grape alcohol (200 proof or 100 percent alcohol) is the best alcohol to use. Never use denatured alcohol, such as methyl or isopropyl alcohol, because it is poisonous and can cause blindness.

Making Alchemical Compounds

Alchemical compounds are preparations in which the life force has been purified and preserved using the operations of alchemy. And by following the following procedures, you can make safe and effective alchemical products right in your own kitchen.

The first step in making an alchemical compound is to choose a plant with the desired signature or properties you desire. A free online version of the *Alchemical Properties of Herbs and Foods* is available at www.alchemylab.com/guideto.htm. It lists the planetary and elemental associations for hundreds of plants and foods. An online version of *A Modern Herbal*, first published in 1931, can be found at www.botanical.com/botanical/mgmh/comindx.html. It contains the medicinal and culinary properties and folklore of hundreds of herbs. A good reference book for this purpose is Paul Beyerl's *Compendium of Herbal Magic* (Phoenix Publishing, 1998), which lists the planetary associations and magical properties of over 200 herbs. (See Appendix A for information on these and other recommended books and websites).

You can grow your own herbs, get them fresh locally from supermarkets or natural food stores, or order them dried and packaged. After you have secured the plant material, discard any thick stems or discolored leaves. Then wash the material to remove any dirt, mold, or insects. Be sure to thoroughly rinse and dry it. If you use prepackaged herbs, this step is usually not necessary.

If your plant material is fresh, you must dry it. Do this by hanging whole bunches from strings with leaves down or suspending plant pieces in a mesh bag in direct sunlight. You may use a commercial food dehydrator if you keep the temperature below 105°F (40°C) to avoid scorching. The drying time depends on the thickness of the stems and leaves and on the ambient temperature. To test if drying is complete, break a piece to see if it snaps easily without bending. Seal the dried material in clean plastic bags or gasketed screw jars, such as jelly jars or canning jars. Properly label the containers and store them in a cool, dark, dry place until you are ready to proceed.

You can make many different kinds of preparations from the plant material. The simplest is an infusion, which is similar to making tea. The volatile components of the dried flowers and leaves are extracted by pouring boiling water over them. Decoctions are a step beyond infusions and are used for plant parts like berries or roots that are harder to extract. Decoctions are boiled longer to reduce the plant parts to a soft consistency, which allows the essences to seep out into the hot water. Infusions and decoctions can be taken hot or cold, added to other preparations, or made into syrups by adding sugar or other thickeners.

def•i•ni•tion

Essential oils are the volatile, oily components of plants, trees, and grasses. They are found in tiny sacs or glands located in the flowers, leaves, roots, bark, or resins of a plant.

Ointments are made by simmering the plant material in wax or fat. The resulting decoction is a solid mixture or balm. You can make creams and lotions by simply mixing the *essential oils* of plants in water with an emulsifying agent, such as beeswax or egg whites, that helps disperse the oil.

You can extract essential oils from plants by using one of four methods: steam distillation, expression, solvent extraction, and entfleurage. In steam distillation, the extracted oil is mixed with the water that condenses by passing hot steam through the material. In the cold expression process, the fresh oil is extracted by squeezing, pressing, or compacting the plant material. In the solvent extraction method, the oil is dissolved in a volatile solvent that is mixed with the plant material. When the solvent is evaporated, it leaves the oils behind. Entfleurage is a longer process involving the dissolution of the oils in heated animal fat. Alcohol is then added, and the oils are recovered by distillation.

Two recommended guides to making and blending essential oils at home are *Aromatherapy: A Complete Guide to the Healing Art* by Mindy Green and Kathi Keville and the *Complete Book of Incense, Oils, and Brews* by Scott Cunningham. A wide range of entfleurage and oil distilling equipment is available from www.crucible.org. (See Appendix A for details.)

Making Tinctures

The most popular alchemical preparation is the tincture, which extracts the active essences of plants in potencies that far exceed those that infusion or decoction can achieve. True alchemical tinctures are always made using the spagyric process (see Chapter 15) although many commercially available tinctures do not follow rigorous spagyric procedures and are actually just infusions.

Preparing tinctures is not really difficult, but remember that alchemical work in general is slow, careful, and deliberate. In fact, the phrase "haste makes waste" was originally a motto of medieval alchemists. Remember to allow time for your feelings and intuitions to catch up with the thoughts that are guiding your work. The alchemist is an important part of any alchemical experiment, and the purity of the intention and attention of the alchemist affects the quality and potency of the finished product.

Before you can begin the tincturing operation, you must complete a process the alchemists called "preparing the menstruum." The menstruum is a particular type of solvent (usually alcohol) that was thought to have the power to dissolve and coagulate at the same time. The idea comes from the medieval belief that the egg or fetus takes its life and form from the menses, which dissolves in the process. In the writings of alchemists, the menstruum was often referred to as the Mercury of the Philosophers or Sophic Mercury.

It's necessary to prepare the menstruum, because alcohol and other solvents are usually prepared by high-temperature fractional distillation, and it was felt that high temperatures depleted a substance of its Celestial Fire or spirit (see Chapter 7). Remember that Celestial Fire is one of the four grades of fire and is carried by the Element of Air. To replace the Celestial Fire lost during the preparation of the alcohol, you must perform what the alchemists called "animating the Mercury."

This simple meditation involves slowly pouring the alcohol into an open beaker or glass while warming it very, very gently. The heat of holding the glass cupped in one's hands is usually considered sufficient. Pouring the spiritually depleted alcohol into an open glass allows it to replenish itself by breathing in the Celestial Fire in the air. This is the same idea in gourmet wine tasting when wine from a bottle is poured into a wine glass and gently swirled. This allows the wine to breathe before being consumed.

The following step-by-step procedure is for making spagyric tinctures. As an example, we will be using the herb lemon balm (*Melissa officianalis*). Lemon balm is a refreshing, sweet-smelling herb associated with the heart, the sun, health, love, and nurturing. Its Element is Fire, and its ruling planet is Jupiter. A favorite of alchemists, Avicenna and Paracelsus recommended it for heart problems and as a tranquilizer. Modern physicians have prescribed it for psychiatric problems, as an antiviral treatment for cold sores, and to ease symptoms of colds and flu.

Before you begin, download the charts of planetary hours from www.crucible.org/ PDF_Files/Planetary_Charts.pdf. Then follow these steps:

1. Begin working with lemon balm during the planetary hour of its ruling planet Jupiter. By consulting the planetary charts, we find that this is immediately after sunrise on Thursdays. The planetary hours for Jupiter occur in the eighth,

fifteenth, or twenty-second hour after sunrise on Thursdays. During the planetary hour, start with meditation or by praying that the mysteries of lemon balm may be revealed to you and that a sacred place be created in your heart and laboratory.

2. When you feel ready, take about an ounce (52 grams) of the dried herb in your hand and begin crushing it by hand, then move on to using a mortar and pestle or coffee grinder. This is the maceration operation when you reduce the material to a powder. During this phase, focus on the idea that you are breaking up the herb to release its divine essence.

3. Place the powdered herb in a clean jar, and then slowly, with focused intent, pour about 4 ounces (120 cc) of alcohol over the herb until it is saturated with fluid but the jar is not over two-thirds full. Tightly seal the jar. If you use a metal lid, cover it completely in wrap before screwing it on.

4. Wrap the sealed jar in cloth or foil to protect it from light, and place it in a warm location, such as near a radiator, furnace, or water heater. Be careful that the temperature does exceed 105°F (40°C), or the tincture may lose life force.

5. Because the liquid cannot escape, an inner circulation or distillation begins as the fluid inside evaporates as it warms up and condenses again. This natural circulation is responsible for the tincturing process, and the color becomes darker with each passing day. In alchemical terms, the coloration is the extraction of the Sulfur (or soul essence) from the Salt (plant matter) by the Mercury (spirit or alcohol).

6. Shake the jar vigorously once or twice a day, and continue this process for two to three weeks until the color of the tincture is considerably darkened. Treat the jar as your unborn Philosopher's Child, and do not let anyone else handle it. At this point, you are in a symbiotic relationship with this plant; both your own soul and the soul of the plant are working together to give birth to a living tincture.

7. After the color of the liquid is sufficiently dark, let the jar cool completely before opening it. If you open the jar when it is warm, some of the volatile essences will escape. Pour the solution into a clean bottle, and press out any remaining liquid from the mass of remaining plant matter. Using coffee filters and a funnel, filter the solution until it is no longer cloudy. Save the filtered dead plant material and remaining liquid for use in making the elixir in the next section.

Store your tincture in a cool place out of direct sunlight. Shake the tincture well before using it. As a calmative and general health tonic, take two to seven drops of the lemon balm tincture up to three times a day. The drops may be placed on the tongue or dissolved in tea, water, or other beverages. To treat cold sores, you can apply the tincture directly to the skin.

You can add tinctures to bath water, mix them with essential oils, or add them to ointments and lotions. Many people rub tinctures into the skin, where they are rapidly absorbed. However, be aware that tinctures can dry and stain the skin. You can also use tinctures to add scent or to anoint magical tools or jewelry with the desired planetary signatures.

> **Thoth's Tips**
>
> Each tincture brings its natural signatures into your body. Remember that tinctures are considered living compounds that respond to your conscious direction and intent. Visualization and meditation on the planetary energies will help release and disperse the healing energies of tinctures.

Making Elixirs

Alchemists considered an elixir a more potent form of extract than a tincture because the elixir carried the resurrected body of the plant. Making an elixir involves purifying what is left of the plant matter after the initial tincturing process and adding it back into the original tincture. The alchemists saw this as restoring the original body (or Salt) of the plant in a more perfect or spiritized form.

The remains of the plant material we saved from making the tincture in the previous section are a depleted mass of waste material the alchemists referred to as the phlegm and feces. They also called it the *Caput Mortum*, literally the Dead Head. It is the completely dead body or expired Salt of the plant. This seemingly worthless material eventually becomes the elixir, and we see how to accomplish this in the following step-by-step procedure:

1. Place the Caput Mortum in a heatproof bowl or steel pot, and cover with a wire screen. Because you have removed the tincture, contact with metal is no longer a concern. Next, use a match or butane fire lighter to ignite the material. Because of the smoke generated, it is best to do this initial burn outside or under a kitchen exhaust fan. Let the dead plant matter burn itself down to ashes.

2. Let the ashes cool; then take them from the initial combustion and grind them into a fine powder using a mortar and pestle. Place the powder in a heatproof dish or crucible, and heat in your oven at the highest possible temperature until it has turned grayish white.

From the Alchemist

Alchemists discovered that if they heated the ashes for prolonged periods (sometimes over a week) at high temperatures (above 1100°F or 600°C), the ashes turned snow white and finally transformed into a deep red color. Thus, the process of making the elixir mimicked the progression of the three phases of the work: Black, White, and Red. Gray-white ashes are sufficiently pure for most alchemical work.

---

3. Remove the ashes and let them cool; then grind them into a still finer powder. The finer the ash particles, the easier to get the whitest or purest ashes.

4. Store the purified ashes in a clearly labeled container. This is the purified Salt of the plant.

5. At the correct planetary hour for the plant, slowly pour the original tincture over the purified ashes in a new container. If the tincture is still living, you should hear a slight fizzing sound. Gently swirl the mixture, and then tightly seal the container. Shake vigorously for at least a minute or two.

6. Put the container with the ashes and original tincture near a low heat source in a darkened area or place in an incubator. Shake three times daily. The purified ashes (the Salt) will eventually absorb the living essences in the tincture. The alchemists called this the digestion phase.

7. After three or four weeks, pour off any remaining liquid, leaving the Salt residue in the container. Seal the container again, and let it stand unshaken in an incubator or in a warm spot out of direct light.

8. After two or three weeks, open the container, and let the material completely dry up. Carefully scrape this regenerated Salt out of the jar, and then grind it to a fine powder. Store this powder in a clean opaque or dark-glass jar.

The elixir powder is now ready for use. The color of the powder attests to its potency. Gray powder is the weakest; white is moderately strong; and red powder is the strongest elixir possible. It can either be kept dry and used as a powder or mixed with ethyl alcohol in dark-glass bottles to make a powerful tincture.

Elixirs are generally used like tinctures with similar awareness and intent on the part of the user. However, while tinctures work physically through the body, elixirs work from Above through spirit. Elixirs are extremely pure essences that carry the highest vibrational energy of the herb from which they are made. Therefore, elixirs are often taken after preparing the body and mind by cleansing and meditation. Like tinctures, two to seven drops are taken up to three times a day. The drops may be placed directly on the tongue or rubbed into the skin over the body's energy centers or chakras. Elixirs may take more time for their effects to be noticed than tinctures; however, the effects last much longer and are believed to initiate physical changes in the body.

Elixirs are also used to add spiritual energy to the environment or during rituals. Adding a few drops of an elixir in the corners of a room or in a circle are thought to purify and protect the area. Placing a few drops on a bell or gong before striking it is said to resonate the spiritual energy of an elixir throughout a room.

To alchemists, the preparation and use of an elixir is a sacred process. The elixir, which literally means from the ashes, represents the Phoenix-like regeneration of the plant into a new body. This dead body (or the salts of the plant) has been resurrected through the sacrifice of the life force of the tincture. If the connection is strong enough between the alchemist and the plant, then a corresponding change is possible that makes the elixir magically regenerative for the alchemist, too. This connection between the alchemist and the elixir is the basis of stories of alchemists living for hundreds of years.

The Least You Need to Know

- You don't need a big laboratory or special equipment to practice alchemy.

- Alchemical compounds are different from other preparations in that they carry the living essences of the plants from which they are made.

- Only tinctures made by using the spagyric method are genuine alchemical preparations.

- The sealed-jar method is the easiest and most direct method of making alchemical tinctures.

- Make the elixir by purifying the dead waste materials of the tincturing process and recombining them with the finished tincture.

- The colors of the ashes used to make elixirs progress through the same black-white-red pattern as the overall stages of the work.

Chapter

17

Working with the Planetary Metals

In This Chapter

- ◆ The correspondences between Saturn and lead
- ◆ The correspondences between Jupiter and tin
- ◆ The correspondences between Mars and iron
- ◆ The correspondences between Venus and copper
- ◆ The correspondences between Mercury and quicksilver
- ◆ The correspondences between the moon and silver
- ◆ The correspondences between the sun and gold

Of all the signatures of the planetary powers expressed on Earth, the purest and most powerful are in the metals. Each of the seven planets of alchemy has its corresponding metal: Saturn produces lead; Jupiter, tin; Mars, iron; Venus, copper; Mercury, quicksilver; the moon, silver; and the sun, gold. And in alchemy, each planet and its corresponding metal share the same cipher.

Researchers have documented the uncanny relationship between planets and their metals many times. In the late 1920s in a series of impressive experiments, Lilly Kolisko of Germany's Biological Institute showed that changes in the relationships between planets are reflected in changes in the chemical behavior of metals on Earth. For example, during a moon-Mars alignment, mixtures of iron and silver compounds tend to be more active.

More recently, researcher Rudolf Hauschka demonstrated that the relative speed of a planet in the sky is directly proportional to how electrically conductive its corresponding metal is. For instance, Saturn has the slowest apparent speed across the heavens, and lead has the lowest conductivity of the metals; the moon has the fastest speed, and silver has the highest conductivity. Statistical studies of the fluctuations of the prices of the metals also show a connection between the planets and their metals. For instance, during conjunctions of the moon and a planet, the value of the corresponding metal falls, while during a conjunction of the sun and a planet, the value of the corresponding metal rises. Other planetary events have also been shown to have an effect on the value of their corresponding metals.

In order to understand the mystery of the planet-metal relationship, let's look at each of the seven metals of alchemy to discover their deepest signatures. Also we'll review the correspondences between the planets and the metals and try to understand how the alchemists worked with the metals to transform them.

Saturn's Metal: Lead

While the alchemists considered lead the lowest of the base metals, they treated it with a great deal of respect because lead was said to carry all the energy necessary for its complete transformation into gold. To the alchemists, the ancient metal was a powerful "sleeping giant" with a dark and secret nature.

Lead is indeed an ancient metal, a stubborn metal known for its durability and resistance to change. Lead products dating from 7000 B.C.E. are still intact, and lead water pipes installed by the Romans 1,500 years ago are still in use today.

Lead is the heaviest metal and a boundary of heaviness for all matter. All the metals beyond lead (of greater atomic weight) disintegrate over time by radioactive decay and transform back into lead. Geologists measure the age of radioactive rocks by how much lead they contain. So radioactive decay is really a process of Saturn that introduces a new characteristic in the metals—that of time. No natural process is more unalterably exact than radioactive decay, and atomic clocks are based on this leaden process. In many ways, lead carries the signature of Saturn's Father Time.

Lead ores lack the slightest water content, and lead does not react with water in any way. Lead also resists many acids, including the traditional "liquid fire" of the alchemists—sulfuric acid. In fact, lead bottles are still used to store the highly corrosive acid.

> **From the Alchemist**
>
> Actually comparatively little lead exists in the earth's crust, but the thing about lead is that once you make the metal, it never goes away. More than half the lead in the world today has been around for centuries and is being recycled over and over.

Lead and Silver

Lead has a strange relationship with the noble metals. In the periodic table, lead is in the same group as gold, and when it occurs in nature, it is always found with gold and silver. In fact, the chemical symbol for lead (Pb) is from the Latin word *plumbum*, which refers to liquid silver. We derive our words plumbing and plumb bob from the use of lead in those applications.

The most common ore of lead is galena (lead sulfide), which also contains the noble metals of silver and gold. The amount of galena processed for lead produces enough silver as a by-product to make galena the leading ore of silver as well.

In the smelting of silver, lead plays an important role by forming a layer over the emerging molten silver and protecting it from combining with air and splattering out. The volatile molten lead covering is gradually burnt away until only the pure silver metal "peeks out from the veil of lead" (in the smelter's terminology) in a stabilized form. Thus, lead protects and even sacrifices itself for the nobler metal.

Saturn Signatures in Lead

Fresh-cut lead looks just like silver, but the silvery luster quickly fades as if the metal were dying before our eyes. Lead metal is very soft and can be easily gouged with a fingernail. Lead, also a sluggish metal, is the slowest conductor of electricity and heat, the least lustrous, and the least resonant.

Lead's saturnic signature of lethargy is expressed not only in its being the heaviest metal but also in its tendency to form inert and insoluble compounds. No other metal forms as many. Lead reacts with more chemicals than any other metal; however, instead of producing something new and useful, lead "kills" the combining substance by making it inert, insoluble, and unable to enter into further chemical reactions.

Another of Saturn's signatures of lead is its ability to "dampen" or absorb energy. Unlike other metals, when lead is struck, the vibrations are immediately absorbed, and any tone is smothered in dullness. Lead is an effective sound-proofing medium, and thin lead sheets are used extensively in the walls of high-rise buildings to block the transmission of sound. Thick pads of lead are also used in the foundations to absorb the vibrations of street traffic and even minor earthquakes.

Lead is truly a destroyer of light and is known for its ability to absorb all types of radiation. Lead sheets are widely used in roofing to block solar rays, and lead foil is used to form lightproof enclosures in laboratory work. Added to high-quality glassware, lead crystal, it absorbs light reflections and makes the glass clearer. Sheets of lead are impermeable to all forms of radiation, including high energy X-rays and gamma rays. Lead is the perfect shield against radioactivity, which is why it is used to transport and store radioactive waste.

Lead Poisoning

Lead is poisonous to all forms of life. Young growing plants are adversely affected by even the smallest trace amount of lead in the soil as it accumulates in the roots of plants and slows down the breathing process.

Lead poisoning in humans is known as saturnism, and symptoms include lack of energy, depression, blindness, dizziness, severe headaches at the back of the head, brain damage, attention deficit disorder, antisocial behavior and anger, atrophy of muscular tissue, excess growth of connective tissue resulting in rigidity, rapid aging, and early death. Lead accumulates over time in the bones of the human body where it can never be flushed out.

Children are especially vulnerable to lead poisoning, and it is believed to be an important factor in stillborn fetuses. Children with more than just 0.3 parts per million of lead in their blood suffer a significant slowing of brain function. Lead in paint has caused mental retardation and premature aging in thousands of children.

Many research studies link lead exposure to anger and violence, especially in adolescents. One recent study conducted by Colorado State University of all counties in the United States revealed that the murder rate in counties with the highest lead levels was four times higher than in counties with the lowest levels of lead.

The Hidden Promise of Lead

To the alchemists, however, lead was still the metal of redemption and transformation. They knew that fire ruled lead, for the metal had an extremely low melting point and was easily separated from its ore by roasting in an open flame. The metal itself melts in a candle flame. Lead is very sensitive to heat, expanding on heating and contracting on cooling more than any other heavy metal.

The wonder of lead is that hidden deep inside the gray, dead metal is a tiny, eternal spark that is the seed of its own resurrection. In the eyes of alchemists, this made lead the most important metal despite its unattractive darkness. For dull lead and gleaming gold are really the same thing, only at different stages of growth or maturity.

> **From the Alchemist**
>
> Lead has an amazing property that few people know about. When made into a fine powder, lead erupts spontaneously into flames. Powdered lead metal must be kept in a vacuum to keep it from catching fire. Otherwise, it ignites all by itself and burns down to a bright yellow ash. The alchemists were right; lead truly does carry the fire of its own transformation!

Jupiter's Metal: Tin

To the casual observer, tin seems like a more perfected form of lead. In fact, the Romans called tin *plumbum album*, or white lead. Like lead, tin resists weathering and does not oxidize. Tin utensils buried underground or lost at sea in sunken ships shine like new when unearthed after hundreds of years. Like lead, tin is endlessly recyclable. Tinkers were gypsy craftsmen who wandered from neighborhood to neighborhood in Europe melting down old tin kettles and utensils and recasting them.

Natural tin metal is known as *stannum*, the Latin word for tin which also gives the metal its chemical symbol (Sn). Natural tin is extremely rare and is found with gold and copper deposits. Most tin comes from its sparkling ore cassiterite (tin oxide), which has been an important source of tin for thousands of years. In ancient times, the metal was considered semi-noble and was used for jewelry in Babylonia and Egypt.

But unlike lead, tin has pleasing acoustic effects and is used in the making of bells. It has a highly crystalline structure, and due to the breaking of these crystals, a "cry" is heard when a tin bar is bent. For many years, large tin sheets were used in theaters to simulate the sounds of thunder, which is very appropriate because Jupiter is the god of thunder.

Tin metal has only a few practical uses, and most tin is used in a variety of useful alloys. The development of bronze, an alloy of 5 percent tin and 95 percent copper, marked a new age of advancement known as the Bronze Age. Most solder is a combination of tin and lead; pewter is also an alloy of tin and lead. Other tin alloys are used to make tin cans and tin roofs, and a thin layer of tin applied to other metals provides protection from corrosion.

Jupiter Signatures in Tin

Oddly, the distribution of tin on Earth follows an ecliptic angle to the equator that is the exact track of the orbit of Jupiter slicing through the planet. Even stranger, these jupiterian forces seem to form tin veins that follow a distinctive zigzag pattern through the rocks that resembles a lightning bolt. This is no haphazard effect but an astonishing confirmation of Jupiter's energy expressed in the distribution of its metal on Earth.

The German philosopher Goethe was fascinated by the distribution of tin and suspected it might explain how all the metals were arranged in the earth through the distant effects of their corresponding planets. "A remarkable influence proceeds from the metal tin," he wrote. "This metal has a differentiating influence, and opens the door [to a mechanism] through which a way is provided for different metals to be formed in primeval rocks."

The Tin Plague

In the late Middle Ages, a curious "tin plague" began as growths on organ pipes in European cathedrals, where it was thought to be the work of the devil trying to disfigure God's work. This tin plague started as white blisters that spread until all the tin metal "sickened" and disintegrated. The plague spread to tin roofs and became a serious problem during Europe's frigid winters.

We now know that the impurities of aluminum and zinc found in tin made in the Middle Ages caused its crystalline structure to change when it was heated or frozen. This caused the tin metal to break down into a white powder that appeared to eat away the metal and had the ability to "infect" other tin surfaces it came in contact with.

Mars's Metal: Iron

Iron is an abundant element in the universe and is even found in the stars in considerable quantity because iron nuclei are very stable. Iron is the most prevalent metal on Earth and the second oldest metal used by man, after lead. Known in prehistoric times, it was smelted by the Egyptians at least as far back as 1500 B.C.E., and iron arti-facts from Asia have been found that are 5,000 years old.

Our word iron comes from the Anglo-Saxon word *iren*, a word derived from an earlier word meaning holy metal because it was used to make the swords used in the Crusades. The chemical symbol for iron is Fe, from the Latin word for iron, *ferrum*, which means to create, form, or bear forth.

Iron is very reactive and forms compounds immediately, so pure iron does not occur in nature. The purest iron on our planet actually comes from outer space in the form of meteorites, which are usually alloys of nickel and iron.

One of the many ores of iron is iron sulfide, also known as pyrite or Fool's Gold. Its beautiful golden luster has often been mistaken for the gleam of gold nuggets, and it has been frequently found in genuine gold deposits. Like gold, iron pyrite carries the golden signature of the sun, and a flattened round variety called the "Pyrite Sun" is prized for its esoteric properties.

Remarkably, the iron sulfide structure of Fool's Gold is exactly the same as the lead ore galena (lead sulfide). The only difference is that a pair of sulfur atoms in pyrite replace a single sulfur atom in galena. This pair of sulfur atoms disrupts the stubborn four-fold symmetry of the more ancient galena ore and produces a stunning transfor-mation into Fool's Gold. In esoteric terms, in the evolution of the metals, the appear-ance of the sulfur compound of iron (Fool's Gold) has freed the lead archetype of its stubborn materiality and set form, and this notable transmutation is marked by the signature of gold.

Iron's Love for Carbon

European alchemists noticed that when they dropped bits of charcoal into molten iron, the iron hungrily "devoured" the charcoal to produce what we now call cast iron. While pure iron was soft and malleable, the new metal was hard and brittle. By controlling the amount of charcoal introduced, it was possible to produce steel, whose characteristics lie between the extremes of pure iron and cast iron.

The alchemists deduced that iron had a profound love for carbon, with which it could form the nobler and stronger metal, steel. Our modern attitude toward iron is much less romantic. Nearly all iron produced today is used in the steel industry, which transforms iron into steel in carbon-based, forced-air blast furnaces. This process is one of the most significant industrial processes in history and resulted in iron (as steel) becoming the most common metal on the planet.

Iron also has a passion for other metals, each of which adds different qualities to the iron to produce unique forms of steel. The alchemists viewed these other metals as spiritual brothers of iron and named them accordingly. Cobalt was associated with the "kobolds" or mischievous gnomes who lived deep in the earth and were said to harass miners. The alchemists considered cobalt an earthier and more primitive form of iron.

Nickel was associated with the "nixies" or underwater spirits. The alchemists viewed nickel as the watery brother of iron, which expressed its watery nature in its shiny liquid surface and in the sea-green compounds it produced. Manganese was the fiery brother of iron because it produced fiery red salts. Added to iron, manganese produces extremely hard and dry steel. Shiny chromium was considered iron's sister. Chromium restores the shiny liquid look of pure iron to steel. Later alchemists found they could produce steel almost as hard as diamonds by adding tungsten and vanadium to iron.

Mars Signatures in Iron

The influences of the planet Mars in its metal iron are obvious. Throughout its history, iron has always served man's will in his weaponry or in the industrial conquest of nature. In classical mythology, the Iron Age is the final epoch of the world, marked by war and degenerate selfishness.

The expression of Mars in our world seems to be in the struggle for material possessions in which only the fittest, or perhaps richest, survive. If the predominance of the iron archetype in our culture continues, we can only expect a further distancing from nature and mechanization of life. Some nature-oriented civilizations, such as the Druids, were aware of the spiritual dangers of iron and actually forbid its use in their culture.

In the Hermetic teachings, the incarnating function of iron was meant to assist cosmic or spiritual elements to enter the sphere of gravity and matter. But when iron becomes too predominate, it becomes destructive to life and tends to rigidify and mechanize living systems. "The Mars impulses at work in iron," noted researcher Rudolf Hauschka, "are the carriers of the forces of embodiment, but these forces lead to mummification if they become too active and overwhelm the system."

Tread Carefully

Be careful in working with the signatures of iron on the personal level. While an iron will and aggressive tactics are often required to succeed in our culture, over the long run the energies of iron tend to make you brittle, suspicious, and unforgiving. Martian energies must always be balanced with the compassion and understanding of Venus.

The alchemists were certainly aware of the hidden signatures of iron and the social implications of the Iron Age. Several alchemists warned of the spiritual dangers of iron, even though they recognized it was a necessary stage in the Great Work and that the iron phase eventually led to the "transformation of the body into the Spirit-Become-Form." In *Alchemy*, Titus Burkhardt quoted several alchemists who warned of the dangers of the Iron Age. One described it as "an active descent of the Spirit into the lowest levels of human consciousness, so at this stage of the Work, the Spirit appears submerged in the body and as if extinguished in it."

Venus's Metal: Copper

The discovery of copper dates from prehistoric times, and copper beads dating back to 9000 B.C.E. have been found in Iraq. Copper pottery dating from 4900 B.C.E. has been unearthed in Egypt. Copper is found in its metallic state in nature and has been mined for thousands of years. The name and chemical symbol (Cu) for copper comes from the Latin word *cuprum*, meaning "the island of Cyprus," which was one of the main copper mining areas in the ancient world. Actually, the island took its name from the Assyrian word for copper, *kipar.*

Copper was used so early partly because it was so easy to shape. Methods for refining copper from its ores were discovered around 5000 B.C.E., and the Phoenicians and Sumerians made all their tools and weapons from copper. Then, around 3100 B.C.E., Egyptian alchemists discovered that when they mixed copper with other metals, the resulting alloys were harder than copper itself. For example, both brass (a mixture of copper and zinc) and bronze (a mixture of copper and tin) are harder than copper. The discovery of bronze changed the evolution of mankind, and the Bronze Age began around 2100 B.C.E.

Copper is a reddish-brown metal with a bright metallic luster. In the periodic table, it is in the same group as gold, and like gold, it is remarkably ductile and can be pressed into extremely thin sheets and strands. Copper is an excellent conductor of both heat and electricity.

Venus Signatures in Copper

The alchemists described Venus, copper's planetary source, as dressed in a blue cloak over a red gown. This is a reference to the observation that copper burns with a blue-green flame with sporadic flashes of red. Molten copper is a sea-green color, and copper tarnishes with a green color.

Copper has always been associated with beauty and harmony. Egyptian women used the powdered copper ore malachite to beautify their eyes. Copper pigments make wonderfully colorful paints and ink, and much of the color in birds comes from the presence of copper in feathers. Some birds, such as the alchemically symbolic peacock, contain as much as 6 percent copper in their feathers.

The Love Affairs of Copper

Copper combines readily with most other elements to form alloys or complex salts. In fact, copper is so ready to form unions with other substances that the alchemists called the metal *Meretrix Metallorum*, "Harlot of the Metals."

Copper shows a special love for sulfur, and geologists agree that copper and sulfur have been locked in an embrace in the bowels of the earth since primordial times. Copper sulfate, known as "Blue Vitriol" to the alchemists, is one of the most beautiful and useful compounds formed by copper. It dries into a white powder when exposed to air but rapidly returns to its beautiful blue crystals when exposed to water. Unlike lead and iron ore, copper ore has a great affinity for water, and copper salts, such as copper sulfate, contain as much as 35 percent water.

Veins of copper run extensively throughout the planet like veins of blood in the human body, and the metal has many applications in the modern world, as wiring, electrical components, and tubing. Nearly all coins in the world contain copper. In addition to copper pennies, our dimes and quarters are about 85 percent copper. Even the nickel is 75 percent copper. Most modern copper production is from sulfide ores containing little copper but quite a bit of iron, which is another element copper likes to spend time with.

The signatures of copper are very important in working with all the metals, especially iron. Copper tends to balance and elevate the energy of metals, and it symbolizes the importance of the feminine influence in the Great Work. As shown in the following illustration, the work requires a cooperative effort between the male and female energies not only in the lab but also on the spiritual level shown in the upper half of the drawing. The male and female alchemists in the drawing represent masculine and feminine ways of working with the substance at hand. The union of these two ways of being in the world is absolutely necessary to success in alchemical transformations.

Working with the archetypal energies.

Mercury's Metal: Quicksilver

The silvery liquid metal mercury was known as quicksilver to the alchemists. The only metal that is liquid at room temperature, it is the heaviest natural liquid on the planet. According to alchemical theory, all the metals began in the liquid state on our planet, but only mercury was able to remain true to its original innocence and resist taking on a final form.

Mercury can be found in its natural state pooled in caves and rock formations. It was known to ancient Chinese and Hindus before 2000 B.C.E. and has been found in Egyptian tombs dating from 1500 B.C.E. Mercury was first used to form alloys with other metals around 500 B.C.E. and became the object of much speculation and experimentation among the Alexandrian alchemists.

Mercury the metal is actually named after Mercury the planet. The chemical abbreviation for mercury is "Hg" from the Latin word *hydrargyrum*, meaning "watery silver." In the Orient, the cipher for mercury is an eight-spoke wheel. Today, mercury is used in thermometers, barometers, diffusion pumps, and many other laboratory instruments. It is also used for mercury switches and other electrical apparatus, for making batteries (mercury cells), in pesticides, and in antifouling paint.

Cinnabar (mercury sulfide) is the primary ore of mercury. The word cinnabar comes from the Persian word for "dragon's blood." The mineral is a beautiful scarlet-red, semi-precious, and used as a high-grade paint pigment known as vermillion. Early metal workers and alchemists considered the affinity between mercury and sulfur in cinnabar a fundamental and magical principle.

The Romans mined cinnabar for its mercury content, and it has been the main ore of mercury throughout the centuries. Some of those ancient Roman mines are still being mined today. Cinnabar is often found with deposits of quartz, stibnite (antimony), and pyrite (Fool's Gold).

From the Alchemist

In nuclear experiments carried out in the 1990s, a mysterious form of mercury known as "red mercury" was discovered. Early reports noted it was the densest matter ever found, but suddenly the government clamped a lid of secrecy on the project. It has been noted that the properties of red mercury make it ideal for a suitcase-size, nonradioactive neutron bomb, as well as a possible source of nearly endless energy. To add to the intrigue, rumors circulated in the 1980s that natural deposits of red mercury had been discovered in Grenada, Iraq, and Russia.

Mercury is a relatively poor conductor of heat and yet is extremely sensitive to it. Mercury expands and contracts in a direct linear relationship to temperature, which is why it is used in thermometers. It is an average conductor of electricity in its liquid state but becomes one of the best conductors known (between copper and gold) when frozen.

In its chemical reactions, mercury acts as a harmonizer because it serves as a catalyst that combines chemicals with opposing properties and speeds up reactions. The power of mercury to balance diverse substances makes it useful as a mediator in explosive devices, and a mixture of mercury and nitric acid (mercury fulminate) makes a reliable detonator for explosives. Mercury is also used in the making of nuclear bombs as a mediator in the detonation process.

Mercury Signatures in Quicksilver

Mercury moistens and dissolves other metals the way water dissolves salt, and for this reason, the alchemists believed it was the key to the transformation of the metals. The dissolved alloys of mercury are called amalgams, and the ease and speed with which mercury amalgamates with gold makes it of primary importance in the recovery of gold from its ores.

Mercury dissolves gold, silver, copper, tin, lead, zinc, cadmium, and all the alkaline metals, but does not affect iron or any members of the iron family, such as nickel and aluminum. The alchemists thought this antipathy between iron and mercury stemmed from the two metals diametrically opposed signatures. Iron represents the mechanical processes of structuring and control, while mercury represents the living processes of growth and mobility.

Since ancient times, mercury has stood for the life force and the light of awareness in matter. In the writings of alchemists, it is often referred to as *mercurius vivens* (living mercury). Because of its signatures of life and growth, mercury has long been associated with twisted serpents, such as in the Staff of Hermes, the medical caduceus, Oriental fighting dragons, shamanic serpents, and even the structure of DNA. All these symbols allude to the fact that the metal mercury somehow carries the principle of life.

Strangely, mercury exhibits a "breathing" pattern when heated almost to its boiling point; at that point it starts sucking in oxygen and produces a yellow-red oxide. Upon further heating, the process reverses, and the mercury expels the oxygen like a metallic lung. This odd characteristic of mercury led chemist James Priestley to discover the element of oxygen.

The Dual Nature of Mercury

Mercury has always had a dual nature and was often referred to as the *rebis*, or double thing, by alchemists. While mercury is a symbol of the life force, it is also intimately connected with the forces of death and decay. While some mercury compounds are therapeutic, others are extremely poisonous. Mercury metal itself is toxic, and its fumes can be lethal.

Organic mercury compounds are especially dangerous because they can be readily absorbed into the human body. Methyl mercury is a lethal pollutant from industrial waste found in rivers and lakes, and mining and the use of mercury in commercial products have increased the organic mercury content of our environment to ten times its natural level. High concentrations have been detected in shellfish and tuna, as well as other aquatic species, and mercury compounds from soil are detectable in nearly every kind of food.

Tread Carefully _____

Do not be seduced by the lure of mercury into handling mercury metal. Open containers of mercury emit poisonous yet completely odorless fumes at room temperature. The threat increases significantly under warmer conditions. If mercury is spilled, it breaks up into scores of tiny balls which dramatically increase the surface area and the amount of vapors released. Health authorities consider even small amounts of mercury metal toxic.

In the body, mercury follows the blood and nerves and goes right for the brain. In a demonstration of mercury's affinity for gold, one eighteenth-century English alchemist put a gold coin in his mouth and then stuck his big toe into a saucer of mercury. Within thirty minutes, the liquid metal had traveled to his mouth and coated the gold coin in a swath of silvery mercury. Unfortunately, he was able to perform his stunt only a few times before he died of mercury poisoning.

Mercury poisoning attacks the consciousness and spirit of a person. Symptoms begin with problems in concentration and attention and progress to anxiety, agitation, excessive emotions, impaired motor function, impaired memory, depression, hallucinations, tremors, slurred speech, and mental retardation. The mental deterioration caused by mercury is known as erythism and was first diagnosed among nineteenth-century hat makers who used a mercury compound to kill bacteria in felt and fur hats. The syndrome became known popularly as "Mad Hatter's Disease."

The Moon's Metal: Silver

Silver has been known since ancient times and is mentioned in Genesis. People knew how to separate silver from lead ore as early as 3000 B.C.E. It has always been popular in jewelry and for coinage, but in the past 150 years, the demand has skyrocketed due to photographic and industrial uses.

Our word silver comes from the Anglo-Saxon word *siolfur*, which was their name for the metal silver. The origin of the chemical symbol for silver (Ag) comes from the Latin word *argentums*, meaning silver. Alchemists associated silver with the moon, which they called Luna and designated the Queen of alchemy. They used the name *Luna Philosophorum* to refer to the planetary spirit of silver.

Pure silver has a brilliant white metallic luster associated with the moon. Contrary to popular belief, silver does not tarnish when exposed to pure air or water vapor; it only tarnishes in the presence of sulfur compounds in the air or to ozone. Silver has the highest electrical and heat conductivity of all metals but also has the peculiar property of reflecting electricity and heat without being affected by it. In other words, heat and electricity pass directly through silver without leaving much behind in the metal.

Silver is usually found with deposits of lead and copper. And silver forms the most organic or living crystals of all the metals, which is to say that silver crystals tend to grow into structures that resemble living plants and animals rather than the more mechanical mineral crystals formed by lead and iron.

Lunar Signatures in Silver

Like the moon, silver comes to life in reflected light. Used in the making of mirrors, the lunar metal is the best reflector of visible light known. Silver nitrate, silver bromide, and many other silver salts are photosensitive. In photographic film, the crystals of the silver nitrate actually are rearranged through the action of light.

Silver has other lunar signatures. When melted and hardened again, trapped oxygen is expelled in gas eruptions that leave behind a lunar surface pocked with craters.

In alchemy, the moon and its metal were always associated with the soul. On the psychological level, the lunar powers represent the subconscious self, of which the conscious self is a reflection. "The moon and silver were considered to be analogous to the soul in its state of pure receptivity," summarized Hermeticist Titus Burckhardt, "whereas the soul transmuted and illumined by the spirit was analogous to the sun and the metal gold."

The Moon's Influence Over Silver

The moon is associated with the tides and water, and its influence over the oceans draws silver to it. Most of the silver metal on our planet is now dissolved in sea water.

It has also been shown that the behavior of silver nitrate in filter media varies with the phases of the moon. Researchers have even documented disturbances caused by lunar eclipses.

The Sun's Metal: Gold

Gold was known and considered sacred from earliest times, and Egyptian inscriptions dating back to 2600 B.C.E. describe gold. Around the world, nearly every culture associated their supreme god or goddess with gold. For many centuries only the images of gods graced gold coins, until Alexander the Great began the trend of rulers' images appearing on gold coins in 330 B.C.E.

The chemical symbol for gold (Au) comes from the Latin word *aurum*, meaning gold. The alchemical cipher for gold is a rendition of the sun, and gold was considered a kind of congealed solar light. Sol is the King of alchemy, and his royal purple color is the indicator of gold particles in solution.

Pure gold metal found in nature seems to like the company of the purest white quartz and is also found mixed with deposits of pyrite (Fool's Gold) and a few other sulfur minerals. Gold rarely unites with any other substance, although it does form compounds with tellurium sulfides and a few other sulfur compounds.

> **From the Alchemist**
>
> One ounce of gold can be stretched into a single wire 35 miles long or beaten to just a few atoms thick.

Still highly valued, gold is used as coinage and is a standard for monetary systems in many countries. Gold is extremely ductile and malleable and relatively easy for artisans to work with, so it is used in making jewelry and artwork and also in dentistry, electronics, and plating. Because it is an excellent reflector of infrared energy (such as what emerges from the sun), gold is used to coat Earth satellites, interstellar probes, and windows of modern skyscrapers.

Solar Signatures in Gold

Gold is an aloof and stubbornly pure metal when it comes to reacting or even associating with lesser elements. That signature explains many of the chemical characteristics of gold. Unlike other metals, no plants contain even trace amounts of metallic gold, and there are very few gold ores because the noblest metal never alloys with baser metals. It only alloys with silver, although it makes an amalgam with mercury.

Gold embodies an inner equilibrium of forces that make it pretty much indestructible. Gold never tarnishes, and whether found buried in the ground, at the bottom of the ocean, in an ancient tomb, or in the ring on your finger, it always looks the same. It is the most flexible, enduring, and beautiful of all metals. The immortal metal is endlessly recycled, and all the gold known today is very nearly equal to all the gold that has ever been mined.

Sol Philosophorum was the name the alchemists gave to the archetypal principle of the sun, the refined essence of heat and fire expressed in the metal gold. According to the medieval alchemists, Nature continually seeks to recreate the perfection it achieved in gold, and every metal yearns to become gold. Gold is at the head of the metals, and alchemists paired it with what in their mind was the strongest and purest planet, the sun.

The Sun's Influence Over Gold

Chemist Lilly Kolisko performed experiments with gold chloride and showed its chemical behavior coincided with events that altered the strength of the sun, such as the weakening in solar forces during solar eclipses or their increase during the summer solstice.

Moreover, she found that both silver compounds and gold compounds seemed to be equally influenced by the sun. In the case of silver, the structure or patterns changed, whereas with gold, the colors changed. Silver shapes moved from jagged spikes to smooth rolling forms, but the colors remained hues of gray, while the basic shape of gold patterns remained the same, but the colors changed from brilliant yellows to violet and reddish-purple hues.

This work, which others have duplicated, presents an amazing confirmation of how the King and Queen of alchemy, the archetypal Sol and Luna, work together. The female lunar principle represents soul and form, and the male solar principle represents spirit, energy, and light.

The Least You Need to Know

- ◆ The powers of each of the seven planets are represented on Earth in the seven metals of the alchemists.
- ◆ Lead contains the fire of its own transformation.
- ◆ Tin carries the complementary cosmic powers to balance lead.
- ◆ Iron and copper are the King and Queen of the metals.
- ◆ Mercury, with the power to dissolve and balance all the other metals, was considered the principle of transformation in the metals.
- ◆ Silver and gold are the universal archetypes of Soul and Spirit, which were known as Luna and Sol to the alchemists.

Part 5

Spiritual Alchemy

Changing lead into gold was only a metaphor for a larger process that involved the rejuvenation of the body, the integration of the personality, and the perfection of the human soul. Though they spoke of retorts, furnaces, acids, and chemicals, the alchemists were really talking about changes taking place in their own bodies, minds, and spirits. One of the central ideas in alchemy is that no transformation is complete and lasting unless it occurs simultaneously on all levels of reality—the physical, the mental, and the spiritual. This distinction is what makes alchemy a unique discipline that combines the methods of science, psychology, and religion. On the spiritual level, alchemy seeks to unite the opposing essences of soul and spirit in an operation known as the Sacred Marriage. The product of this union is the Philosopher's Stone, which in spiritual alchemy is the embodiment of a permanent state of perfected consciousness.

18

Mental Alchemy

In This Chapter

- Turning to Salt
- The First Matter within us
- The Four Elements in people
- Planetary forces in the personality
- The father of modern alchemy
- The three phases of mental alchemy

Mental alchemy is the use of alchemical techniques and operations on the psychological level in an attempt to perfect one's character and personality. This is different from spiritual alchemy in that mental alchemy focuses on the existing aspects of the personality and deals with psychological forces in personal transformation. Spiritual alchemy, on the other hand, deals with the universal forces of soul and spirit as they are expressed in individuals (see Chapter 19).

To alchemists, the mental or psychological work took place primarily in the material realm in the Salt of the personality. In the work of personal transformation, the psychological operations are usually completed during the conjunction while the spiritual operations don't culminate until the final coagulation, which is the fixation of spirit in a new body or incarnation.

Interest in mental alchemy began in the eighteenth century as people realized that the operations and matter of alchemy could be interpreted in psychological terms. At the time, there was great interest in curing mental illness and alleviating the day-to-day phobias and neuroses that dominated people's lives.

The Salted Personality

The basic problem in personal alchemy is that on the spiritual and mental levels, many individuals become more rigid and less alive as they grow older. For example, many people stubbornly cling to set judgments and outmoded beliefs that limit their range of experience in the world. In the alchemist's view, we all gradually turn to Salt as we mature. In alchemy, Salt is the principle of the crystallization of energy into set structures. To retrieve that energy, the original Salt (our personality) must be dissolved and purified so that it better reflects the essence of who we really are.

In other words, as we pass through the trials and tribulations of existence, we form judgments and beliefs that limit or structure our experience. We compromise ourselves and our integrity to conform to the dictates of society, and we end up carrying psychological baggage composed of rejected and suppressed feelings, emotions, thoughts, and desires.

Of course, this natural process of adulteration is no fault of our own. It is just how we learn to survive in the world and fit into human society. However, it is also where the work of mental transformation must begin.

Tread Carefully

In alchemy and psychology, suppressed or rejected material is called the "shadow" (in Latin, umbra). This material often retains some of its life force and can become a threat to successful transformation. It's like a hidden contaminating energy that develops in the work. On the personal level, we develop a shadow personality in which the rejected material still lives on in the darkness of our subconscious minds. That subconscious material has a mind of its own and is the source of many psychological problems when it conflicts with our conscious goals and preferred behavior.

The First Matter in People

Psychologically, the First Matter is identical with the dark, irrational forces of the subconscious mind. Like the First Matter of the universe, the First Matter within us contains all the potential energy and dynamic oppositions necessary to fuel our transformation and achieve the goal of the Great Work.

In the mental work, the First Matter to be transformed is the shadowy and chaotic subconscious mind. It is located in the vessel of the human mind, and that is where the work begins. However, the awakened subconscious is a surprisingly powerful force that can generate all kinds of negative energies in the personality. That's why the work of mental alchemy must take place in the hermetically sealed vessel of the mind in the inner laboratory. The energies must be contained and worked on without contaminating the personality or interfering with its functioning in the world. In analytical psychology, the sealed vessel symbolizes the cooperative efforts and confidentiality between the patient and therapist.

Sealing the vessel confines all the potentially dangerous psychic matter inside, but as heat from the fires of intense introspection increases, the pressure inside the psychic vessel builds. Jungian therapist Louise von Franz described this process: "It is the torture of fire, intensifying the psychological process. One is roasted, roasted in what one is—for you roast in what you are yourself and not in anything else; one could say that one is cooked in one's own juice."

Just as in the laboratory work, with too much liquid at this stage, the matter tends to putrefy. In mental alchemy, liquid is symbolic of emotions and feelings, so the idea here is to divorce oneself from the intense emotions associated with the contents of the psyche and work more with fire, which is symbolic of the light of objective consciousness. This internal heating results in an evaporative process, in which the emotional energy is slowly driven off. This also removes the original impurities, leaving behind a purer solution of self with which to work.

This is the general principle behind working with the chaotic and often threatening energies of the First Matter of the subconscious in mental alchemy. This process of recognizing and isolating the First Matter is the first step in alchemy, and the work proceeds through the three phases of alchemy with which you are already familiar (see Chapters 11 through 13).

The Four Elements in People

In mental alchemy, the structure of one's personality is based on the Four Elements and originates from the creation of ego out of the chaos of the subconscious, just as the fourfold structure of the universe was created by the action of the Four Elements emerging from the First Matter.

As you know from Chapter 7, the Four Elements were believed to be present in the form of humors that made up a person's temperament or personality. The Fire Element was expressed in the Choleric humor, the Water Element in the Melancholic humor, the Air Element in the Sanguine humor, and the Earth Element in the Phlegmatic humor.

The Four Elements in people are also expressed as positive characteristics or virtues, and negative characteristics or vices. For example:

◆ The virtues of Fire are courage, daring, and enthusiasm, while the vices of Fire are anger, jealousy, and vindictiveness.

◆ The virtues of Water are compassion, love, and creativity, and the vices of Water are instability and spinelessness.

◆ The virtues of Air are diligence, dexterity, and optimism; the vices of Air are frivolity, boasting, and squandering.

◆ The virtues of Earth are endurance, strength, and patience, but the vices of Earth are laziness, dullness, and boredom.

Psychologist Carl Jung saw the Four Elements as archetypes existing in the collective subconscious and thus present in everyone. He called them functions. The Fire Element is expressed in the function of intuition; the Water Element is expressed in the function of feeling; the Air Element is expressed in the function of thinking; and the Earth Element is expressed in the function of sensation.

Jung considered Fire and Air the active, masculine Elements and Water and Earth the passive, feminine Elements. In Jungian psychology, the degree of development of each of the Four Elements in our conscious mind balanced with the subconscious retention of the remaining elements determines our personality and attitude.

In both psychology and alchemy, the goal is to develop a balance of the elements within the individual. As far back as Empedocles (490–430 B.C.E.), philosophers noted that those who have near equal proportions of the Four Elements are more intelligent and have truer perceptions of reality.

Success in mental alchemy requires balancing the elements within one's psyche. And the relationships of the elements within us—whether they oppose or complement one another—determine whether we feel basically happy and balanced or develop neuroses, phobias, and other psychological disturbances.

According to Jung, when two opposing elements encounter each other in the personality, there are three possibilities:

1. They may generate psychic energy.

2. They may neutralize each other.

3. They may combine.

In alchemy and psychology, the third case is the most important, for it represents the conjunction of opposites that results in a transcendence of conflicting polarities.

> **Thoth's Tips** _____
>
> Sometimes it's easier to relate to the Four Elements on a personal level. Two books that help you do that are *The Four Elements of Change* by Heather Ash and Vicki Noble, and *The Four Temperaments* by Dr. Randy Rolfe. See Appendix A for details.

The Planets in People

According to the principles of mental alchemy, the planetary forces are present in our individual personalities. We reach enlightenment by conquering—understanding and controlling—the archetypal energies each planet represents.

In the cauldron of our personality, the sun is what gives us the desire to transform in the first place. In a sense, the sun wants pure spiritual energy and a new more perfect identity. The moon, on the other hand, wants physicality and experience. Mercury wants to find inspiration and higher love. If we were to personify these planetary powers, we might portray the sun as the Creator, the moon as the Nurturer, and Mercury as the Thinker.

These first three planets represent primordial desires that carry the signatures of the noble metals gold, silver, and quicksilver. They also represent the Three Essentials of Sulfur (sun), Mercury (Mercury), and Salt (moon) within us.

The outer planets and base metals are unbalanced and unperfected. Venus suffers from too much Water and needs focus and intention. Mars suffers from too much Fire and needs compassion and understanding. Jupiter suffers from too much spirit and needs grounding and restraint. And Saturn is too materialistic and structured; it needs growth and expansion. If we were to personify these planetary powers, we might characterize Venus as the Lover, Mars as the Warrior, Jupiter as the Philosopher, and Saturn as the Teacher.

Jung and Alchemy

Swiss psychiatrist Carl Gustav Jung has been called the father of modern alchemy for his efforts to revitalize the ancient art and apply it to mental alchemy. Jung began a lifelong study of the subject after he discovered the images and principles of alchemy surfacing in the dreams and compulsions of his patients.

Jung eventually accumulated the largest library of original alchemy texts in Europe and spent many years trying to decipher the writings of the alchemists. He came to appreciate alchemy as a dynamic system of inquiry into the nature of the subconscious. "Alchemy, as a nature philosophy of great consideration in the Middle Ages," he said, "throws a bridge to the past and their gnosis, and also to the future, the modern psychology of the unconscious."

Jung's interest in alchemy was kindled not only by the thoughts and dreams of his patients, but also by his own personal experiences. Long before he discovered alchemy, Jung had the same repeating dream that held a clue to the structure of the human mind. He dreamt that right next to his house was a huge addition or wing that he had not known about. He was amazed that the strange structure was there all the time and he had not realized it. In his dreams, Jung explored the mysterious addition to his house and finally realized the rooms contained things from his subconscious that he had rejected or locked away there.

Then, in 1926, Jung had a dream that opened the door to understanding the strange addition in his inner house and shaped the focus of his studies for the rest of his life. He had been intensely searching for a framework for his work with the subconscious but could find no modern discipline—including the psychology of the time—that was powerful enough to encompass the subject. In this unusually powerful dream, he was being held captive in time in the seventeenth century. "Later I understood that this dream was referring to alchemy," he wrote, "for in the 17th century alchemy reached its climax." Jung felt the dream was telling him that the subconscious would reveal itself by an in-depth study of medieval alchemy.

Jung's exhaustive studies revealed that the operations of alchemy were at work in the human mind. It was an astonishing discovery that confirmed the alchemists' teaching that the principles of alchemy were universal and took place on all levels of reality.

As depicted in the following figure, the operations of alchemy are like a stairway leading to the perfection of the inner person. The blindfolded person in the lower right corner has not yet discovered the path of alchemy, while the person to his left is trying to tell him that there is life in the dark caves of the mountain. This hidden life is the subconscious mind, and its contents are symbolized by rabbits who live underground.

The psychological operations of alchemy.

Jung saw that the First Matter in people is the subconscious mind, and that it is the subject of transformation in mental alchemy. According to Jung, the Philosopher's Stone in mental alchemy is the perfection of the personality. This natural alchemical process is the gradual transformation from a false, fragmented, and distorted personality into a whole or integrated personality in which psychic elements and energies are balanced.

From the Alchemist

Carl Jung was a true alchemist who introduced alchemy to the modern world. "Only by discovering alchemy," he said, "have I clearly understood that the unconscious is a process and that ego's rapports with it and its contents initiate an evolution—more precisely, a real metamorphoses—of the mind."

The Black Phase of Mental Alchemy

As in other kinds of alchemy, the blackening is the first sign that the processes of mental alchemy are beginning. The Saturn signatures of depression and melancholia arouse suspicions that all is not right and cause us to slow down and examine our inner life.

The blackening is always seen as the death of the First Matter or the removal of life and energy from it. In psychology, it is the death of old habits, attitudes, relationships, unhealthy attachments and dependencies, and the withdrawal of psychological projections in which we blame others for our own predicament.

Primary among these factions taking shape within the First Matter is the shadow, which is the inferior part of the personality that lives in the darkness. Think of the shadow as those mental elements that are incompatible with the chosen conscious attitude. In mental alchemy, these rejected elements coalesce into a "splinter personality," which is a concentration of subconscious energy that the alchemists likened to a threatening dragon. To defeat that dragon and keep it from taking control of your life, the shadow and dark aspects of yourself must be brought to light, confronted, and assimilated into consciousness.

All the unpleasant feelings of guilt and worthlessness must be suffered through in this alchemical process of mortification. Both in the lab and in the mental work, this is a dangerous period during which poisonous vapors are released and vessels explode due to overheating. On the psychological level, the operations of calcination and dissolution are necessary to differentiate one's ego from the shadow and to reinvent oneself on a higher level that psychologists call "the Self."

Carl Jung clarified how the mental work proceeded for medieval alchemists: "The profound darkness that shrouds the alchemical procedure comes from the fact that although the alchemist was interested in the chemical part of the work, he also used it to devise a nomenclature for the psychic transformation that really fascinated him." Although the alchemists lacked the modern psychiatric system of classification to describe this inner transformation, they invented their own unique terminology that applied to all levels of their work.

The White Phase of Mental Alchemy

At the moment of the death of the shadow and the splintered personality during the Black Phase of mental alchemy, the White Phase begins to unfold. A person rises up from depression and reports feeling suddenly relieved, refreshed, and optimistic.

It is the daybreak of the new personality free of its gross and rejected parts. Psychic energy is no longer shared between the inner forces of light and darkness and is now becoming fully available to the resurrected self. The matter has suffered through the Black Phase and starts coming back to life. This moment is highly rewarding in both the practical laboratory work and in the work in the inner lab.

The focus of the White Phase in mental alchemy is a washing or purification of psychic contents separated out from the Black Phase. This takes place entirely in the twilight of daybreak in a mix of rational thoughts and irrational feelings in one's own mind, or in free-flowing conversation in the office of a therapist. There is no more reason to hide your dirty linen, because you have freed it of its contaminating guilt. During this separation process, the opposing forces and essences of the psyche are clearly discerned.

If the opposing essences remain separated and generate new energy, the energy will be used up in some sort of creative endeavor, such as an artist giving his inspiration a new form. If these essences simply merge and neutralize each other, no new energy is produced, and the merging is considered an alchemical stillbirth. If, however, the opposing essences unite in a fertile marriage of opposites, then a new element is born that incorporates the essences of both. This is the alchemical conjunction, the transcendence of conflicting polarities in the creation of a higher form known as the Philosopher's Child. This is the product of the operation of conjunction, and if it survives, it grows into the perfected Philosopher's Stone.

Thoth's Tips

The overall plot of the *Harry Potter* books by J. K. Rowling is a three-part drama that follows the three phases of alchemy. The long Black Phase culminates in *Harry Potter and the Order of the Phoenix,* in which everything Harry attempts goes wrong, ending in the death of Sirius "Black," his beloved godfather. The White Phase takes place in *Harry Potter and the Half-Blood Prince,* which centers on the death of Albus Dumbledore. Albus is Latin for "white." The final Red Stage culminates in the final book, *Harry Potter and the Deathly Hallows,* in which Harry's friend Rubeus Hagrid is forced to take part in a death march to celebrate the "slaying" of Harry. *Rubeus* is Latin for "red." At the end of the series, as at the end of the Great Work, conflict is resolved and the subject of the work is perfected.

The Red Phase of Mental Alchemy

If the White Phase concludes in a successful conjunction of opposites, then the Red Phase of alchemy begins. This is the true sunrise of the mental work, when all forces and elements have been assimilated into conscious awareness.

If, however, there are unassimilated subconscious elements or the ego raises its ugly head as pride, then the matter is still contaminated and cannot proceed without further purification. This often happens both in the lab and in the mental work and initiates a period of putrefaction similar to the Black Phase. The length and intensity of the putrefaction depends on the degree of contamination.

If the putrefaction of all remaining traces of impurities is successful, then the life-giving operation of fermentation begins. In mental alchemy, fermentation is the introduction of spiritual forces into the personality, which gives us a sense of purpose and new energy for life.

A process of mental distillation begins as we try to assimilate the spiritual forces from Above and unite them with the forces of the personality from Below. This is sometimes called the "Vertical Work," and it is exemplified by the "Circulation of the Light" meditation we discussed in Chapter 13.

As the Red Phase of alchemy proceeds, the process of coagulation begins naturally. Once the level of purification in distillation reaches a certain stage, the Red Stone will form all by itself. The true key to the Stone—and the last operation over which the alchemist has any control—is distillation. The process of distillation—whether in the lab or in the mind—is really a process of gradual multiplication of powers, an amplification of energy that eventually condenses into a completely new material.

The Least You Need to Know

◆ Mental alchemy is the use of alchemical techniques to perfect the personality.

◆ The First Matter in people is the chaotic and powerful subconscious mind.

◆ Each of the Four Elements is expressed in mental functions common to all people.

◆ The planetary forces in people are archetypal energies that determine our temperament and personality.

◆ Carl Jung is considered the father of modern alchemy.

◆ The Black, White, and Red Phases take place on the psychological level of transformation as well as in the alchemist's laboratory.

Chapter 19

Alchemy of the Soul

In This Chapter

◆ Taming the dragons of alchemy

◆ The light of the True Imagination

◆ Kinds of alchemical meditation

◆ Secrets of the Azoth drawing

Spiritual alchemy, which focuses on the perfection of the soul, began in ancient Egypt with efforts to connect the pharaohs with their divine nature and later developed into the Hermetic teachings that evolved into alchemy. Spiritual alchemy seeks to transform and perfect the immortal essence that is in all of us.

Most alchemists would argue that alchemy has always been a spiritual discipline that delved into metallurgy and chemistry, only to find in nature a universal pattern of transformation that could be applied to the spiritual work. Just as alchemists try to awaken the metals to their true nature in gold, so do spiritual alchemists try to awaken the soul and body to their spiritual nature.

In spiritual alchemy, the transformation of lead into gold is analogous to spiritual progress. The base metals have yet to mature into the incorruptible perfection of gold, just as the common person has not yet achieved her full ripeness of spiritual embodiment.

So the Great Work, which is the creation of the Philosopher's Stone, is not simply about turning lead into gold, nor is it about the production of the elixir of life to gain immortality. The Philosopher's Stone represents a level of achievement, a touchstone of proof indicating the alchemist has already succeeded in the inner work of spiritual transformation.

The Dragons of Spiritual Alchemy

No symbol in alchemy captures the energies encountered in spiritual work better than that of the dragon. Alchemists both East and West believed in dragons, if not in the real sense, then certainly as archetypal energies embedded in the very fabric of the universe. In fact, if we do not understand the nature of the dragon, much of the advanced alchemical wisdom will be beyond our grasp. So the first step in spiritual alchemy is to seek out the dragon.

Where do we find a dragon? Anywhere—the dragon is in everything. Its scales are in the bark of trees; its claws gouged out the great canyons. The dragon's roar is heard in the thunder, and its forked tongue is the lightning. The dragon is a composite of the features of many animals and represents the chaotic matrix of nature of which our lives are part.

Dragons derive their power from the primordial First Matter from which all things spring. Unleashing the dragon into the world is one of the primary goals of alchemists. To alchemists, the dragon represents boundless unstructured energy and the primordial life force. An old alchemical saying advises: *Opponere draconem est prehendere vitam.* (To face the dragon is to seize life.)

Facing the dragon occurs during the Black Phase of alchemy (see Chapter 11). Accepting the dragon as part of our lives is difficult for most people. The dragon is the underlying chaos in our lives, our culture, and our bodies that is part of the unknown, part of the dark side of the universe. Spiritual leaders, from prehistoric shamans to Buddha and Christ, all began their spiritual journey by realizing how much chaos and suffering are in the world.

Once you muster the courage to face the dragon, you can do nothing but accept it. Surrendering to the dragon begins during the White Phase of alchemy (see Chapter 12). During this stage of purification, you must acknowledge both the chaotic powers in the world and also the chaos within yourself. Part of this purification is the realization that the dragon is never all good or all bad. You have to suspend judgment to accept the powers of nature and realize that the universe is not just about you and your comfort. A greater pattern exists, and the energy of the dragon is what fulfills it.

The last step in dealing with dragons is the most dangerous. It is the act of unleashing the dragon, which marks the Red Phase of alchemy (see Chapter 13). In alchemy, the dragon destroys any structure or Salt, any gross elements that exist in a person's spirit. If you are free of falsity, devoid of ego, and pure of spirit, there is a chance the dragon will not devour you.

Oddly, the real trick to unleashing the dragon is not to confront it but to disappear before it notices you. "Be still," the alchemists advised. "Rest in the arms of the dragon." In spiritual alchemy, if you can quietly merge with the primal energies of the universe, the dragon's powers will follow the light of your own mind.

The True Imagination

In Hermetic philosophy, the light of mind directs the transformation of energy into matter. The same principle of divine light manifesting the whole universe from the chaos of the First Matter works in each one of us. This principle is the source of the alchemists' fascination with what Paracelsus called the True Imagination.

The True Imagination of the alchemists should not be confused with daydreaming or fantasy. In his writings, Carl Jung referred to it by the Latin *Imaginatio* to differentiate it from the common concept of imagination. True Imagination actually envisions the subtle processes of nature and connects with the divine archetypes. It is the concentrated awareness of real imagining.

From the Alchemist
"The concept of *Imaginatio*," said Carl Jung, "is the most important key to understanding the Opus." Jung believed that the True Imagination of the alchemists had nothing to do with fantasy, memories, or dreams. As hard as it was for him to risk his reputation as a psychologist, Jung admitted that the True Imagination connects with something real that exists on a more subtle level than our everyday lives. He described this subtle level as an intermediate realm between mind and matter, in which subtle bodies (called "psychoid elements") manifest themselves in a mental as well as a material form.

According to Paracelsus, the True Imagination "leads life thus deciphered back to its spiritual reality, and it then takes the name of meditation." What he meant was that the True Imagination envisions the divine source of anything, and the primary way to access it is in meditation. This hidden reality is always present, but the eyes of ordinary men do not see it. Only the mind's eye of the purified intellect and the force of the True Imagination can perceive the true vision of which the alchemists spoke.

The True Imagination attempts to capture the essence of things "as god dreams them." Therefore, when Hermetic writers speak of "seeing with the eyes of spirit," they are describing a process that penetrates into the mystery of things beyond their outward appearance.

Alchemical Meditation

Most often the methods recommended by alchemists for entering the True Imagination consisted of prolonged and silent invocation of divine powers. Sometimes a person's "inner angel" or "good angel" was invoked. In their meditations, the alchemists were seeking to find the "angelic ray" that unites the world of forms with the divine ideals that are the source of everything.

In the Hermetic view, the creation of the universe took place through meditation—the focusing of the light of the mind of God. "All things have come from this One Thing," says the Emerald Tablet, "through the meditation of One Mind." The source of the One Mind is the same for everyone and can be found in meditation.

Meditation was very important to the alchemists and was even part of their practical laboratory work. However, during the heyday of alchemy in the Middle Ages, the concept of meditation was a dangerous idea to talk about. Just saying that people could make contact with the divine through private meditation and prayer was enough for the Church to burn a person at the stake.

In general, the meditations of alchemists are marked by three *magisteriums* or accomplishments. These three accomplishments made Hermes "Thrice Greatest" and correspond to the three levels of reality—the physical, the mental, and the spiritual. Lunar meditations work on the physical and bodily level. Solar meditations work on the mental and psychological level. And Stellar (or cosmic) meditations work on the level of spirit and the divine or cosmic powers.

◆ Lunar meditation is cultivating the stillness and the darkness within to discover the deeper essence we all possess. It is an introverted journey to the underworld of matter and body to seek out the spark of light trapped there that is our essence. During lunar meditations, we plumb the depths of soul in a deeply relaxed state that seeks connection with subconscious or dormant powers.

◆ Solar meditation is a more extroverted journey into the realm of light and consciousness. During solar meditation, we attempt to break the shackles of ego and cultural controls to seek higher consciousness. By exposing the self-deception in our thoughts and using mantras and other meditation gimmicks to lull our everyday ego mind into submission, we purify and increase our personal consciousness.

◆ Stellar meditation requires the merging of Lunar and Solar consciousness in the most powerful of all the alchemists' tools. By retrieving the sparks of light trapped in our bodies and uniting them with the light of consciousness freed from egotistical control, we create a brilliant beacon to the universe.

Tread Carefully

Don't confuse alchemical meditation with other meditative or relaxation techniques. Alchemical meditations are about harnessing spiritual forces for transformation and manifestation. Alchemical meditation is also different from other forms of meditation because it is an active instead of a passive activity. Alchemical meditation seeks to actually work with the transcendental powers, and the object is not always just to relax the mind.

Through stellar meditation, we attempt to connect with the source of all spiritual power, the One Mind of the universe. This state requires a truly free and purified consciousness, free of psychological, genetic, and social restraints to our being. A higher presence that becomes our true guide in alchemical transformation fills the void created by this death of our worldly connections. And it is at this level of mind that Thoth/Hermes is said to speak to us directly.

The Azoth of the Philosophers

As an example of one of the many meditative emblems used by alchemists in their spiritual work, let's look at a drawing known as the Azoth of the Philosophers, which the legendary German alchemist Basil Valentine published in 1659. The word "Azoth" is another name for the First Matter. The "A" and "Z" in the word convey the idea of something complete and all-encompassing—everything from A to Z.

The diagram, shown in the following figure, is arranged like a mandala (a geometric circular emblem used to focus meditation), and at its center lies the face of a bearded alchemist at the beginning of the Work. Like looking into a mirror, this is where the adept fixes his attention to begin meditation. The downward-pointing triangle super-imposed over the face of the alchemist represents Water in the sense of divine grace pouring down from heaven.

The schematic body of the alchemist is shown in perfect balance with the Four Elements as depicted by his arms and legs. His right foot is firmly planted on Earth and his left is in Water. In his right hand is a torch of Fire, and in his left hand an ostrich feather symbolizing Air.

The alchemist also stands balanced between the masculine and feminine powers in the background. Sol, the archetypal sun King, is seated on a lion to his right; Luna, the archetypal moon Queen, is seated on a great fish in the ocean to his left.

Sol holds a scepter and a shield, indicating his authority and strength over the visible world, but the fiery dragon of the rejected contents of his subconscious waits patiently in a cave beneath him. Luna holds the reins to a great fish, symbolizing her control of the forces of nature, and behind her is a chaff of wheat, which stands for her connection to fertility and growth. The bow and arrow she cradles in her left arm symbolize the wounds of the heart and body she accepts as part of her existence.

Between the legs of the alchemist is a smaller triangle labeled *Corpus*, meaning "body." The five stars surrounding it indicate that the body also contains the hidden Fifth Element, the invisible Quintessence or life force.

Where the head of the alchemist should be, there is a strange winged caricature. This represents the Ascended Essence, the essence of the soul raised to the highest level in the body. Touching the wings of the Ascended Essence are a salamander engulfed in flames on the left side of the drawing and a standing bird on the right. Below the salamander is the inscription *Anima* (Soul); below the bird is the inscription *Spiritus* (Spirit).

The Three Essentials of *Spiritus, Anima,* and *Corpus* (Spirit, Soul, and Body) form a large inverted triangle that stands behind the central emblem of the alchemist. Together they symbolize the archetypal energies the alchemists termed Sulfur, Mercury, and Salt.

The Azoth of the Philosophers.

The Operations of the Azoth

The seven rays placed in a circular pattern around the body of the alchemist indicate the progressive level of transformation. Numbered from one to seven, these contain the cipher of the corresponding planet and metal. Next to each ray is a circle containing a scene, which elaborates on the meaning of the operations performed at that stage.

The Ray of Saturn

Looking at the figure, you can see that the first ray in the Azoth is the black ray labeled number one. Representing the beginning of the Ladder of the Planets, it is marked by the cipher that stands for both the metal lead and the planet Saturn, which is the archetypal situation at the beginning of the Work. The square symbol for Salt, also shown in the first ray, indicates the Work begins in the unredeemed or imperfect matter.

The first circle (between rays one and two) shows a black crow perching on top of a skull. Next to it is the Latin word *Visita*, which means "to visit or start a journey." Black crows are symbols of the initial Black Phase of alchemy, during which the subject of transformation is purified by breaking it down during mortification and calcination.

The Ray of Jupiter

The second ray is marked with the symbol that stands for both the metal tin and the planet Jupiter.

And the corresponding second circle depicts the black crow watching itself being dissolved. The word on the outer ring near this circle contains the word *Interiora*, referring to the interior or innermost parts. The operation at this stage is a further process of mortification known as dissolution.

From the Alchemist

Meditating on the Azoth drawing could get you in a lot of trouble in the Middle Ages. It was decreed that all attempts to reach the divine, including prayer and meditation, had to be done through the Church. Furthermore, the downward-pointing triangle that covers the alchemist's face at the center of the diagram represents divine energy raining down from heaven. This implies that the face of God and the face of the alchemist are the same. Such blasphemous ideas explain why this drawing was circulated secretly among alchemists for many decades before being published.

The Ray of Mars

The cipher signifying both the metal iron and the planet Mars marks the third ray of the Azoth, which is also marked with a smaller symbol denoting Sulfur, one of the Three Essentials of alchemy. Iron and sulfur come together chemically in vitriol or sulfuric acid, the aggressive liquid fire of the alchemists.

The third circle depicts the alchemical operation of separation. The black, earth-bound crow splits into two white birds that retrieve the saved remains from the earlier operations.

This is the first coming together of soul and spirit and represents the beginning of the White Phase of purification. In the ring above this circle is written *Terra*, meaning "of the earth" and referring to the real essences being separated out from the dregs of matter at this stage.

The Ray of the Sun

In the fourth ray, the cipher stands for both gold and the sun.

The fourth circle depicts the twin birds of soul and spirit leaving the earth together, lifting a five-spiked crown which represents the Fifth Element or Quintessence recovered from the preceding operations. At this point in the Work, the operation of conjunction begins, which recombines the saved essences of soul and spirit into a new, living incarnation.

In the ring above the fourth circle is inscribed the word *Rectificando*, which means "setting things right." This is the turning point in alchemy, when the matter begins the process of spiritization.

The Ray of Venus

The Azoth's fifth ray is marked with the cipher that stands for both copper and Venus.

The fifth circle is under the inscription *Invenies* (you will discover). In this operation of fermentation, the essences of soul and spirit come together into a new life, which is the beginning of the Red Phase of empowerment. The corresponding circle shows the birds of soul and spirit nesting in a tree, brooding over the alchemical egg.

The Ray of Mercury

In the sixth ray, the cipher for the metal mercury (quicksilver) and the planet Mercury appears, as well as an identical smaller symbol indicating the principle of Mercury in the Three Essentials.

Distillation is the operation at this stage, which is represented in the sixth circle by a unicorn lying on the ground in front of a rose bush. According to legend, the unicorn runs tirelessly from pursuers but lies meekly on the ground when approached by a virgin. The virgin is the purified matter at this stage, which has returned to a state of innocence and potential.

Above the circle is the word *Occultum*, meaning "secret or hidden," because the essences at this stage are carried invisibly by the distilling waters.

The Ray of the Moon

The seventh ray contains the symbol that stands for both the metal silver and the moon, the level of manifestation in the Azoth.

The seventh and final circle shows an androgynous youth emerging from an open grave, with the Latin word *Lapidem*, the Stone, on the outer ring next to it. This stage of the operation is coagulation, in which the Philosopher's Child is born. The resurrection of the soul is accomplished by bringing together only the purest essences of one's body, soul, and spirit under the guiding light of meditation.

From the Alchemist

There is a hidden message in the Azoth drawing. The Latin words in the outer ring spell out a summary of what has taken place: *Visita Interiora Terra Rectificando Invenies Occultum Lapidem* (Visit the innermost parts of the earth; and by setting things right [rectifying], you will find the hidden Stone). The first letters of these seven Latin words spell out the word "VITRIOL," which is a natural form of sulfuric acid. This liquid fire is the fundamental agent of change in most alchemical experiments and also symbolic of the Secret Fire that drives the spiritual perfection of the alchemist.

The Least You Need to Know

◆ Spiritual alchemy focuses on the perfection of the soul.

◆ Dragons in spiritual alchemy represent the archetypal powers of the First Matter.

◆ The True Imagination connects with the hidden realities of the universe.

◆ The three kinds of alchemical meditation are Lunar, Solar, and Stellar.

◆ The Azoth of the Philosophers drawing contains a coded formula for the creation of the Philosopher's Stone.

Chapter 20

The Sacred Marriage

In This Chapter

- ◆ The sacred marriage on the personal level
- ◆ The child of the sacred marriage
- ◆ Alchemy of the Eucharist
- ◆ The three marriages
- ◆ The psychology of the sacred marriage

In alchemy, a marriage of two different substances is known as a *conjunction*, which literally means to "join with." For instance, we can view the merging of silver and mercury to form silver amalgam (commonly used in dentistry) as a conjunction.

The combining or conjoining of substances that takes place during conjunction usually produces a new substance with its own characteristics, and this new substance or compound is called the Child of the Conjunction. Most often in alchemy, the Child of the Conjunction is viewed as a hermaphrodite, a gross melding of the characteristics of the original substances.

When the conjunction involves the union of living essences or archetypal energies, the event is very powerful and produces a totally new incarnation of energies known as the Stone. At this level of the Great Work, the product of the marriage is known as the Philosopher's Child.

If the essences involved in conjunction are the primal immortal essences of soul and spirit, the event is very special indeed. Known as the sacred marriage, it is the most important event in alchemy. Whether in the laboratory work, the mental work, or the spiritual work of alchemy, the sacred marriage is considered the crucial turning point in the transformation of the matter.

The Sacred Marriage in You

The sacred marriage on the personal level is the marriage of the sun and the moon within, the union of your own spirit with soul to produce a new empowered presence. The alchemists saw this as a passionate coming together of the Elements Fire and Water, an act of inner love that united all the opposing forces within a person.

> **From the Alchemist**
>
> In the *Gospel of Thomas,* Jesus described the sacred marriage in very alchemical terms: "When you make the two One, and when you make the inside like the outside and the outside like the inside, and the Above like the Below, and when you make the male and the female one and the same, then you will enter the Kingdom of God."

The sacred marriage is the creation of a whole new personality from the essences of soul and spirit we have discovered within us, and it takes a lot of courage, passion, and devotion to succeed in uniting them. Conjunction is what we experience when we fall in love with another person, and it is also the communion we feel with all of nature. But when it deals with the essences of soul and spirit within us, it becomes the sacred marriage.

The Inner Marriage

Though they often depicted the sacred marriage as outright sexual intercourse, the alchemists were trying to describe inner experiences. They realized that no matter how fervently one desires to possess the qualities of soul and spirit recognized in another person, romantic love often fails. However, it is possible to bring together those same essences of soul and spirit that we fall in love with in another person together within ourselves. "That which failed to become two in one flesh will succeed in becoming two in one spirit," noted one spiritual alchemist. "Earthly lovers, however greatly they may love," wrote another, "must be distinct and separate from one another; but you pour yourself so utterly into the soul's essence that no part of you remains outside."

Among the most disturbing images of the sacred marriage are those that describe it as an act of incest or masturbation, and some medieval churchmen even accused alchemists of advocating lewd behavior. In the view of Carl Jung, the symbolic incest is the descent into or the penetration of the subconscious. The mother is the subconscious, and the son is the conscious. The marriage is a return to the womb of the mother. For most Hermetic writers, such scenes were metaphors for the inner union that took place between the alchemist's own soul and spirit.

The primary symbol for the sacred marriage in alchemy is the six-pointed star, in which the two interlocking triangles signify the union of opposites. The triangle pointing upward is the alchemical cipher for Fire and symbolizes spirit, God, the sun, and the masculine ego. The triangle pointing downward is the cipher for Water and symbolizes soul, the goddess, the moon, and the feminine unconscious. Sometimes the symbol also stands for the child of the sacred marriage or the Philosopher's Stone.

Birth of the Philosopher's Stone

As we have seen, alchemy uses many opposing concepts, like Fire and Water, sun and moon, Mars and Venus, lead and gold, dryness and wetness, warmth and cold, volatile and fixed, matter and spirit. The union of these opposites constitutes a conjunction.

Many laboratory experiments confirmed the idea that something new was born from the conjunction of some substances. For example, in an ancient experiment known to Alexandrian alchemists, mixing potassium nitrate and sulfuric acid produces a blue-colored solution of *aqua fortis* (literally "strong water" or nitric acid) that can be used to separate silver from gold. In the reaction, a solid residue precipitates out of the solution like a child being born from the womb.

Potassium nitrate was also known as cubic-saltpeter and was often referred to simply as natron, which represented the principle of Salt in alchemy. Sulfur was obtained from vitriol, the highly symbolic chemical known as the Green Dragon. That the mixture of these two archetypal substances would produce a child in precipitation was considered highly significant by early alchemists.

In the following figure, we see a depiction of the formation of the precipitate or Stone from the marriage of opposites. The two dragons represent the opposing lunar and solar forces of conjunction. Their heads are twisted backward as they seek out the complementary solar (masculine) or lunar (feminine) energy that will complete them. This natural urge to find balance in the embrace of our opposite is what makes the world go 'round. This act results in the birth or precipitation of the Stone, which is shown as the round ball on which the dragons perch.

The marriage of opposites.

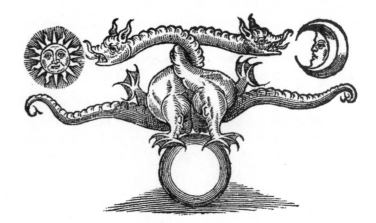

In the same way precipitates form in some chemical reactions, the Philosopher's Stone is formed during the sacred marriage, which is the union of the divine spirit with the soul and finally with the body. According to some authors, the Great Work has been accomplished when the divine spirit has been brought down to impregnate the soul with light. This act results in the purification and assimilation of the physical body, so that spirit, soul, and body unite to form a new or resurrected body of light.

Thoth's Tips

For an example of a diabolical conjunction, read *The Goblet of Fire* by J. K. Rowling and pay attention to the alchemy between Harry Potter and Voldemort. After Harry falls into the abyss, he encounters Voldemort, who quickly incarnates into a murderous spirit and forces Harry into a duel. But their duel is really a marriage of opposites. Voldemort's motivation is complex. He wants Harry's blood, not to kill the child but to take Harry's powerful spirit into himself. On a subconscious level, the dark Voldemort wants to force himself to connect with the solar light through the Philosopher's Child—Harry Potter.

The Sacred Marriage in Christian Alchemy

Christian alchemy began in the Middle Ages in the writings of alchemists, who saw parallels between the work of alchemy and the life of Christ. Christ was viewed as the Philosopher's Stone and was referred to in many treatises as simply the *Lapis* or Stone.

Christians view the sacred marriage as the union of one's soul with the eternal spirit of Christ. Christ consciousness is born out of that union, and Christ himself, as the Philosopher's Stone, then becomes the magical touchstone that transforms one's life.

In Christian alchemy, every event in the life of Christ is a metaphor for operations in the Great Work. The virgin birth and nativity of Jesus represent the birth of the Philosopher's Child, and his subsequent separation, conjunction, fermentation, and sublimation produced the essence of the Divine Life that is available for all of us.

The Holy Sacrament is believed to contain the most profound secrets of spiritual alchemy and is said to offer anyone a way to experience the transformation of the soul. Out of this mystical marriage, Christ as the Philosopher's Stone is born again within the worshipper. *Transubstantiation* is the Christian term for the process of alchemical transmutation.

According to Christian alchemy, all three phases of the Great Work were played out in the last three days in the life of Jesus. The Black Phase of alchemy was Christ's suffering on Calvary; the White Phase was his lingering death on the cross; and his resurrection was the perfection of his soul in the Red Phase of alchemy.

In both Gnostic and Christian alchemy, the place where the supreme mystery of the sacred marriage occurs is called the bridal chamber. The *Gospel of Philip* instructs the initiate that he will receive the heavenly light in the bridal chamber. "If anyone does not receive the light while he is here," it warns, "he will not be able to receive it in the other place, for when he leaves the world he has already received the truth."

def•i•ni•tion

Transubstantiation is the mystical process of becoming the body of Christ in the sacrament of the Eucharist. Worshippers partake of the bread, which is the body and nature of Christ, and of the wine, which is the blood and life force of Christ, and become one with Him. The accompanying rituals of the sacrament transform the bread and wine into vehicles of spiritual power.

The experience one receives in the bridal chamber has something to do with the resurrection of the soul. For instance, in the Gnostic text "The Exegesis of the Soul," the feminine soul falls from heaven and is entrapped in the physical world. She returns to heaven by incest with her brother in a mysterious bridal chamber. "And when she had intercourse with him," says the text, "she got from him the seed that is the life-giving spirit, and this is the resurrection that is from the dead."

The Three Marriages in Alchemy

Some alchemists claim that three conjunctions in alchemy correspond to the Three Magisteriums or accomplishments of the Great Work. The first marriage in the work of transformation is the Lunar Marriage or *unio mentalis*, Latin for "union in the mind." This marriage occurs when the soul separates itself from the body or when the alchemist becomes conscious of these as two separate entities. This occurs when the soul and the spirit unite and become separated from the body. It is like a voluntary rejection or death of the body in relation to the united soul and spirit.

The second or Solar Marriage occurs when the united soul and spirit (the *unio mentalis*) unites with the body, which has now been completely purified by the spiritual or solar energies. The third and final union is the Stellar Marriage in which the body-soul-spirit unites with the *unus mundus* (the One World).

The *unus mundus* is the whole universe seen as One Thing, which contains all of the potential of the First Matter on the first day of creation. The idea is expressed in the alchemical motto "All is One." This is the cosmic marriage or the union of "everything we are" with "everything that is." The body at this level is the Salt of the Stars, the Astral Body, or the body of light.

The Sacred Marriage in Psychology

Carl Jung titled the last book he wrote *Mysterium Coniunctionis* (Latin for *Mystery of the Conjunction*). He considered it his most important book, and scholars are still amazed at the depth and intuitive grasp of the principles of alchemy he showed in this work.

The book focused on the marriage or archetypal union between the powers of Sol (the sun) and Luna (the moon). Jung used the alchemical term *Hierosgamos*, Latin for "sacred marriage," for this event.

Jung felt that one alchemical text in particular defined the archetype of the sacred marriage. Called the *Rosarium Philosophorum* (*Rose Garden of the Philosophers*), this manuscript first appeared in the 1550 edition of an anthology called *De Alchimia* (*The Alchemy*).

The *Rosarium* depicts the sacred marriage in a series of 20 woodcuts showing Sol and Luna in various stages of conjunction. As the sacred marriage progresses, the male essence or Sol, representing spirit or energy, merges completely with the female essence or Luna, representing soul or matter.

As depicted in the *Rosarium*, this union is achieved through coitus or the sexual union of Sol and Luna. Their lovemaking symbolizes the mystical union of opposites. The bride represents the soul or incarnate self, and the bridegroom represents the spirit or disincarnate self.

The product of this sacred marriage, the child of Sol and Luna, is a new archetype known as the Divine Child or Divine Androgyne. This is the same archetype as the alchemical hermaphrodite or *Rebis* (the double thing).

In Jungian psychology, the inner marriage of the opposites within the psyche, which include masculine and feminine, conscious and subconscious, divine and human forces, gives birth to the Self. The Self is the archetype of wholeness in a person. According to Jung, the realization of the Self archetype is the real goal of the alchemical quest.

There is no doubt that Carl Jung's interpretation of alchemical symbols proved very powerful. His discovery of alchemy completely changed his life and inspired a whole new therapy known as depth-psychology.

In the garden of Jung's home in Bollingen, Switzerland, stands a large cube-shaped monument inscribed by Jung in his own hand with alchemical symbols. This square stone symbolized Jung's work in the world. In his last dream before his death, Jung saw a huge round stone engraved with the words "And this shall be a sign unto you of wholeness and Oneness." For him, it was the Philosopher's Stone and a sign that he had followed the right path in life.

The Least You Need to Know

- A conjunction is a union of two substances or forces.
- The sacred marriage is a conjunction of the essences of soul and spirit.
- The three marriages in alchemy are Lunar, Solar, and Stellar.
- In psychology, the child of the sacred marriage is the integrated Self.

Part 6 Modern Alchemy

People in all walks of life are discovering that the images and methods of alchemy have great meaning in the everyday world, and alchemy is synonymous in our culture with the idea of positive growth and change. Leaders in such diverse fields as business, psychology, and the arts are eager to apply the ancient operations of alchemy to release new creative energy into their work. Readers of the mega-selling *Harry Potter* series are spellbound by its magical characters and alchemical themes, which author J. K. Rowling freely admits she borrowed from alchemy books dating back over five hundred years. Quantum physicists and scientists working in many other fields muse about the "New Alchemy," in which consciousness is seen as a force of nature—just as the alchemists believed.

Chapter 21

Alchemy and Medicine

In This Chapter

- ◆ The search for the elixir of life
- ◆ Accumulating the energy of life
- ◆ The cures of Paracelsus
- ◆ The healing properties of metals

The obsession to change base metals into gold was not the only goal of the alchemists. They also sought to discover the panacea or universal cure for all diseases. Also known as the elixir of life, Alkahest (universal solvent), or Azoth (universal remedy), this medicine would carry the power of the Philosopher's Stone to transmute and perfect or cure anything.

Alchemists have always provided natural remedies for a variety of ailments because they possessed a powerful arsenal of herbs and compounds with knowledge of how they acted in the body.

The Life Force

According to alchemists, health can be measured by how much life force is available in the body. This life energy has been called by different names in various traditions, and alchemists as far back as 3000 B.C.E. have tried to understand the life force. The Egyptians associated it with the symbol of the Ankh, which is an ancient cipher for the morning star, planet Venus. The Taoist alchemists named it Chi; the Hindus called it prana; and the European alchemists associated it with the Quintessence.

In alchemical terms, the body is actually a special state of matter that might best be described as "spiritmatter" to reflect the fact that it is animated matter infused with a life force of its own. Whatever it is called, the alchemists treated this special energy of life like a chemical ingredient. They believed they could separate it from living matter and actually add it to their experiments just like any other chemical. In fact, many medieval alchemists actually claimed to have created little animated beings called humonculi by adding the life force ingredient into batches of chemicals. Alchemists believed they could use this same separated energy to heal disease and rejuvenate the body, and therefore attempted to capture its essence in their elixirs.

The life force is the source of the undifferentiated energy that is available for the transformations of cells and the life of the organs. In alchemy, the cells and organs are thought of as vessels of transformative energy in the body, and each organ is associated with a planet or astrological sign that describes this energy.

Paracelsian Medicine

Foremost among the alchemists devoted to healing was Phillipus Aureolus Theophrastus Bombastus von Hohenheim (otherwise known as Paracelsus, whom we've met in earlier chapters). Born in Switzerland in 1493, he entered the University of Basel at the age of 16 and studied alchemy, surgery, and medicine. He developed into an iconoclastic genius and is considered the first modern medical scientist.

Paracelsus pioneered scores of medical techniques and is the founder of modern methods of antisepsis, wound treatments, and pharmacology. He was the first person to treat and understand the causes and symptoms of syphilis, and he treated epilepsy as a disease and not an affliction caused by demonic possession as the Church insisted. He also was the first person to consider environmental factors as the cause of disease, and noted that dust and vapors caused lung afflictions among miners. He introduced the use of opium narcotics, mineral compounds, and medicinal mercury preparations.

Paracelsus taught that physicians should seek to find ways to stimulate the body to heal itself and not use drastic measures that weakened the body, such as bloodletting. He felt that everything carried a divine image of its perfect state that could be accessed for healing.

He called this divine inner principle the *Archaeus*, from the Greek word for ancient. The Archaeus is the oldest part of a substance's First Matter that goes back to when it was just an ideal form or thought in the divine mind. It is the source of health that presides over the growth and well-being of every living thing.

Paracelsus believed that everyone had an inner star or astral body that could be accessed to embody a state of perfect health and immortality. This new body was the source of a heavenly medicine beyond matter.

"The divine power is the heavenly medicine," Paracelsus said. "It accomplishes what no natural force can accomplish. There is no field on earth in which heavenly medicine grows or lies hidden, other than the resurrected flesh or the 'new body' of man. Only in the 'new body' have all its words force and efficacy here on earth. This heavenly medicine works according to the will of the man of the new birth. For it does not operate in the mortal body, but only in the eternal body."

> **From the Alchemist**
>
> "Death," proclaimed Paracelsus, "is the enemy of our body, of our health, the enemy of medicine, and of all natural things. God has made known this enemy to us and also how and by what means we can escape it. For there is no disease against which there has not been created or will be discovered a medicine which cures and drives it away. So there is always one thing that can be placed over against another in this world."

Paracelsus is said to have discovered a miraculous remedy he called the Azoth, which is an ancient name for the universal solvent or cure. In the work with metals, the Azoth is the first principle or mercurial essence from which all the metals arose, and it has been described as a fiery water or electrical plasma that contains all the archetypal powers of the metals. As we saw in Chapter 19, the Azoth drawing is a meditative emblem that attempts to systematically transform these powers within the alchemist.

Paracelsus said his Azoth acted like a universal remedy or *alexipharmakon* (counter poison), and he kept it close at hand at all times. Strange confirmation of this comment comes in portraits of Paracelsus commissioned in the early sixteenth century. In the paintings, the pommel of the sword on which Paracelsus rests his hand bears the inscription "Azoth."

Paracelsus was a tireless defender of his ideas. He traveled extensively and was ruthless in his attacks on charlatans and puffers. He died in 1541 in a small room at the White Horse Inn in Salzburg, Austria, and his body was buried nearby in St. Sebastian Cemetery. Sick and troubled people still visit the old church cemetery to seek a cure at his gravesite. Paracelsus, definitely more appreciated after his death than while he lived, became known both as the "German Hermes" and the "Father of Modern Medicine."

Healing with the Metals

The Azoth was thought to be a universal cure because it embodied all the archetypal energies of the metals. Alchemists believed these energies, which originated with the planets, governed our lives, relationships, and health in invisible ways. Over the centuries, these alchemists developed a powerful arsenal of metallic remedies.

In the following figure, we see an alchemist preparing his medicine. All the necessary components are shown. Through the window we witness the cosmic energies of the sun and moon coming together Above, while the alchemist points to a plant from which he has isolated the essence, which is symbolized by the cipher for Mercury. The work is accomplished using the fire in his furnace to his right and the Secret Fire within him. This inner fire of the alchemist is symbolized by the lion (Leo) devouring a serpent. The serpent is the classic symbol of the life force, which the alchemist sublimates and sacrifices for his medicine during the final stages of the work.

An alchemist prepares his cures.

Healing with Lead

Although lead is poisonous, alchemists have always tried to tame it and use it to tap into the Saturn energy that supports and enhances the structures of life. Saturn and lead rule the spleen, skeleton, and bone marrow.

Oil of Lead was one preparation made by alchemists that sought to capture the signatures of lead to heal. Made from the ashes of incinerated lead and powdered lead ore (Galena), which were dissolved in a strong vegetable alkali, this metallic solution was then fermented, and a fiery red oil resulted. The astringent oil was rubbed into the skin to encourage the growth of bones after breaking, strengthen the skeleton, prevent the atrophy of muscles and connective tissue, and stimulate the spleen, as well as increase one's patience and stop visions and hallucinations.

In the "like cures like" philosophy of homeopathy, lead is used to treat sclerosis, the hardening of bones and arteries, which is the hallmark of old age and a signature of lead. The homeopathic name of lead is *Plumbum metallicum.*

Healing with Tin

Tin carries the preserving qualities of Jupiter. Flowers last longer in tin vases, and food has remained preserved in tin cans for over a century. Jupiter rules growth, the metabolic system, the liver, and the enrichment of the blood from food. In the Middle Ages, sick people were served food on a tin plate and drinks in a tin vessel to help them regenerate and recover their strength. Today, we know that tin acts as a bactericide and pesticide and plays an important role in the regeneration of skin and many of the structuring processes in the growth of cells in the body.

The alchemists made an Oil of Tin that ruled the liver, cartilage, and muscles. They made the oil by incinerating metallic tin and dissolving the ashes in a strong vegetable alkali. The solution was then fermented, and the result was a black tarlike substance they called the Oil of Tin. They used this oil to treat jaundice, hepatitis, cirrhosis, ovarian cysts, acne, water retention, and obesity. It was taken internally to cure parasites and relieve constipation, and it was also an antidote for mercury poisoning.

The homeopathic form of tin is called Stannum, a remedy which is said to strengthen and regenerate muscle and brain tissue. It is also a remedy for problems with the joints and connective tissue of ligaments and cartilage. Stannum is beneficial in liver disease and is used for congestion, hardening, encephalitis, and other illnesses where the balance of fluids is upset.

The powers of Jupiter in tin are accessed in magical rituals and spells to promote abundance, prosperity, and success in business; attract what you desire; increase energy; and promote regeneration and rejuvenation. Amulets and talismans representing Jupiter are made of tin or tin-bearing pewter and charged with Jupiter's signatures. Jupiter's energy is said to be transmitted by lightning and the thunderbolt, which is the primary symbol used in rituals. For instance, in Tibetan Buddhist ceremonies, the *dorje* (or thunderbolt) is the stylized magical instrument or wand of jupiterian powers.

Healing with Iron

Iron is a vital constituent of plant and animal life and the key component of hemoglobin in the blood. The Mars archetype in iron rules the blood, adrenal glands, genitals, and immune system. Mars's effects are stimulation and toning of the blood and immune system and make one more aware of the functions of the organs and body.

Oil of Iron purifies the blood, heals wounds and cuts, soothes the gallbladder, stimulates the pancreas, helps ulcers, strengthens bone marrow, enhances instincts, cures impotency, and gives physical energy. The oil was produced from iron oxide ore. The black, sticky ore was first purified and made soluble and then distilled slowly to release its thick, oily soul. It was considered one of the most powerful oils and was never used more than 40 days.

Common homeopathic iron preparations are pure iron (*ferrum metallicum*) and iron phosphate (*ferrum phosphoricum*). Their therapeutic properties are stimulation and toning.

Iron and steel are used in rituals, magical spells, talismans, and amulets to promote energy, strength, determination, will-power, and aggressiveness. They are also used in fertility rites; new beginnings and undertakings; and for speed, power, and courage. Iron ornaments or jewelry (such as the iron cross) are thought to carry these same characteristics.

Healing with Copper

The origin of the alchemists' glyph for copper and Venus is the Ankh, the symbol for the life force used by the Egyptians. The healing powers of copper metal are legendary. One of the most popular copper cures was the legendary Powder of Sympathy, a form of copper vitriol which was carried in European apothecaries for nearly 300 years. It was considered a miracle cure for wounds of all types and was endorsed by physicians throughout Europe.

The odd thing about the Powder of Sympathy was that it never touched the patient. Blood and bandages from the wound were placed in a bowl of water containing a handful of copper vitriol powder, and the copper solution healed by sympathy. Believe it or not, patients immediately reported a cooling effect that diminished pain and resulted in rapid healing of the wound.

We know that copper metal kills germs, fungi, and algae, and a copper coin dropped into a vase of flowers or aquarium will keep the water fresh longer. Florists sometimes provide copper salts in small plastic bags for this purpose. Many older hospitals still have copper doorknobs that were believed to help prevent the spread of disease.

Copper plough tips do not dry out soil as iron ploughs do, and some farmers use fine copper filings to "charge" the soil or produce more powerful compost. Experimenters have discovered that copper wire or tubing twisted into an open circle (ends overlapping but not touching) and placed around a tree or plant seems to enhance growth and prevents disease.

Thoth's Tips _____

Copper metal can be applied directly to afflicted areas. To alleviate the symptoms of influenza, medieval physicians would prescribe rubbing the forehead with a piece of copper twice daily. Copper metal or powdered copper was also rubbed on sore joints to ease the pain of arthritis, neuralgia, and rheumatism—a tradition carried on today in the therapeutic wearing of copper bracelets.

The alchemists used copper pans and cauldrons to infuse their extracts and tinctures with Venus energy and were aware of the possible copper salts that could be formed. Using copper pans and utensils in the kitchen reduces the risk of passing germs onto food, and copper pans distribute heat evenly and cook foods faster and more thoroughly. However, copper combines readily with many substances and could form poisonous compounds with the wrong ingredients. For example, cooking salty foods in copper pans can cause a green corrosion called verdigris to form. Verdigris is copper acetate, which is a poisonous compound used to kill fungus.

Copper has been shown to assist in arthritis, diabetes, pregnancy, and diseases of the kidneys and thyroid. It is also very helpful in healing wounds and trauma from accidents and surgery. Copper is abundant in the female sex organs, and some studies even suggest copper in the body is used up during sexual intercourse. Copper is also present in gallstones, which medieval physicians blamed on lack of sexual activity.

The alchemists believed that deficiencies of copper in the body caused thyroid problems, sexual dysfunction, poor circulation, cramps, aneurysms, multiple sclerosis, epilepsy, and even mental illnesses. Some modern evidence suggests that copper deficiencies result in symptoms of aging, such as gray hair, skin wrinkles, crow's feet, varicose veins, and saggy skin.

Copper is a necessary chemical in venous blood that carries toxic substances to the excretory system. In sea creatures, such as snails, mollusks, crabs, and squid, copper takes the place of iron as the chemical of the blood and respiration.

Oil of Copper was used to treat a wide variety of problems, including blood pressure abnormalities, low energy, impure blood, kidney and liver problems, skin infections, and heart problems. It was made from crushed copper ore and the ashes from incinerated copper metal, which were dissolved in a strong vegetable alkali alchemically and fermented. The green oil was then separated out by distillation.

Homeopathic copper is used to treat leg cramps and children's growing pains in general, as well as for convulsions, diabetes, and to stimulate the kidneys. Homeopaths use copper under the name *Cuprum metallicum*.

Copper is used in rituals, spells, and amulets to promote love, sensuality, and positive relationships of any kind. Copper is said to increase one's personal magnetism and attraction to the opposite sex, increase psychic abilities, and give insight into the plant kingdom and nature in general. In some Wiccan ceremonies, copper objects are used in ritual copulation ceremonies to ensure the fertility of the land.

Healing with Mercury

Despite its poisonous properties, mercury was the main ingredient in many Eastern remedies. In his travels through India, Marco Polo observed that many people drank a concoction of mercury and sulfur twice monthly from early childhood with no observable ill effects. They believed the drink gave them longevity. Some Tantric alchemists in India still take metallic mercury in place of food as an elixir of life, although they caution that the body must be perfectly attuned and strengthened to tolerate the metal.

In Indian alchemy, mercury is called *rasa*, which refers to the subtle essence that is the origin of all forms of matter. The chaotic First Matter from which the universe sprang is called the *Rasasara* (Sea of Mercury), and the craft of alchemy is referred to as *rasayana* (Knowledge of Mercury).

A variety of mercury oils and elixirs have been created and used over the centuries. The most famous was the rasayana Oil of Mercury known as Makaradhwaja Oil. It was used as a rejuvenative tonic for the nervous system, lungs, liver, lymphatic system, and the brain. Makaradhwaja was used to treat paralysis, nervous disorders, tuberculosis, cancer, and immuno deficiencies.

The oil was also used to treat mental dullness, increase awareness and psychic powers, aid in developing verbal abilities, and enhance the powers of solar and lunar herbs. It is believed to relieve obsessions, fixed ideas, and deep depression. When combined with animal essences (such as musk), the oil was considered a powerful sexual tonic. The average treatment routine with Makaradhwaja, repeated on a yearly basis, lasts for about a month and usually works best in the coldest months of the year.

Tread Carefully

Never handle or attempt to ingest mercury. Metallic mercury is a poisonous heavy metal and is considered very toxic. Do not expose yourself to open mercury containers, including small amounts such as broken thermometers, because the poisonous vapors are completely odorless. The mercury remedies described here are presented only for educational purposes and are not intended for consumption.

The production of Makaradhwaja Oil is fascinating. It was made from purified medicinal mercury which had been processed to absorb the healing essence of copper. This mercury was alchemically compounded to purified sulfur. The resulting substance was a bright red "exalted" cinnabar. On being exposed several nights to the full moon, it resolved itself into a blood-like oil by "attracting the universal spirit of the world in the form of corporified light."

The most fantastic legends have grown up around members of the Bhairavi cult, who are worshippers of a wrathful form of Lord Shiva. They are rumored to live hundreds of years through the alchemical use of Makaradhwaja and other mercury-based compounds. Some are said to have obtained immortality by freeing their minds and overcoming their innate addiction to time.

Statues used in rituals in the Bhairavi cult display some of the side effects of using mercury compounds to extend life. They are statues of grotesquely mutated, other-dimensional beings who are supposed to be what successful candidates taking the mercury elixirs really look like.

Western alchemists make an Oil of Mercury by distilling metallic mercury seven times and quenching it each time in lime. Then it is dissolved in warmed spirit of niter and the salt extracted and boiled in vinegar. The vinegar is distilled away leaving the salt, which is washed in rainwater and fermented in pure grape alcohol. The alcohol is then distilled off, which leaves behind a fragrant oil of mercury. It is said to purify the blood, sweat, and urine, and cure all venereal diseases and many other illnesses. Only four or five drops are taken per day.

Because of the dangers of mercury, silver replaces it in mercurial rituals and talismans. Magical spells invoking mercury archetypes deal with improving communication, trade, commerce, transport, progress, change, travel, mental clarity, learning, thinking, memorizing, test results, writing and speaking, and powers of persuasion.

Healing with Silver

Silver is a powerful antibacterial and has been used in healing since 4000 B.C.E. The Persians kept their "healing waters" in silver vessels to leach silver atoms into the solution. Egyptians used a form of a silver wrap for wounds. Druids lined their drinking bottles with silver metal for a disinfectant.

Medieval royalty held a substantially higher immunity to bacteria than a commoner due to the fact that they dined with silverware, ate off silver plates, and drank from silver chalices. Even soldiers in World War I were known to swallow a whole silver dollar to ward off infection from wounds. Before refrigerators were invented, a silver coin was kept in milk to keep it from going sour.

Today, hospitals put silver solution drops in newborn babies' eyes to prevent infection and use a cream of 1 percent silver sulfadiazine, known as Silvadene, as a highly effective treatment for burn patients.

The therapeutic effects of the lunar metal are sedation, coolness, and moistness. Moon-ruled plants affect the subconscious mind and are useful for hypnosis, breaking bad habits, and dealing with unwanted desires. Lunar elixirs are used to reduce karma and also to rekindle an interest in family matters and relationships. They are said to increase sensitivity and imagination and a fondness for domestic pursuits in general. Medical astrology places the female reproductive organs, menstruation, the breasts, hormonal imbalances, the stomach, and the watery body-fluids under the control of the moon.

Oil of Silver was used to treat disorders of the brain and cerebellum, reduce stress, balance emotions, improve memory, treat nervous disorders and epilepsy, and improve both melancholia and mania. The oil was also used as a physical purgative and mental purifier.

Oil of Silver is said to affect the subconscious mind, help one see into the past clearly, remove fears and blockages, allow one to unwind, produce homey feelings, give a feeling of grace and sensitivity, and enhance imagination. Two popular homeopathic medicines derived from silver are *Argentum nitricum* and *Argentum metallicum*.

A permanent suspension of microscopic silver particles in water is known as colloidal silver. It has been documented since 1887 as an effective antibiotic against anthrax spores, and silver solutions were regularly given in the early twentieth century to knock out bacterial, viral, and fungal infections like pinkeye, ringworm, bronchitis, bladder infections, hepatitis, yeast infections, allergies, sinusitis, and many more common ailments. In fact, colloidal silver was able to fight over 650 diseases without any known side effects or drug interactions.

Tread Carefully

Do not overuse silver colloids or compounds. Since 1975, the FDA has discouraged the use of silver colloids because intensive, long-term use of silver preparations can lead to argyria, a condition in which silver salts deposit in the skin, eyes, and internal organs. This results in the skin turning a permanent ashen-gray color. Most cases of argyria occurred during the preantibiotic era, when silver was a common ingredient in nose drops and other over-the-counter preparations.

Silver is used in rituals, magical spells, and talismans to invoke moon-goddesses and in "drawing down the moon" ceremonies. The lunar forces are thought to control the female force, cycles, emotional and hormonal imbalances, the reflecting or neutralizing of negativity, dreams and intuition, psychic work, and psychic abilities. It is said wearing silver jewelry will improve fertility, emotional balance, and hormonal stability. Silver is also believed to improve the assimilation of food, which is why young children are traditionally given a silver fork and spoon to eat with. Water from silver chalices is thought to contain the lunar archetype and is used in rituals accordingly.

Healing with Gold

Gold has been used for both spiritual and medical purposes as far back as ancient Egypt. Over 5,000 years ago, the Egyptians used gold in dentistry and ingested it for mental, bodily, and spiritual purification. The ancients believed that gold in the body worked by stimulating the life force and raising the level of vibration in the body. In Alexandria, alchemists developed a powerful elixir known as liquid gold, which reportedly had the ability to restore youthful characteristics.

In ancient Rome, gold salves were used for the treatment of skin ulcers, and gold leaf still plays an important role in the treatment of chronic skin ulcers. Paracelsus developed many highly successful medicines from metallic minerals including gold. In medieval Europe, gold-coated pills and "gold waters" were extremely popular. The waters were known as "aurum potabile" (drinkable gold). Some were solutions of pure gold particles, while others contained no gold at all but were solutions of sulfur compounds.

Alchemists mixed powdered gold into drinks to comfort sore limbs, and today, it is widely used in the treatment of rheumatoid arthritis. In the 1900s, surgeons regularly implanted a five-dollar gold piece under the skin near an inflamed joint, such as a knee or elbow. In China, peasants still cook their rice along with a gold coin in order to help replenish gold in their bodies, and fancy Chinese restaurants put 24-karat gold-leaf in their food preparations.

Chrysotherapy (from the Greek word for gold) is the name given to healing with gold. The alchemists believed that gold represented the perfection of matter and that its presence in the body would enliven, rejuvenate, and cure a multitude of diseases. Gold never corrodes or even tarnishes, is completely nontoxic, and exhibits no interactions with other drugs. The atoms of gold spin in a right-handed direction, which is opposite to all the other heavy metals. This makes it difficult for gold atoms to unite with other atoms to form compounds. Because gold is so inert, it is well tolerated in the human body.

Physically the sun and gold rule the heart and circulation and the distribution of bodily heat. Its herbal therapeutic uses are as a tonic, heating agent, antiarthritic, and antiulcer. While no plants or herbs contain metallic gold, gold the metal is used to treat a variety of degenerative diseases including cancer.

The gold salt disodium aurothiomalate is administered intramuscularly as a treatment for arthritis. Metallic gold solutions have been used to inhibit or prevent the pathogenic progression in rheumatoid arthritis that damages cartilage, bone, and other connective tissues. Gold is also thought to create a beneficial balancing and harmonizing effect on the heart, improving blood circulation, rejuvenating sluggish organs (especially the brain), and assisting the digestive system to function smoothly.

In medical astrology, the sun rules the physical heart and the eyes as mirrors of the soul. The sun also controls the circulatory system and the central energy system of the spine. Because they carry the signature of the vitality principle on the cosmic level, solar herbs can be of seemingly miraculous aid in cases of apathy, lethargy, and unproductivity. Solar herbs also heal inferiority complexes, bolstering people and giving them a sense of purpose beyond the norm.

Several oils of gold are made by alchemists, although with any gold product, one should be aware of the extravagant claims sometimes made for it. Simple Oil of Gold is said to work for leukemia patients and most afflictions of the heart. It is also recommended for teenage growing pains, physical deformation, vertigo, and circulation problems.

The Red Oil of Gold was used as a circulation aid, heart tonic, blood purifier, regenerative of brain cells, and protector of bones and joints. It was used to treat rheumatism and arthritis, uremia and multiple sclerosis, to cure cancers and syphilis, increase vitality, and balance metabolism. Psychologically, it even was thought to cure a weak will, give ambition, restore courage, and increase creativity.

The formulae for making gold compounds tend to be very obscure and sometimes outlandish. For instance, the recipe for Dr. Anthony's "Famous Aurum Potabile" contains the following directive: "Take the urine of a healthy man drinking wine moderately; put it into a gourd which you must stop close, and set in horse dung for the space of forty days."

One inscrutable recipe for Oil of Gold calls for "calcinated gold fused into a colorful glass with special alchemical salts elaborated from a phosphoric principle and combined naturally with the universal spirit which contains corporified light or astral fire. When exposed several nights to the full moon, this glass dissolves by attraction into an oily thick paste."

Pure colloidal gold, which has a royal purple hue, was first prepared in 1857 by the famed English scientist, Michael Faraday, and many uses were found for the amazing solutions of "activated gold." Historically, colloidal gold has been found useful in cases of glandular and nervous unbalance because it seems to help rejuvenate the glands and stimulate the nerves. Colloidal gold also helps regulate body temperature.

Thoth's Tips

If you want to ingest gold, make sure the metal is at least 99.99 percent pure. Edible gold flakes are used in Chinese cooking and are sold in gourmet cooking stores. The German schnapps Geldschlager also contains gold flakes. Gold colloids also contain pure gold particles.

In general, colloidal gold has a balancing and harmonizing effect on all levels of body, mind, and spirit. It is used to improve mental attitude and treat unstable mental and emotional states such as depression, melancholy, sorrow, fear, despair, anguish, frustration, suicidal tendencies, seasonal affective disorder, poor memory, poor concentration, and many other unbalances in mind and spirit. Because it works to balance mental extremes, it has unpredictable effects in people with bipolar or manic-depressive disorders and is not recommended for their use.

Colloidal gold has been shown to relieve attention deficit disorder and improve mental focus. In the nineteenth century, colloidal gold was commonly used in the United States to cure alcoholism, and today it is used to reduce dependencies on other compounds besides alcohol, such as caffeine, nicotine, and carbohydrates. According to many studies over the years, colloidal gold increases mental acuity and the ability to concentrate.

The signatures of gold are invoked in rituals, magical spells, and talismans concerning solar deities, the male force, authority, self-confidence, creativity, financial riches, investments, fortune, hope, health, and worldly and magical power. Gold jewelry is said to improve self-confidence and inner strength.

The Least You Need to Know

- The life force is an ingredient in alchemical preparations.

- Paracelsus introduced a form of Hermetic medicine that incorporated many modern techniques.

- Each of the seven metals of alchemy carries planetary signatures that can be used in healing.

- Colloids are permanent suspensions of minute metallic particles in water and have been used in healing for over a century.

Chapter 22

Social Alchemy

In This Chapter

- ◆ Alchemy in the everyday world
- ◆ Alchemical transformation of relationships
- ◆ Alchemical transformation of the workplace
- ◆ Money as the First Matter of the modern world

Social alchemy is the application of alchemical principles and operations in relationships and for the general welfare of society. Its aim is to take alchemy out of the exclusive fraternities and brotherhoods of secret initiation and put it into the public light.

This general application of alchemical ideas to everyday life and situations is something medieval alchemists would not have expected and probably not approved of. For them, the principles of alchemy were too powerful to share publicly.

But times have changed, and alchemy is the buzz in such diverse areas as business and finance, art and education, bureaucracies and government, personal development and the media, and in relationships and the workplace. The revolutionary ideas of social alchemy are inspiring many individuals to become seeds of gold in the world, and the new motto of alchemy is, to quote Gandhi, "Become the change you wish to see in the world!"

The Alchemy of Relationships

The first level of social alchemy is found in personal relationships. This application is based on the realization that the same alchemical processes that the alchemists observed in their laboratories are at work in the maturation of the individual person. Those same principles surface in relationships between individuals.

Consequently, the inherent alchemical forces that build up between people can be harnessed to transform failing relationships into living, productive pairings in which both partners can grow into a unified whole that is often bigger than the sum of its parts. The opposing essences in relationships are what drive the alchemy between people.

Often the mental or physical conjunction we are seeking with friends and lovers is a subconscious effort to complement our deepest essence and attempt to find our soul mate. Loved ones are mirrors of our own souls, reflecting unexpressed qualities that are within us but that we need to reclaim as our own.

Unfortunately, maintaining the alchemical fires in a relationship is a full-time job. Through intimacy, we gradually realize that the other person is not the perfect embodiment of the soul mate that we had expected. Feelings get polluted; thoughts turn poisonous; and the relationship itself becomes toxic. At this point, the relationship can be saved and kept alive in only one way, and that is through the permanent purification and fundamental transformation offered by the operations of alchemy.

Calcination in Relationships

Starting with calcination, the elements of ego from which the poisons are being released must be exposed and burnt away in the fires of awareness. These poisons are made up of past judgments, unforgiven mistakes, pointless criticism, and endless complaining.

Thoth's Tips

You might want to review the operations of alchemy discussed in Part 3 (Chapters 11 through 13). The symbolic, psychological, and laboratory correspondences of the operations I presented will give you a deeper understanding of the alchemy of relationships and how they can be transformed.

The typical toxic reaction to these poisons is the formation of habits that tend to numb feelings and distance the partners from one another. Preoccupation with outside activities, partying with friends, consuming hobbies, drinking, and watching television are all possible escapes from facing the toxicity and removing it from the relationship. Poisons build up in any relationship just like they do within one's personality, and if they are not burnt away, they pollute the entire environment.

Dissolution in Relationships

Dissolution is a way to remove pollutants by assimilation. Tensions, contagious moods, and hurt feelings must be defused and dissolved before they take hold, and the little dramas and trumped-up crises must be drowned in the waters of genuine caring before they take shape. Hardest of all to dissolve are patterns of emotional, sexual, and physical abuse that arise in many relationships. The effects of passive-aggressive tactics such as the infamous "silent treatment" are just as difficult to remove, because these poisons eat deep into a partner's dignity and self-esteem.

Sometimes, in order to save the relationship at all costs, total dissolution takes place as the partners completely surrender individual identities and take on the will and traits of the other. In alchemical terms, such a dissolved relationship is stillborn and can no longer be transformed. That is why it is so important to see the toxins as existing in the relationship and not in the individuals.

The goal is to transform the relationship, not each other, for the opposing essences we share with one another is what fuels the entire relationship. Once these purified essences surface and are divided and identified in alchemical separation, they can be brought together in a new conjunction.

For instance, one partner may have qualities of imagination and inventiveness lacking in the other, while the other may have practical knowledge and a down-to-earth emotional base that grounds them both. Both partners realize that by validating the other, they support themselves. Then, in conjunction, the best of each partner is saved and united into a shared Quintessence that offers new hope and promise for the couple.

Fermentation in Relationships

However, no matter how optimistic the conjunction, traces of past pain and ego invariably find their way into the newly formed and reoriented relationship. Putrefaction is a natural process that develops in the course of even the best relationships as each partner compromises, surrendering aspects of his or her own personality for the survival of the couple. The black mood that sometimes results can cause an extinction of all interest in the relationship, and the partners must act to keep things alive at this stage, or they will slip back into a toxic relationship.

At this point, fermentation is the only way of saving the pairing. Whether through the help of friends, a marriage counselor, the birth of a child, the starting up of a company, or shared meditation sessions, the individual essences in the relationship must be exposed to outside or even transcendental spiritual forces to introduce something completely new, genuine, or sacred into the relationship.

By moving the focal point of the relationship from the mundane concerns of everyday survival to some higher ground, the relationship itself can be raised. Gradually, the partnership blooms, and one learns to trust what he sees in the mirror of the relationship and act on it. Thereby, the partners look within themselves, not only to their partners, for growth and true transmutation.

Distillation in Relationships

In the ensuing distillation phase of rebuilding a relationship, both partners learn how to look past their own and each other's personality flaws to the beauty and innocence of individual essences. The objectivity acquired during distillation is what purifies and concentrates the energies of the relationship.

The partners have finally moved past blame, shame, and games and have refined their relationship to the point where they are able to share hurt feelings without anger by reopening their hearts in mutual trust. In marriages, sexuality reaches a higher level in a true mixing of masculine and feminine essences that can lead to *Tantric* enlightenment.

def•i•ni•tion

Tantric refers to the concepts of Tantra, which is an Asian form of spiritual alchemy that is based on the idea that the universe we experience is the concrete manifestation of divine energy. The Tantric practitioner attempts to channel that energy through rituals, contemplation, and secret sexual practices.

Coagulation in Relationships

In the final coagulation, the opposing forces in the relationship are balanced and solidified into a living third thing—the Stone—from which each partner takes his or her due and grows stronger in its reflected energy.

Every relationship seeks to build this third presence or Stone, which allows each partner to keep his or her own identity while sharing in the traits and energies of the other. Psychologically, the Stone is the solid footing experienced in a successful relationship or marriage resulting in new confidence, creativity, and peace of mind for both partners.

Creation of the alchemical Stone in a relationship is the only way the toxins and pollutants of everyday life can be eliminated on an ongoing basis to prevent them from building up, to keep them from stifling and diverting the vital energies that keep any relationship alive.

The Relationship Laboratory

To apply these alchemical principles to your own relationships, begin by taking a good, hard look at a deep relationship you have already shared with someone. Try to start with a relationship that is over and done, so you might have a greater sense of objectivity that you can develop and apply to a present or future involvement with someone.

Unfortunately, most contemporary people fail at keeping the fires burning in the athanor, which can be viewed as the shared heart of the relationship. It doesn't help that the modern world is generally missing its opportunity to use the power of love to transform our lives, because we are kept busy thinking about so many other things. We simply have too much on our plates, too many possibilities, too many products, and too much entertainment.

However, if we look at the songs of the troubadours, the writings of the romanticists, or the poetry of the Sufi alchemists, we realize this was not always the case. Sometimes we have to stop and remind ourselves of the power of love in the world. In Sufism, alchemy is a creative and passionate journey with another person in which the love generated is the transformative tool. Rumi, a thirteenth-century spiritual alchemist who lived in Persia, expressed this concept when he wrote: "Love is that flame which when it blazes up, burns away everything except the Beloved. There remains but God, the rest has gone. Bravo, oh great, idol-burning Love!"

We must be brutally honest in examining our relationships, because they contain important lessons whether or not they last. Analyze a past relationship without placing any blame on any one partner. Try to trace exactly what happened to dampen the fires, and why all the love exchanged at the beginning of the relationship was taken back by the end of it. Finally, trace the alchemical processes in the relationship and the order in which they occurred. What could have been done alchemically to rekindle the relationship or end it in a nondamaging way?

In the following illustration, which is from the *Splendor Solis* series, we see an expression of the power of love to balance and deepen our experience of being alive in both our personal relationships and on the social or group level. Above in the heavenly realm is the archetype of love, Venus, riding in a chariot drawn by two lovebirds with Cupid at the reigns. Below in the manifested world are scenes of people dancing, singing, playing games, and conversing, while in the privacy of the surrounding woods are couples embracing. At the center is a retort in which the peacock, symbol of fermentation and new life, spreads its feathers.

The fermenting power of love.

Alchemy in the Workplace

The next level of social alchemy is in the workplace. As an alchemist, your changing-lead-into-gold mindset can perform miracles on all levels of everyday life, and your place of employment is the ideal place to start. The survival-of-the-fittest basis of capitalism does not mean that you, as an alchemist, cannot work within the system and transform the workplace into a creative and nourishing environment.

The truth is that companies that are run with integrity and creative freedom are faster to react and hardier in the long run than any organization based on greed and bureaucracy. As an alchemist, you should focus on the alchemical factors of joyful work: finding your life's purpose, creating spiritual products and franchises, liquidating cumbersome assets, developing conscious investing, and transforming the workplace.

Also examine your relationship with money and identify any hard feelings or jealousies associated with it. Your goal is to set up an alchemical relationship with both the workplace and the financial rewards it provides—just like the alchemists did with the metals—to manifest gold in your life and become fully alive whether you are at home or at work.

Calcination in the Workplace

The transformation of any organization begins with calcination, and the target of this fire is the dross and unessential salts that form in companies. Much of the friction that fans the fire comes from ego. Because ego is not a team player, it is constantly seeking control of all available resources, including energies that could be better applied to personal and organizational transformation.

Calcination continues on the corporate level by focusing on methods that eliminate bureaucracy, the greater ego of the organization. Traditional bureaucratic structures take on a life of their own and soon become the identity of the whole organization, so the goal is to transform these entrenched bureaucracies into intelligent organizations that make full use of the energies and insights of all employees. Only companies with this type of freedom and sense of community can be reborn and survive for any time in the marketplace.

Dissolution in the Workplace

Overcoming egocentric control, whether in an individual's personality or in the bureaucracy of an organization, requires a decentralization of power and the creation of a free-flowing environment. The process of dissolution originates from a kind of creative interplay between worker and work that has long been ignored in modern corporations.

But this process cannot take place unless the worker exerts some control over the outcome of her work. The goal is to show modern managers how to "let go" and recognize that the workers, not the system, make an organization soar to excellence.

Dissolution continues on the management level by identifying those managers, departments, and processes that serve as bottlenecks to the creative flow of energy. Sometimes this requires establishing an independent team or accepting the input of a maverick manager who has the confidence and honesty to look at the workplace from a fresh viewpoint. Careful consideration is given to ensure that the "bottlenecks" are not vital checkpoints and can be eliminated without adversely affecting the organization.

Separation in the Workplace

Separation involves freeing the living essences isolated within the organization in the operations of calcination and dissolution. Successful calcination has freed the company's spirit, and dissolution has released its soul. Only by recognizing and isolating these two fundamental ingredients can the work of transformation proceed.

In most companies, spirit is concentrated among managers, and soul is concentrated among the workers. Indeed, employees' loyalty and their creative energy are the soul and lifeblood of a company. This vital energy can be increased in an organization by exercising the Golden Rule of Management: treat your people like you would like to be treated. Managers who are too busy or too proud to recognize jobs well done only sow the seeds of less productivity; and managers too insensitive to acknowledge employee's problems will themselves receive no sympathy.

One practice that restricts the growth and balance of living essences in an organization is the traditional method of compensation, which is usually based on tenure and entitlement rather than performance. Over the years, employees build up a sort of internal equity just by being around for a long time, finding specialized niches in the organization, or getting to know their bosses on a social level. In most cases, such employees have become "essential" just by working there a long time and knowing their job well. In other cases, however, employees feel they do not have to contribute anymore and know the ropes well enough to get away with doing the minimum work.

Alchemical pay practices attempt to form a positive partnership between employees and the performance of the organization for which they work. Employees should be rewarded in ways that reflect not only their own performance but also their organization's overall success. Hiring and personnel practices should aim to balance the levels of soul and spirit in an organization. Rightsizing, not blind downsizing, is the tool of the separation phase of corporate transformation.

Conjunction in the Workplace

Conjunction as a corporate operation attempts to balance the opposing essences of soul and spirit in an organization and redirect them toward a unified vision of success. Just as the alchemists tried to get the forces of spirit to descend and the forces of soul to ascend and materialize in the reality of the sacred marriage of essences, so the modern manager can work with these corresponding organizational realities.

Within the individual manager and employee, spirit and soul combine to create a feeling intellect, which is the development of an intuitive attitude. In the organization, intuitive managers create an enlightened mission, which is the development of corporate vision.

From the Alchemist

In her book *Alchemy at Work* (see Appendix A), Cassandra Eason writes: "Intuitive powers can enable us to tune into the hidden needs and feelings of fellow workers, employers and employees, thereby becoming aware by signals even deeper than non-verbal indicators of the right time to propose change or new ideas and the right time to hold back. We can empathize with others, sensing when to ease their workload and when we can push productivity ahead."

In simplest terms, the new conjunctive vision is the articulation of the image, values, direction, and goals that will guide the future of the organization. This down-to-earth approach also involves ascertaining the capabilities of competing forces and identifying other environmental influences.

Unfortunately, the new vision is just like any other corporate plan or goal at this stage: we must give it life to make it happen. Often an erosion of energy occurs after the conjunction phase, which is something we have all experienced while working on a project.

At this point, managers should focus on negative or challenging issues that may have been deliberately ignored or swept under the carpet. These are the hidden signatures—the concealed potential of things, events, and people—that directly challenge the outcome of a project but which we often ignore.

Fermentation in the Workplace

The aim of the fermentation phase of the transformation of a company is to teach managers and employees how to bring life to their work and their work to life. The first step in this process requires the acceptance that higher values do have a place at work. Managers and employees must swallow their pride, forget personal ego, and open up to the insight and inspiration that others can offer. "By denying that spirituality exists in the workplace," notes Wally Amos (founder of the Famous Amos cookie company), "we are denying the essence of who we are and the substance that helps us create success."

Practical methods for achieving corporate fermentation begin by teaching the managerial alchemist how to achieve departmental goal agreement, give and receive feedback, deliver and digest tough messages, and have frank discussions about learning and development with subordinates. These critical skills are developed by applying practical methods of on-the-level communication, in which discussions are characterized by directness, respect, shared responsibility, and purpose.

The goal is to create a management culture that fosters the flow of relevant data, eliminates barriers to essential communication, and orchestrates the flow of information in order to make the correct decisions. Managers also need to learn how to contain the anxiety provoked by learning or new experiences, so they are able to question fundamental assumptions and engage in true dialogue that is part of the life-giving fermentation process.

Personal development, meditation, consciousness-raising, discussion, training, and experiential learning techniques are some of the methods a manager can use to develop a living awareness, which is his most valuable asset. This kind of flexible awareness fosters group synergy, which is defined as new energy for the group itself that empowers the team and gives it identity. In fact, the real purpose of management is to tap into the magic of group synergy.

The role of the alchemical manager is to interact with people in a way that cuts through barriers to energize and empower individuals to participate fully in their jobs. This kind of manager is a spiritual warrior, who protects the group culture while at the same time cutting through unproductive or sabotaging patterns to get to what enhances and fulfills the group purpose.

Distillation in the Workplace

Distillation in an organization involves inventing new ways to work smarter, not harder, by eliminating debilitating emotional barriers to productivity. For instance, worry or anxiety in the workplace environment depletes the life force of the organization. In many cases, worry is a perverted mental game we play to try to produce desired outcomes without working. We worry as a substitute for action. Some people worry to gain sympathy or acceptance, while others worry to brace themselves for anticipated pain. Many managers worry simply because they think it is their duty. The hidden connection between worry and indecision is what cripples the organization.

Many managers are considered indecisive because they simply fail to take action, yet in truth, it's the other way around. Indecisiveness and worry cause the inaction, yet to take more action, one has to make more decisions. It's an endless loop of arrested consciousness. Managers must accept the essential chaos we are all faced with in trying to transform something. Sometimes it's necessary to make decisions with incomplete information just to get the ball rolling on a project. Later, as more facts become available, it may be possible to tailor the project to fit changing conditions.

The acquisition of this confidence and professional attitude, based on the objective assessment of a situation, is the distillation of management. In fact, the process of distillation can be applied to all levels to purify the life force of the organization. Distillation overcomes barriers to productivity and unties emotional knots in individuals and the organization. Successful distillation means that both personal emotions and bureaucratic structures no longer interfere with creativity within the organization.

From the Alchemist

Many people experience distillation as a state of consciousness known as "flow," where concentration is so focused that one is totally absorbed in an activity, at the peak of one's abilities, free of personal problems or any sense of time restriction. While such feelings are often associated with sports, music, or the arts, they also surface quite often in the business environment. One study of nearly 5,000 Americans showed that three times as many people experience "flow" while at work than at home.

Coagulation in the Workplace

The paradoxical yet triumphant fusion of opposing qualities is what the alchemists called the Philosopher's Stone, which is formed during the process of coagulation. For example, Sam Walton, the late founder of Wal-Mart (the most profitable corporation in the world), embodied three paradoxes:

1. He was relentlessly focused on winning, yet he was totally flexible, willing to try anything and to drop whatever did not work without a second thought.

2. He was ingeniously creative but always ready to copy anything that had worked for someone else.

3. He was one of the best motivators who ever lived, yet constantly checked up on everything anyone did.

If all Walton had was a relentless drive to do things his way, he could have made all the common mistakes of any other entrepreneur, such as sticking with an idea long after it was no longer working or motivating people, only to have them scatter their energies in a thousand different directions. The combination of Sam Walton's paradoxical traits made him unbeatable.

The goal of coagulation is to create such paradoxical unions that are more powerful and durable than either component. This greater paradox is what the alchemists saw as the union of Fire and Water, or the fusion of masculine and feminine ways of knowing. Such paradoxical thinking generates unusual viewpoints, leading to a broader-based understanding of the true nature of a particular problem or opportunity.

The key to high levels of performance and dealing effectively with problematic situations is to consciously use all sides of one's core paradoxes at once. For the modern manager, this is an alchemical trick well worth learning. This type of thinking sometimes produces moments when things come together in an almost unbelievable way, when events that could never have been predicted seem to conspire to help us reach our goals. Psychologist Carl Jung named this ability "synchronicity," which he defined as meaningful coincidences or significant patterns of chance that seem to align with our own thoughts or contribute to our progress toward reaching goals.

In quantum mechanics, reality has been defined as a collection of "intermediate states in a network of interactions." The same definition applies to the modern business environment. The only way of organizing this chaos is in how we interpret the relationships between the individual components of the network. In alchemistic management, the leaders of the organization are not tied to a specific behavior or set response but are alive and responsive enough to focus on the changing relationships between people, events, and positive and negative influences throughout the organization.

Transforming the Workplace

So, to put it all together, the alchemical transformation of a company or organization follows the same operations that alchemists used to transform any substance. The alchemical formula consists of seven operations, which are usually performed consecutively but may, in fact, be performed in any order depending on the situation. These operations are:

1. **Calcination**   An operation of fire in which artificial structures, blind habits, and bureaucracy are burnt away.

2. **Dissolution**   A cooling-off period that dissolves the ashes of the previous operation, making the situation fluid.

3. **Separation**   A filtering process to find the essential ingredients, i.e., personnel and markets needed for survival.

4. **Conjunction**   The recombination of the saved elements from previous operations to bring it all together.

5. **Fermentation**   Seeking outside inspiration through retraining employees or an infusion of new talent.

6. **Distillation**   New objectivity and goal setting that raises the entire organization above past greed, feuding, and personal transgressions.

7. **Coagulation**   Integrating and revivifying the organization to make it all happen.

Using these methods in a combined effort by managers and employees, which are the spirit and soul of an organization, can transform the workplace through the initial throes of resistance to its crowning rebirth as a new entity, in which essential participants work together in an integrated, focused, living, and highly adaptable team for the mutual benefit of everyone.

Wealth: The First Matter in Society

The most important stage of social transformation begins, as it did amongst the alchemists, with the search and accumulation of the First Matter. In alchemy, the First Matter is that amorphous, chaotic, potential energy that is shaped into something physically real by the focusing of mind or consciousness. In the modern cultural climate, nothing fits the description of First Matter better than the vitriolic green stuff that is the "almighty dollar." The great and undifferentiated potential of money is what turns our dreams and images into concrete reality.

Tread Carefully _____

Talking about money may seem materialistic, but there's nothing inherently evil or unspiritual about money. Like the First Matter, the chaotic and impartial substance of money can be used for good or evil. When accumulated with avarice and greed, money takes on the attitude of its possessor and becomes a force of lies and evil-doing, as it has in many unscrupulous corporations. But when accumulated with compassion and understanding, money can become a source of spiritual power, whether in an individual's life, in a business, or in society.

Freedom is the Hermetic basis of capitalism and the basis of the founding principles of America as developed by the Freemasons. The idea of freedom not only applies to individuals, but to markets as well. Prices should be free to fluctuate through the natural pressures of supply and demand. Anyone should be able to start a business, and competition and innovation should be encouraged. These precepts create an extremely alchemical environment.

Money is simply a form of social power and transformation. If money is the agent of transformation in the everyday world, then the First Matter of money is a vital principle in every alchemist's life. It makes no sense to disenfranchise ourselves from the accumulation of money because we feel spiritual, as long as we work to accumulate wealth in an alchemical way without doing harm to others. Actually we do not have to be wealthy to have wealth. Simply not spending, not consuming, not overindulging, and being satisfied with what we have can dramatically increase effective wealth.

Furthermore, accumulating money offers practical training in the application of alchemical principles in the real world. The fact is that money makes us free to pursue alchemy. The medieval alchemists had patrons and benefactors to support their work, but that is no longer the case. Sometimes a little mercuric sorcery is required just to survive on a day-to-day basis.

As social commentator George Bernard Shaw demonstrated in his plays, the poor are uncultured and unrefined because they lack money, not because something is lacking within them. The problem is that they do not have the resources to gain the freedom to pursue transformation. The same situation was true of every alchemist, whose first steps in transformation were always toward freedom and independence in the world in order to focus on the Great Work.

So money, although much misunderstood in our culture, can be a vehicle for personal and social transformation. But alchemically, the personal relationship we have to money determines how it functions in our lives. Many of us have wounds around money that keep us stuck and prevent money from flowing naturally through our life. We must keep in mind that money, as the First Matter, can manifest as energy, security, intention, clarity, commitment, and vision, enabling the highest aspirations and ideals.

The Least You Need to Know

- We can apply the principles of alchemy to personal and social relationships of all kinds.

- We should adapt the sequence of operations in alchemy as the requirements of the situation demand.

◆ The goal of alchemical transformation in society is to make our relationships real and living.

◆ We can view money as the First Matter of modern civilization.

Chapter 23

The Science of Magic

In This Chapter

- Future science and magic
- The mysterious properties of light
- The new alchemy of quantum physics
- Twentieth-century scientists/alchemists
- Alchemical projection of consciousness
- The natural alchemy of evolution

Alchemy is a spiritual technology that merges the methods of science in the physical realm with the Hermetic teachings of the spiritual realm. Alchemists have developed theories, distinct operations, and unique equipment designed to work with spiritual energies. As an ancient science of soul, alchemy seeks to reveal the essences of time and space that are the fundamental truths of the universe.

Modern science, in its search for a grand unified theory of the universe, seeks the same things as the alchemists. With advances in quantum physics that incorporate the powers of consciousness in the fabric of the cosmos, alchemy and science are becoming more and more alike in their theoretical foundations.

Magic, too, has evolved along these same lines. Of course, I'm not talking about the tricks of stage magicians, but rather referring to the ancient tradition of magic—sometimes called Magick—that developed from the Hermetic teachings. In this tradition, the focusing of consciousness in will and intention is the force that transforms reality.

With the development of chaos magic in the last 50 years, the theories of magic approach the same theoretical basis as alchemy and modern science. Chaos magic emphasizes the power of the consciousness of the practitioner as opposed to the invocation of elemental forces or spiritual energies. Developed in England in the 1970s, the discipline teaches that both subjective experience and physical reality can be changed through a highly focused mind. A key belief in chaos magic is that there is no such thing as an objective truth outside of our perception, and therefore, all things are true and possible. This mercurial mindset is very empowering, and the philosophy behind chaos magic is very alchemical.

The basic technique in chaos magic is the development of a highly purified state of one-pointed concentration known as the gnostic state. A single thought experienced in the gnostic state is quickly released or forgotten and sent to the subconscious mind, where it is enacted into reality through unknown means. As we have seen, the chaotic subconscious mind is very much like the First Matter of the alchemists, and as such, is the source of all creation on all levels.

The Science of the Future

It has been noted that any future science will be indistinguishable from magic to those of our present time. This is exactly what is happening in alchemy. The ancient traditions of alchemy and magic are merging with modern science in a greater discipline that recognizes the mystery inherent in the universe and acknowledges that consciousness is a force in nature. This new alchemy has become the science of magic.

Early Hermetic writings remain some of the oldest and most sacred texts ever written, and throughout history the Hermetic teachings have influenced visionary philosophers and scientists. The secret truths of ancient Hermetic philosophy and the evolving perspectives of modern psychology and physics validate alchemy as a true means of understanding the workings of the universe. Alchemy is a truly unique discipline that combines science and religion and attempts to work on all levels of reality at once.

Of course, some proponents have always wanted to keep science a purely material discipline and alchemy a purely spiritual discipline. However, this approach weakens both disciplines. Certainly, for alchemy there can be no separation of spiritual and practical work because their combination is the basis of the craft.

From the Alchemist

In his book *The Philosopher's Stone,* philosopher Israel Regardie, a highly respected author of many books on the magical tradition and an active member of the Golden Dawn (an influential magical order founded in the late 1800s), documented his belief that alchemy was strictly a spiritual and psychological tradition that had no connection with the laboratory work of the medieval alchemists. However, after being initiated into alchemy and learning the laboratory work, he recanted his earlier view and admitted that both the practical and spiritual methods of alchemy were rooted in the same laws of nature and complemented each other.

Science can be seen as a more modern, secularized version of alchemy. The Egyptian origins of alchemy come from a time when there was no difference between science and religion, when there was just one true philosophy for the whole world. The Hermetic tradition attempts to hold true to that perennial philosophy and preserve the central mystery of creation, while science seeks to eliminate it. In that respect, we can only hope that the magic of today becomes the science of tomorrow.

The major criticism alchemists have of the scientific method is that it is based on argumentative instead of intuitive methods, and that the search for truth gets side-tracked in arguing about the details. For alchemists, true science is knowledge of nature acquired slowly by meditation. "Sciences are acquired only by study, by meditation, and not by dispute," said the alchemist-monk Antoine-Joseph Pernety. "Learn a little at a time; repeat often the same study; the mind can do all when concentrated upon one sole thing, but nothing when trying to embrace too many."

The Mystical Nature of Light

The common catalyst that seems to dissolve the boundaries of alchemy, magic, and science is light. Whenever alchemists, magicians, or scientists talk about the nature of light, it seems they are talking about the same thing.

Early Theories of Light

In ancient India, light was considered a subtle element out of which emerged the gross elements of creation. According to texts dating back to 500 B.C.E., light consists of particles of energy that make up all matter. Indian theorists knew that the sun was at the center of the galaxy and that the moon and planets shined by reflecting the light of the sun. They also knew that white light was composed of colors that they called "the seven rays of the sun."

About this same time, the Greek philosopher Empedocles postulated his theory of the Four Elements that viewed light as fire traveling at high speed. This fire was carried in humans and shone out of their eyes making sight possible. Around 300 B.C.E., Euclid wrote *Optica*, which was the first scientific study of light. He described the laws of reflection mathematically and postulated that light traveled in straight lines.

In his *Book of Optics*, the Arabian alchemist Alhazen (965–1040) disputed the idea that light originated from the eyes and said instead that it was caused by light rays emitted from the sun or lamps that struck the eyes. He theorized that light was streams of minute particles that traveled at a very high but finite speed. He described the laws of refraction or how light behaves in a lens and also invented a primitive camera.

The Alchemical Rebis

French philosopher René Descartes (1596–1650) believed that light traveled in the unseen plenum, which was the subtle substance or etheric First Matter of which the universe was composed. He demonstrated that light behaved like a wave and concluded that refraction could be explained by the varying speed of light in different media. As a result, Descartes is considered the father of the wave theory of light.

Alchemist Isaac Newton promoted the particle theory of light when he postulated that light was composed of corpuscles of matter emitted from a light source in all directions at once. Newton published these ideas in his book *Opticks* in 1704.

Actually, Newton's alchemical studies suggested that light might exist in two states at once, as both wave energy and particle matter, although the idea seemed too controversial for his time. "The changing of bodies into light and light into bodies," noted Newton, "is very comfortable to the course of Nature, which seems delighted with transmutations."

Newton's intuition told him that light was the alchemical Rebis, the double-headed thing that showed two opposite faces to the world. For thousands of years, alchemists had associated light with Mercury, the paradoxical Rebis. For alchemists, Mercury was light in all its forms: the light of the heavens, the light of our fires, and the light of our imagination and consciousness.

In the following figure, we see a painting from the *Splendor Solis* series of the Rebis toward the end of the work. The Rebis was first created as the Child of the Philosophers during the conjunction of the White Phase, then entered rebirth on a higher level during fermentation, and finally empowered as an independent body during distillation and coagulation during the Red Phase. The white and red wings signify that these processes are complete. The mirror-globe held by the Rebis is the Philosopher's Stone, the magical touchstone of the alchemists. The shining mirror-globe is also a symbol of the light of consciousness and its reflective nature—in other words, the light of consciousness is the Philosopher's Stone.

The Rebis reborn and empowered.

Newton was correct in his assumption that the world was not ready for an alchemical theory of light. Endless quibbling over the nature of light dominated physics for the next century. Dozens of experiments that demonstrated the wave nature of light challenged Newton's corpuscular theory. Finally, in the nineteenth century, James Clerk Maxwell developed a mathematical theory of electromagnetic radiation that included light, and numerous experiments verified his work.

The wave theory was accurate at explaining most optical and electromagnetic phenomena, but a few troubling anomalies remained that could not be accounted for.

One of these was the speed of light (186,282 miles per second in a vacuum), which could not be deduced from Maxwell's equations. Another problem was that the wave theory failed to explain the levels of electricity produced by the photoelectric effect, in which light striking a metal surface generated an electrical current. Still another problem was known as the "ultraviolet catastrophe," in which the spectrum of energy emitted by black bodies or thermal radiators could not be accounted for. Wave theory also had a hard time explaining light pressure or the way light pushes objects in a vacuum.

Finally in 1905, Einstein resolved these problems by returning to Newton's suspicion that light existed as both matter and energy. Einstein combined the wave and particle theories of light in a "wavicle" concept in which photons exhibit wave-particle duality. His theory stated that everything has both a particle nature and a wave nature, and various experiments can be done to bring out one or the other. In other words, the nature of light, or which face the Rebis shows the world, is determined by the conscious choice of the human observer as to which experiment to use in studying light. Some experiments prove the wave or energetic nature of light, while other experiments prove the particle or material nature of light.

Quantum Alchemy

Einstein's work and that of other physicists, including Max Planck, Louis de Broglie, and Richard Feynman, led to the development of a very alchemical new science called quantum physics. The basic premise of quantum physics is that reality is made up of "quanta" or packets of energy from which matter originates. In effect, the efforts of physicists to understand light led to the creation of quantum physics, which is the most comprehensive and accurate theory ever formulated to explain natural phenomena.

> **Thoth's Tips**
>
> Two books by Gary Moring are excellent introductions to quantum alchemy. *The Complete Idiot's Guide to Understanding Einstein* contains a section on alchemy, and *The Complete Idiot's Guide to Theories of the Universe* elaborates on the dual nature of light and other topics I cover in this chapter. (See Appendix A for details on both books.)

The power of quantum physics led to its acceptance by many reluctant physicists. The notion of wave-particle duality was extended to include the electron and electromagnetic phenomena. According to the field of quantum electro-dynamics, when electrons are excited, packets of quanta are released as electromagnetic radiation. These packets of energy or quanta act the same way as a ball hitting a wall but are, in fact, packets of solidified energy.

Modern physicists have also discovered that every fundamental particle of matter has a shadow energy or force carrier particle, and every energy carrier particle has a shadow matter particle. This relationship between matter particles and energy carriers is called supersymmetry.

The most startling revelation of modern quantum theory is another alchemical principle that states the origin of the physical world is in spirit or light and energy. Matter does not exist of itself in the universe but emerges from a quantum foam or First Matter. Atomic particles, which are the basis of all matter, are created out of the underlying strings of pure, wild energy that condense into physical reality.

Even the movement of particles of matter is not what it seems. Particles move in quantum jumps in which they disappear from reality and reappear in another position. The discontinuous motion of atomic particles gets so weird that completely imaginary components must be invented to describe their movement.

It's hard for us to accept such an alchemical explanation of nature, but our mechanistic concept of reality is completely false and has polluted all our thinking and beliefs. No scientific experiment in the history of physics has ever shown that hard material particles exist or can even move. However, now hundreds of experiments prove material particles move by being teletransported through time—disappearing from one place to reappear in another place without moving along a continuous path.

Contrary to what our senses make us believe, the world is not solid and fixed but is constantly being created out of a chaotic, formless, invisible quantum foam that is guided by the conscious expectation of what is there. And this is a more perfect description of the First Matter than any alchemist could ever conceive.

Whether the conscious expectation that creates reality comes from our minds or the divine mind that alchemists called "Mind the Maker" is still open to debate in modern physics. For alchemists, however, the divine light of mind—the same light we share in purified consciousness and the True Imagination—is the fundamental force and ultimate source of creation.

Twentieth-Century Alchemists of Science

In many ways, the insights of quantum physics have humbled modern scientists and forced them to accept an alchemical viewpoint of the universe. The days of the coldly objective and mechanistic search for truth have given way to a gentler science in which human intuition is an important tool.

Albert Einstein (1879-1955)

Albert Einstein was the epitome of the scientist-alchemist and never lost sight of the fundamental mystery of the universe. In 1905, he resolved problems in explaining the speed of light by revising the seventeenth-century model of space and time to account for the constancy of the speed of light. Einstein formulated his ideas in his special theory of relativity, in which the fundamental constants of nature are relative to the conscious awareness of the observer. It is one of the most alchemical treatises of nature ever written.

Einstein also proved an ancient tenet of alchemy that was previously unknown in physics: the fundamental equivalence between energy and matter in relation to light. His revolutionary equation of the universe is $E = mc^2$, where E is energy, m is mass, and c is the speed of light. As noted in Chapter 8, this theorem is a restatement of the three forces of the alchemists in which Sulfur is energy, Salt is mass or matter, and Mercury represents light.

When Werner Heisenberg, while still a brash and aggressive young physicist, came to Einstein for advice, Einstein told him to beware of being too sure of the power of logic alone. Instead, Einstein told him to use his intuition and allow the object of his work—his theory—to speak to him, and let it suggest where he should look and what was of importance in nature.

Werner Heisenberg (1901-1976)

As fate would have it, the overly logical Heisenberg became the one physicist to show that exact measurement and precise logical knowledge in physics is not possible. In 1927, Heisenberg proved that the more precisely the position of an atomic particle is determined, the less precisely its momentum is known, and vice versa. More generally, the act of measuring one magnitude of a particle, whether its mass, its velocity, or its position, causes the other magnitudes to blur.

It is not that we do not have precise enough instruments to measure the magnitudes of subatomic particles. The blurring of exact knowledge of a single particle of matter is a fundamental property of nature. This startling defeat for empirical measurement became known as the Heisenberg Uncertainty Principle and is now a basic tenet of quantum physics.

In quantum physics, the observer is no longer external and neutral to the experiment but becomes part of it, just as the alchemists believed. The outcome of an experiment depends on the view of the person doing the experiment. This concept was extremely unsettling to scientists. It meant that the facts of nature are no longer objectively verifiable and mathematically treatable, and it suggested that the scientific method would never be able to grasp complete and ultimate knowledge of the universe.

Barbara McLintock (1902–1992)

The new scientist-alchemist is epitomized by the work of geneticist Barbara McLintock, who won the Nobel Prize for Medicine in 1983 for her many important breakthroughs including the discovery of so-called "jumping genes."

McLintock devoted her life and all her attention to understanding just one thing—maize. She tried and succeeded in becoming one with her work and discovered the whole universe in an ear of corn. Working like a true alchemist, she identified completely with the substance of her work and connected with the inner life of maize. "Truth," she said, "has a mystical origin both inside and outside myself."

Thoth's Tips

Quantum physicist Fred Alan Wolf has introduced what he calls the "new alchemy," which is a melding of the ideas of the old alchemists and the new scientists to reach a fuller understanding of the connection between mind and matter. Dr. Wolf has written many books on quantum alchemy, including *The Spiritual Universe, Mind Into Matter,* and *Matter Into Feeling* (see Appendix A). You can download free copies of his articles explaining quantum alchemy from www.FredAlanWolf.com/page2.htm.

David Bohm (1917–1992)

Another example of the scientist-alchemist is nuclear physicist David Bohm, who developed the Ontological Interpretation of quantum mechanics in which mind and matter are viewed as opposite polarities in the universe. He demonstrated that electrons possess a "proto-mind" or primitive intelligence that seems to read active information in experiments.

Bohm believed mind had been present in the cosmos from the beginning and was part of the fabric of creation. He also introduced the notion of the Implicate Order, which is the ground or undivided wholeness of the One Mind of the universe from which the manifested world, which he called the Explicate Order, emerges.

Bohm also believed in the alchemical principle of "As Above, so Below." Because we are created of the same matter and in the same way as the whole universe, the truths of the cosmos should be within us. In quiet meditation, Bohm listened to his body and translated sensations of movement and tension into mathematical formulae that provided insights into problems of physics he was working on. Bohm believed that consciousness and the physical brain itself could be transformed by contact with the greater mind of the universe.

Wolfgang Pauli (1900–1958)

One of the greatest scientist-alchemists of the twentieth century was Austrian physicist Wolfgang Pauli, who is considered a founder of quantum physics. Pauli was an intellectual perfectionist, who urged his colleagues to seek deeper truths and became known as the "conscience of physics."

Pauli was so impressed by the alchemical work of Carl Jung that he sought him out and began a collaboration to mathematically prove the effect of consciousness on matter. Pauli was convinced of the effects of mind over matter through his own personal experiences. In fact, the Pauli Effect in physics is when experimental equipment breaks down because of the conscious anticipation of the participants. Pauli had the bizarre ability to disable scientific equipment when he was in the vicinity and delighted in tormenting his fellow physicists with his inexplicable talent.

Pauli came to understand that nature can never be completely reduced to a rigid logic, and researchers must always allow for the unpredictable, the unknowable, and the irrational. He felt that the goal of physics and the Great Work of alchemy was the same—to unite mind and matter. He wanted to "resurrect the spirit in matter" through the inner working of matter and consciousness within the hermetically sealed alchemical vessel.

He spent his life working on the unified field theory in which all the forces of the universe would be explained by one grand theory. He included consciousness as one of the unexplainable forces of nature, and hoped to prove it to his colleagues. Pauli died of cancer in 1958 before he was able to finish his work, and it has been suggested that he died from the Pauli Effect on his own body, which had become the crucial piece of equipment in his grand experiment.

Physicist David Peat commented that Pauli had successfully sealed the forces of matter and spirit into the alchemical vessel but was never able to generate the transforming heat of love to complete the transformation. That indispensable heat of transformation comes from the Secret Fire within the alchemist himself. Indeed, a colleague of Pauli once noted that the element of Eros was missing from Pauli's life.

The Philosopher's Stone of Physics

The Grand Unified Theory that Wolfgang Pauli was working on is now the Philosopher's Stone of science. It is the one theory of everything that will give human beings unprecedented control over the forces of nature.

Physicists have already accomplished the dream of medieval alchemists to change lead into gold. It was relatively easy. In a small particle bombardment vessel in 1965, physicists succeeded in transforming an unstable isotope of lead into a small amount of molecular gold.

Physicists might even have captured the elusive First Matter of the alchemists. At the Relativistic Heavy Ion Collider at Brookhaven National Laboratory, an experiment was performed to try to reproduce the state of matter in the first microseconds after the Big Bang, when the universe was created. Electrically charged gold atoms were accelerated to close to the speed of light and then smashed together.

What the equations predicted was a hot gas made up of quarks and gluons, the primary components of atoms. Surprisingly, what was created was much like the First Matter. Instead of a gas, they produced a primordial liquid of perfect consistency, such that any part was just like any other part. It was made up of pure energy that was 150,000 times hotter than the sun.

The quantum level of reality can be considered more subtle or spiritual than the gross physical level at which we all live. Yet somehow, the alchemists knew that consciousness was the tool through which man could access that invisible level underneath our everyday reality. Like a modern quantum physicist, the alchemist is always looking for the most subtle level of reality, the deepest underlying pattern that explains physical reality.

Alchemy, magic, and modern science are slowly converging on the realization that mind is a force in nature and its purification and perfection are the Philosopher's Stone. Whether the perfection of consciousness is described as the magical touchstone of the alchemists, the power of focused intention of the magicians, or the Grand Unified Theory of the physicists really does not matter. We are ultimately talking about the same thing—the power of mind or spirit over matter.

The Projection of Consciousness

The real power of the Philosopher's Stone was to project perfection into matter, to bring any substance into alignment with the ideal mental image of what it should be. This is how the Philosopher's Stone worked, how it healed and perfected anything. At this point we might be able to draw on the combined efforts of alchemists, magicians, and scientists to develop a workable method of projection.

From the Alchemist

"The Great Work is, above all things, the creation of man by himself," said Hermetic scholar Eliphas Levi in his book *Transcendental Magic*. "That is to say, the full and entire conquest of his faculties and his future; it is especially the perfect emancipation of his will, assuring full power over the Universal Magical Agent. This Agent, disguised by the ancient philosophers under the name of the First Matter, determines the forms of modifiable substance, and we can really arrive by means of it at metallic transmutation and the Universal Medicine."

Actually, alchemists refer to the conscious projection or manifestation of desires as chemicalization, although it has nothing to do with chemicals. It is the alchemist who is changed or chemicalized. The term refers to the use of certain methods to condense one's spiritual powers into external chemicals that can react and have an effect in the real world. The steps in this psychospiritual process are:

1. **Sealing.** The first step in this process is to try to isolate the relevant essences and primal energies and seal them in the vessel of transformation. The vessel, of course, is one's own mind, which must be purified of distractions and outside influences. The work here is in the inner laboratory, and it may take some effort to connect with the archetypal essences of the situation or desire. They must be identified as separate "chemicals" with their own identities and properties.

2. **Agitation.** This is a process of stirring up the energies or bringing them to life in the sealed vessel. It involves visualizations and guided imagery designed to encourage the trapped essences to express and release their archetypal energies.

3. **Combustion.** Having released the volatile inner vapors, they are now set afire with forceful and focused intention. You want to turn up the fire to gain control and direct the energy. It is a time of chaos and inflammation, of unrelenting intrusion of your intention into the vessel. It is the aggressive application of your will over the lesser powers trapped in the vessel. There may even be some

negative counter energy that escapes from the vessel into your environment, which is something to watch out for.

4. **Withdrawal.** The fires of will are abruptly withdrawn and the aggressive focusing of the fires of consciousness is turned off. Total silence without thoughts or emotions must prevail. The essences in the vessel are now cooking in their own heat, digesting in their own juices. There may be a black period of doubt or depression within you, but this is part of the process. To succeed, you must let go without losing interest.

5. **Manifestation.** Slowly the original desire begins to reappear in your life, but you must not rush it or want it too badly. Never talk about it or share the experience with others at this stage. Enthusiasm must be contained. Let the desire gain power slowly. Allow the energy to congeal on its own. This is the pregnancy of your intention, and it must have time to mature in the darkness. Soon, perhaps unexpectedly, your desire will manifest into reality.

The process of projection and manifestation is difficult to master because it requires a lot of inner work and the intense development of willpower, the True Imagination, and the inner Secret Fire. You must give of yourself, for you, too, are an ingredient in the process of manifestation. Once you are able to demonstrate the desire in the world, the ordeal becomes easier.

The Alchemy of Evolution

The alchemists' idea of the mind of nature is very similar to our modern notion of evolution. Over time, nature seems to be perfecting itself. It may take millions of years but eventually a species transforms itself in response to some great need, and a new species, more able to survive in the world, comes into existence.

The Great Work of alchemy has always been to find ways to speed up this natural process of perfection. In the words of the modern French alchemist Jean Dubuis, "Alchemy is the art of manipulating life, and consciousness in matter, to help it evolve, or to solve problems of inner disharmonies."

Alchemy seeks transformation not by mechanically forcing nature to do its will but rather by encouraging certain latent patterns to come alive and grow. The alchemists viewed the growth of minerals, plants, animals, or the evolution of whole species as alchemical processes going on in the laboratory of nature. Indeed, for the alchemist all matter is alive and has the potential for growth and change.

The alchemist believes that everything carries the energetic seed or pattern of its own perfection, and it was the job of the alchemist to resurrect these essences of perfection that are trapped in matter—to bring them to light and allow their full expression in time and space. Alchemists see this guiding pattern of perfection as an inner spirit that exists in all matter, from a dull gray lump of lead to a living human being.

The alchemists' task, therefore, is to speed up nature's work by perfecting substances in the laboratory. Such artificial transmutations by the alchemists were believed to encourage the overall pattern of transformation on our planet and contribute to the evolution of everything, including human beings.

> **From the Alchemist**
>
> "The long work is always Nature's," noted the French alchemist Antoine-Joseph Pernety. "She works simply, by degrees, and always by the same means to produce the same result. The work of Art is shorter; it outstrips Nature. The work of God is done in an instant. Alchemy, properly speaking, is an operation of Nature, aided by Art. It places in our hands the Key of Natural Magic, or Physics."

What makes humans different from ordinary matter is that we can consciously participate in our own process of perfection. In fact, we all participate in alchemy whether we know it or not. We can proceed as alchemists and try to intentionally manifest our perfected nature, or we can spend our lives (or lifetimes) unconsciously cycling through worldly experiences that finally bring inner spiritual resources to the surface. According to this deeper tradition, the gold of alchemy is hastened perfection in the highest sense—the divinization of matter and of human beings.

The Least You Need to Know

- The viewpoints of alchemy, magic, and modern science are slowly converging on a unified view of nature.
- The nature of light comprises contradictory states that the alchemists attributed to the mercurial Rebis.
- The theories of quantum mechanics acknowledge the role of consciousness as an additional force in nature.
- An individual can learn the projection of consciousness to manifest desires in a process called chemicalization.
- The evolution of life can be seen as the alchemical perfection of nature.

Appendix A

Resources

If you'd like to learn more about alchemy, the suggested books and websites in this appendix are a good jumping-off point.

Books

Albertus, Frater. *Alchemists Handbook: Manual for Practical Laboratory Alchemy*. Samuel Weiser, 1974. First modern guide to practical alchemy.

Aromatico, Andrea. *Alchemy: The Great Secret*. Harry Abrams, 2000. An illustrated history exploring alchemy's mix of science, philosophy, art, religion, and magic.

Ash, Heather, and Vicki Noble. *The Four Elements of Change*. Council Oak Books, 2004. Using the Four Elements to create a solid foundation to support your mind, body, and spirit.

Bartlett, Robert. *Real Alchemy: A Primer of Practical Alchemy*. Spagyricus, 2007. Explores experimental techniques for beginning the Work in the laboratory.

Beyerl, Paul. *Compendium of Herbal Magic*. Phoenix Publishing, 1998. Guide to magical properties of herbs; includes planetary associations.

Cavalli, Thom. *Alchemical Psychology*. Tarcher, 2002. Ancient alchemical recipes for living in the modern world.

Cunningham, Scott. *Complete Book of Incense, Oils, and Brews*. Llewellyn Publications, 2002. Guide to preparing essential oils and using them to make incense, balms, and lotions.

Eason, Cassandra. *Alchemy at Work*. Crossing Press, 2004. How to use the ancient arts to enhance your life at work.

Edinger, Edward. *Anatomy of the Psyche: Alchemical Symbolism in Psychotherapy*. Open Court Publishing, 1991. In-depth description of the operations of alchemy in psychological terms.

Goddard, David. *Tower of Alchemy*. Samuel Weiser, 1999. Filled with Hermetic principles that are meant to be applied at the spiritual level.

Green, Mindy, and Kathi Keville. *Aromatherapy: A Complete Guide to the Healing Art*. Crossing Press, 1995. Shows how to use, blend, and prepare essential oils at home.

Hauck, Dennis William. *Emerald Tablet: Alchemy for Personal Transformation*. Penguin Arkana, 1999. Definitive history of the Emerald Tablet and the application of its principles to personal transformation.

———. *Sorcerer's Stone: A Beginner's Guide to Alchemy*. Citadel Press, 2004. Makes alchemy come alive with clear explanations, fascinating anecdotes, and hands-on experiments.

Junius, Manfred. *Spagyrics: Alchemical Preparation of Medicinal Essences, Tinctures, and Elixirs*. Healing Arts Press, 2007. Classic guide to the art of extracting plant essences; includes elixir recipes from famous alchemists.

Linden, Stanton. *The Alchemy Reader: From Hermes Trismegistus to Isaac Newton*. Cambridge University, 2003. Basic writings of the alchemists ranging from Alexandria to the end of the seventeenth century.

Marlan, Stanton. *Black Sun: Alchemy and Art of Darkness*. Texas A&M Press, 2005. Examines the alchemical stage of *Nigredo*, the blackening or mortification from which the true light emerges.

Martin, Sean. *Alchemy and Alchemists*. Chartwell Books, 2007. Basic review of the history and methods of alchemy.

Melville, Francis. *Book of Alchemy*. Barron's, 2002. Presents the seven operations of the Emerald Tablet, as well as an illustrated overview of alchemy.

Miller, Richard, and Iona Miller. *Modern Alchemist*. Phanes Press, 1994. Guide to personal transformation using the principles of alchemy.

Moring, Gary. *The Complete Idiot's Guide to Theories of the Universe*. Alpha Books, 2001. Guide to modern cosmology and quantum physics that lays the foundation for the ideas of modern alchemy.

————. *The Complete Idiot's Guide to Understanding Einstein*. Alpha Books, 2004. Great introduction to modern physics that contains an interesting section on alchemy.

Reich, Wilhelm. *Secret of the Golden Flower*. Harcourt Brace, 1988. Taoist alchemy treatise with wonderful commentary by Carl Jung.

Rolfe, Randy. *The Four Temperaments*. Marlowe & Company, 2002. Understanding the Elements as alchemical humors that allow you to fine-tune your health, career, and relationships.

Roob, Alexander. *Alchemy & Mysticism*. Taschen, 1997. Stunning pictorial presentation of the spiritual practice of alchemy.

Stavish, Mark. *Path of Alchemy: Energetic Healing and the World of Natural Magic*. Llewellyn, 2006. Guide to the teachings of Hermes and their applications in alchemy and healing.

Von Franz, Marie-Louise. *Alchemy: An Introduction to the Symbolism and the Psychology*. Inner City Books, 1980. Inspiring guide to spiritual wholeness that follows the Jungian interpretation.

Whitmont, Edward. *Alchemy of Healing: Psyche and Soma.* North Atlantic Books, 1996. Challenges the methods of mechanical medicine and emphasizes the importance of consciousness in healing.

Wolf, Fred Alan. *Matter Into Feeling: A New Alchemy of Science and Spirit.* Moment Point Press, 2002. Examines the science behind consciousness, memory, dreams, and the "One Mind" concept of the alchemists.

————. *Mind Into Matter: A New Alchemy of Science and Spirit.* Moment Point Press, 2000. Interprets modern physics in terms of ancient spiritual texts from alchemy, the Qabala, and the Eastern traditions.

————. *The Spiritual Universe.* Moment Point Press, 1998. Presents one physicist's vision of spirit, soul, matter, and self in the universe.

Yudelove, Eric. *Tao and the Tree of Life: Alchemical and Sexual Mysteries of the East and West.* Llewellyn, 1996. Decodes the mysteries of the Tao and Kabbalah to show their underlying basis in alchemy.

Websites

http://groups.yahoo.com/group/EmeraldTablet   Emerald Tablet Roundtable is an online discussion group on alchemy and the principles of the Emerald Tablet.

http://groups.yahoo.com/group/Flamel_College   Public online forum for students of Flamel College and others interested in Hermetic topics.

http://homepages.ihug.com.au/~panopus   Paracelsus College Australia was founded in 1984 by Frater Albertus and offers resources in practical and spiritual alchemy.

http://pwp.netcabo.pt/r.petrinus/alchemy-e.htm   The English version of Portuguese alchemist Rubellus Petrinus's website devoted to practical and laboratory alchemy.

www.alchemergy.com   Alchemergy is devoted to modern alchemy as it is applied to personal, social, and global transformation.

www.alchemycode.com   Alchemy Code is devoted to solving the secrets of alchemy and providing reference materials, discussion groups, and chat rooms for people involved in the Great Work.

www.alchemyconference.com   Lists current lectures, workshops, and conferences on alchemy around the world.

www.alchemygallery.com   Alchemy Art Gallery is a visual feast of alchemy engravings, drawings, paintings, sculptures, and other artwork from ancient to modern times.

www.alchemyguild.org   Official website of the International Alchemy Guild (IAG) with over 800 members in 23 countries. Free subscription to the *Alchemy Journal*.

www.alchemykey.com   Alchemy Key is a guide to all kinds of alchemy resources including free ebooks, classes, and other links.

www.alchemylab.com   Alchemy Lab is dedicated to personal transformation and has been described by the *London Times* as "one of the most stunning web archives ever."

www.alchemylab.com/dictionary.htm   The Alchemy Electronic Dictionary offers a fast way to find the meaning of alchemical terms and ciphers.

www.alchemylab.com/guideto.htm   Alchemical Properties of Herbs and Foods Index lists planetary and elemental associations for hundreds of plants and foods.

www.crucible.org   Online catalog of alchemical lab supplies, glassware, chemicals, herbs, oils, tinctures, books, artwork, jewelry, and other Hermetic items.

www.flamelcollege.org   Flamel College offers a wide assortment of alchemy, Hermetic, and esoteric classes mostly taught through correspondence courses.

www.levity.com/alchemy   Adam McLean's huge resource of original texts, drawings, and articles on practical and spiritual alchemy.

www.parachemistry.com   Parachemistry is devoted to practical alchemy and chemistry experiments.

www.rosicrucian.org   Rosicrucian alchemy in the tradition of the Ancient Mystical Order Rosae Crucis (AMORC).

www.spagyria.com   John Reid's website on practical plant alchemy and the art of spagyrics.

www.spagyrium.com   Spagyrium is devoted to the art of spagyrics and the practice of practical plant alchemy.

http://tech.groups.yahoo.com/group/AlchemyGuild   Public discussion group for members of the Alchemy Guild as well as the general public.

http://tech.groups.yahoo.com/group/Alchemy_Student_Forum Public discussion group for serious students and beginners in alchemy.

www.triadpublishing.com Offers the alchemy courses of the now-defunct Philosophers Of Nature (PON).

Glossary

adept   Someone who is initiated into the secrets of alchemy or has passed through an alchemical apprenticeship.

albification   Whitening of a substance by washing, scrubbing, grinding, or bleaching with chemical agents.

alchemy   The art and science of transforming substances, situations, or living things to perfect them.

alembic   The upper part of a still; a stillhead or type of retort. *See* distillation.

aludel   A pear-shaped vessel, open at both ends. Used as a condenser in the sublimation process, it thus came to signify the end stages of transformation. Also called the Hermetic Vase or the Philosopher's Egg.

amalgamation   The formation of an amalgam or alloy of a metal with mercury. This term is sometimes extended to mean any union of metals.

archetypes   Elementary ideas rooted permanently in our consciousness. They are the divine ideals or spiritual essences from which existing objects or situations arise.

athanor   From the Arabic word *al-tannur* (oven), the furnace used by the alchemists. Built of brick or clay, it usually was shaped like a tower with a domed roof and was designed to keep an even heat over long periods of time.

Azoth   Formed from the first and last letters of the English alphabet, which stand for the alpha and omega or the beginning and end of all creation, the Azoth is the ultimate solvent and coagulant that can change anything to its perfected essence.

baths   In alchemy, symbolize the dissolution process in which metals are cleansed and purified.

brimstone   From a German word meaning "burning stone," refers to sulfur.

caduceus   Staff with two serpents entwined in opposite directions around it. The serpents represent the life force, and the caduceus is often shown with two wings that represent the purified or ascended life force.

calcination   An operation in alchemy in which a substance is dehydrated and reduced to ashes in a fire.

cibation   The addition of liquid to the contents of the crucible at precisely the right moment.

cipher   A stylized symbol or glyph used to signify fundamental principles or universal constants.

circulation   The purification of a substance by a circular distillation in a pelican or closed distillation apparatus.

coagulation   An operation in alchemy in which a solution thickens, congeals, or crystallizes into a solid material or body.

coction   The cooking or heating of a substance at a moderate heat for an extended period.

cohobation   A kind of distillation in which the distillate is poured back into its residue; a method of redistillation.

conjunction   The marriage of two different substances.

crucible   The melting vessel of the alchemists. It is made of inert material such as porcelain and can withstand great heat.

cucurbit   The lower part of a still, containing the original liquid. Made of glass or earthenware, it was also known as a "gourd" on account of its shape; a receiver.

digestion   A kind of putrefaction in which the nutrients or essences are reabsorbed; the slow modification of a substance by means of a gentle heat.

dissolution   To turn a solid into a liquid, or a process by which something is mixed with a liquid.

distillation   The process of purifying a liquid by boiling it and condensing its vapors; an operation of alchemy in which volatile essences are separated from solutions.

dross   Scum formed by oxidation at the surface of molten metals; any worthless material that should be removed. From the old English word "dros," meaning dirt or dregs.

essential oils   The volatile oily components of plants, trees, and grasses. They are found in tiny sacs or glands located in the flowers, leaves, roots, bark, or resins of a plant.

exaltation   An operation by which a substance is raised into a purer and more perfect nature. It usually involves the release of a gas or air from a substance.

fermentation   Transformation of an organic substance into new compounds by the action of a ferment such as yeast. In general, the introduction of new life, agitation, excitement, or inspiration into a substance or situation.

filtration   A kind of separation in which material is passed through a sieve or screen designed to allow only pieces of a certain size to pass through.

First Matter   The primordial chaos out of which the universe originated; the first principle or soul of a substance.

fixation   To make a volatile subject fixed, stable, or solid so that it remains permanently unaffected by fire.

Four Elements   The four archetypal principles that emerged from the First Matter: Fire, Water, Air, and Earth.

head   The top of the retort flask used in distillation.

Hermetic   Secret; referring to the teachings of Hermes. "Hermetically sealed" means sealed airtight so no outside influences might corrupt the contents.

iatrochemistry   The use of chemicals or drugs in medicine as pioneered by Paracelsus. Iatrochemists believe that health depends on chemical reactions in the fluids of the body.

impregnation   To saturate thoroughly in order to produce a crystallization or new compound.

inhumation   To bury under the earth; sometimes used to mean any process that buries the active substance in a dark earthy material. Also applied to placing a flask in the warm heat of a dung bath.

karmic The effect of a person's actions on his or her life or next incarnation. Selfless acts and compassion are thought to create good karma.

litharge (or **letharge**) The leftover scum, spume, or ashes of a metallic operation; reddish-yellow crystalline form of lead monoxide formed by fusing and powdering massicot.

magnesia A mystical term to the alchemists that denoted the primordial transforming substance in the universe.

matrass A round-bottomed flask with a very long neck, sometimes called a "bolt-head."

menstruum An alchemical term meaning a solvent or alkahest having both the power to dissolve and coagulate at the same time. Based on the belief that the ovum takes its life and form from the menses, the menstruum was also referred to the as the Mercury of the Philosophers.

mental alchemy The use of alchemical techniques and operations on the psychological level in an attempt to perfect one's character and personality.

microcosm and macrocosm The "little universe" of human physiology, psychology, and society as opposed to the "greater universe" of planetary, cosmic, and spiritual processes.

mortification A process during which the substance undergoes a kind of death and seems to have been destroyed but eventually is revived.

multiplication A process of distillation and coagulation in which the power of transmutation is concentrated; an increase in the amount of the Stone as obtained from its pristine form.

Perennial Philosophy The belief that there are certain universal truths sensed by all sentient beings and common to all cultures and systems of knowledge.

Philosopher's Stone A magical substance or chemical catalyst that would immediately turn any metal into gold. A powder or elixir made from the Stone could perfect or cure anything.

precipitation To cause solid matter to separate from solution or suspension; to cause a vapor to condense and fall or deposit residue.

projection The final stage of coagulation in which the power of transformation is directed toward a body; the final process in making gold, in which the Stone is tossed upon the molten base metal to transmute it.

pulverization   The breaking down of a substance to smaller fragments through repeatedly striking it with a blunt instrument, such as a hammer or mallet.

purgation   Purifying a substance by casting out a gross part of it.

rasayana   A form of Indian alchemy that focuses on mercury preparations and tinctures. It is considered part of the ancient healing system of ayurveda.

receiver   The flask attached to the outlet of the condenser tube during distillation that contains the distillate or distilled product.

rectification   The purification of the matter by means of repeated distillations, the distillate being again distilled.

retort   A spherical container (usually glass) with a long neck or spout used to distill or decompose solutions by the action of heat or acids.

reverberation   To reflect or radiate heat or light. The action of a reverberatory furnace or kiln in which heat is radiated from the roof.

separation   An operation of alchemy in which useful essences are removed from materials by filtration, sifting, ceration, and chemical binding.

signatures   The characteristics plants and other objects share with the planetary powers and astrological events in the heavens.

social alchemy   The application of alchemical principles and operations in relationships and for the general welfare of society.

spagyrics   The applied alchemy of isolating the essences of plants and herbs.

spiritual alchemy   The application of the principles and operations of laboratory alchemy to mental and spiritual processes of transformation.

sublimation   The vaporization of a solid without fusion or melting, followed by the condensation of its vapor in the resolidified form on a cool surface.

Tantra   A form of Asian alchemy that combines elements of Hinduism and mystical teachings to transform bodily energies using mantras, meditations, and erotic rites.

Three Essentials   The trinity of forces that make up creation, named by the alchemists as Sulfur, Mercury, and Salt.

transmutation   The permanent change of one substance into another at the physical or atomic level, as in the transmutation of uranium into lead by radioactive decay.

transubstantiation The mystical process of becoming the body of Christ in the sacrament of the Eucharist. Worshippers partake of the bread, which is the body of Christ, and of the wine, which is the blood of Christ, and become one with Him.

transudation A process that occurs if the essence appears to sweat out in drops during a distillation or when heated.

trituration The reduction of a substance to a powder, not necessarily by the use of grinding but also by the application of heat.

volatile Changing readily from a solid or liquid into vapor. Anything characterized by erratic changeability.

volitilization To cause a substance to pass off into a vapor. Also, tending to erupt suddenly or violently.

Zep Tepi An epoch in Egyptian history over 12,000 years ago when divine beings arrived to share their wisdom and civilize the primitive peoples.

Index

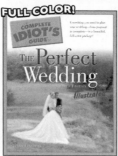

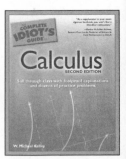

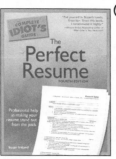
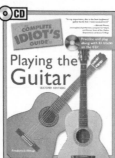